THE LIGHT
OF CHRIST

POPE JOHN PAUL II

THE LIGHT
OF CHRIST

Meditations for Every Day of the Year

Edited by Tony Castle

FOREWORD BY CARDINAL HUME

CROSSROAD · NEW YORK

1113

1987
The Crossroad Publishing Company
370 Lexington Avenue, New York, N.Y. 10017

Copyright © 1981 by Tony Castle

Printed in the United States of America

Library of Congress Catalog Card Number: 81-68527
ISBN: 0-8245-0041-5
      0-8245-0820-3 PBK

242
J2l

FOREWORD
by Cardinal Basil Hume

I am pleased to contribute a Foreword to this collection of daily readings from the addresses, sermons, articles and books of Pope John Paul II. This book renders a service to us all by bringing together under one cover the words of our Holy Father on a great variety of subjects. These words have been delivered to audiences in many different parts of the world, and have been written and spoken under many different circumstances. Nevertheless, whatever the topic, the place or the audience, the underlying thesis remains constant. The Pope's profound belief in the Incarnation and in man's dignity colours his approach to every subject. He expressed his fundamental attitude to life in the opening words of his first encyclical: "The Redeemer of Man, Jesus Christ, is the centre of the universe and of history". From this basic belief comes Pope John Paul's appreciation of the uniqueness and dignity of every human being — created in the image and likeness of God and redeemed by Jesus Christ. This belief and the attitude to people and events that it has engendered in the Holy Father can be perceived throughout this book and, like a golden thread, links the most disparate subjects. It is my hope that everyone who uses this book daily will come to share Pope John Paul's vision.

Basil Hume

Archbishop of Westminster

INTRODUCTION

My search for material for this book took me not only through the pages of *L'Osservatore Romano*, the Vatican newspaper, but also to Cracow, the Pope's own city. This was my first visit to an Eastern European country.

A day or two before departure I discovered that the friends of a friend, who were to accommodate me, had not yet heard of my trip! As the Polish LOT aircraft came in to land at the lush green, secluded airstrip — which doubles for a commando base — and taxied up to the minuscule Cracow air terminal, I was filled with anxiety. Would there be anyone there to meet me? With not one word of Polish to drop back on, I sought out for advice, in the slow-moving queue for Immigration, an elderly Polish priest who was clearly proficient in English. The Immigration controller, who spoke as much English as I did Polish, took mysterious exception to some detail in my papers and handed me over to a huge bearded green-clad Customs man. With the aid of sign language I was instructed to empty out every item of my luggage. The subsequent intensive search would have found the proverbial needle in the haystack — had there been one there! The green giant appeared delighted when he discovered an ancient and battered folder containing details of this book and handed it to a colleague, who bore it off with a satisfied smile. I was next ushered into a private room and ordered to empty out my pockets. Each scrap of paper, and a light-weight novel in my pocket, were zealously scrutinized. A body search followed and then I was left alone to my anxieties and, hopefully, the return of my papers.

All the other passengers had long since departed, with the exception of the elderly priest whom I espied in an adjoining room receiving similar treatment. After a further fifteen minutes or so my papers and folder were thrust at me and I was dismissed with a sweep of the hand.

Bursting through the connecting door to the terminal lounge I discovered, with a great surge of relief, that two Polish priests had been patiently waiting for me for some hours. The younger of them,

Father Edward, who spoke impeccable English, had travelled 150 miles to meet me. His colleague, who only spoke Polish, had come to offer me accommodation at his country parish house at nearby Rybna. The warmth of their welcome and the subsequent hospitality that evening at the priests' house, was in marked contrast to the oppressive and dehumanizing atmosphere at the airport. When I started to recount my experiences Father Edward stopped me with, 'You forget, you are in Poland now.'

In the short car journey to Rybna, Father Edward asked me why I had come to Poland and what my plans were. When I had explained, he pointed out that it made no sense to stay the week at Rybna when the material I sought was in Cracow. It became apparent that the small religious community – Sons of Divine Providence – who were my hosts, were somewhat amazed at this scatty Englishman who had turned up at Cracow airport with nowhere definite to stay, no knowledge of Polish, and no clear idea where material for the book might be found. If and when I found what I was looking for, one asked, how would I know if it were suitable? I explained that I was hoping to find an English-speaking student (Cracow is a university city) who would assist me.

The next morning, Monday, Father Edward drove me the fifteen miles to the city. We went straight to Archbishop's House, where Karol Wojtyla had been in residence as Archbishop and Cardinal, and a curial official rang round various religious houses to find me accommodation. Providentially Monsignor Nowak of the seminary offered me a room. The seminary was only three minutes' walk away, along a broad leafy walk, called The Planty.

I was excited to be staying at the college where Karol Wojtyla had trained as a priest; and further delighted to find that my room looked out upon Wawel Hill, the ancient fortress site on a bend of the Vistula which encompasses both the cathedral and the former royal palace.

The curial office had also made an appointment for me at ZNAK, the Catholic publishing house, whose premises are in a road adjacent to Archbishop's House. Here I learnt to my amazement that ZNAK were just about to publish the collected sermons and talks of Pope John Paul II under the title *Kazania 1962–1978*. The editor generously allowed me to borrow the proofs of the manuscript for five days.

That Monday morning seemed truly miraculous when on our return to the seminary, Father Edward and I met a small group of students, one of whom experimented with a few words of English. Suddenly he dashed off to find his friend, who he said spoke 'English good'. So I

8

met Stan, named after Poland's martyr patron, Saint Stanislaus, who proved an excellent translator, guide and friend. By mid-day on that incredible Monday, I had been accommodated in the Pope's own seminary; found all the material I would need collected in one place; and a keen-to-please translator!

Cracow was proving to be a place of great contrasts. Besides the contrast between the stark officialdom and the gentle warmth of the people, I was to observe and note more in the following few days. For example, the dignity and beauty of the old city and the stark utility of the modern housing developments around Cracow. The leap in design and conception from the eighty old-world Baroque city churches to the breathtaking space-age church at Nowa Huta.

It was July and the city was thronged with thousands of tourists. The majority were clearly from Eastern European countries – I only heard English spoken twice during the week and on both occasions with an American accent – and they crowded into the churches. What was so impressive to an Englishman, who has witnessed tourist behaviour in Westminster Abbey, was the prayerful quiet and respect of these tourists from Communist countries. The city churches of Western Europe are so often locked for fear of vandalism. That week I must have visited about thirty of the eighty Cracow churches and each was open, beautifully cared for and resplendent with flowers. The notice boards revealed that Mass was hourly from five a.m. to mid-day each Sunday!

One evening I spent two hours talking, through Stan, with five of the seminary's 300 students. I learnt that this was only one of several seminaries in Cracow and to cram more in, the students themselves (with professional assistance) were extending the premises. Meanwhile they were trying to manage with four students to a room. One of the students commented on how wonderful it must be to live in Western Europe and have complete religious freedom. 'Yes,' I replied, 'but when there is something to push against people develop and are stronger, when there is nothing they become flabby. The Church is stronger, more vibrant here. If you continue to recruit at the present rate and we continue to decline, you will be sending missionaries to Western Europe and America by the end of the century.'

Within the bastion walls of Wawel Hill, the ancient cathedral and royal palace stand side by side, symbolic of Church and State, the two monoliths, standing side by side within the land of Poland. Within the extremely beautiful cathedral the silver tomb of the martyr bishop Stanislaus – the Thomas Becket of Poland – dominates the nave with its own prominent altar. Before this tomb and altar each year the students from the seminary, at the foot of Wawel Hill, who are ready for the priesthood, are ordained. Their national identity and pride is endorsed as the sacramental seal of the priesthood is bestowed upon them. Before this tomb, Karol Wojtyla was ordained.

After visiting Pope John Paul's birth place and the church where he was christened, I took a forty-minute ride on a local bus to the former concentration camp of Auschwitz or, as it is called now, the museum of Oswiecim. Passing under the same weeping willow and through the same gates as the tens of thousands of victims of forty years ago, and recalling the elderly Polish priest sitting with bowed head at the airport, I realised more fully why Pope John Paul speaks repeatedly of the dignity and unique value of each individual. He tells us that he has visited Auschwitz many times and it is evident that the proximity of that place to his home town has made a marked impression upon him, his spiritual life and his message.

What TV viewer in the western world has not been warmed by his smile and wondered at his empathy with both individuals and crowds? It is almost as though preaching man's dignity as a child of God is not enough for him, he is compelled in his own person, by his warmth and sensitivity, to make up for man's hurt and indifference to man.

My visit to Cracow not only resulted in a number of passages from Karol Wojtyla's sermons and talks from 1962–1978, which you will find for the first time in English in this book, but also in a better understanding and appreciation of this world leader.

Each successive occupant of the See of St. Peter is assured a place in Church history, but this Pope seems set to influence the very course of modern history. In striking contrast he personally sees his mission simply: to proclaim Christ – and him crucified (1 Cor. 2:2). To further this end, adding to his other heavy responsibilities, he drives himself mercilessly with a prodigious output of addresses, sermons and talks. In 1979, for example, he prepared and delivered over 550, all bearing the unmistakable traits of Karol Wojtyla.

It was not only this colossal out-pouring, and the evident and overwhelming love of Christ (2 Cor. 5:14) which prompts it, that impressed me as I prepared this volume, but also the cool logic of his thought, so firmly based upon a deep knowledge, love and appreciation of Scripture. The poverty-stricken Brazilians of the favelas, the youth of Galway and Paris, the black community of Harlem, were all clearly enriched by meeting Pope John Paul; I hope that I too have grown spiritually by exposure to the rich maturity of this mind, as most assuredly will Christians of all traditions, who meet Karol Wojtyla through these pages.

As editor I am responsible for the selection of the passages, the use of italics, the headings and the Scripture text introducing each piece. In many cases, however, the latter are suggested by Pope John Paul himself in the text immediately preceding or following the excerpt.

TONY CASTLE

EDITOR'S NOTE:
As Easter is a movable feast the readings for Lent are arranged with this in mind. The festival readings are gathered at the end of April.

January

GOD SUBMITS TO THE FLOW OF TIME January 1

When the appointed time came, God sent his Son, born of a woman, born a subject of the Law.

(Gal. 4:4)

The year is the human measure of time. *Time speaks to us of the 'passing' to which the whole of creation is subjected.* Man is aware of this passing. Not only does he go through time, but he also 'measures the time' of his passing: time made of days, weeks, months and years. In this human flow, there is always the sadness of farewell to the past and, at the same time, opening to the future.

Precisely this farewell to the past and this opening to the future are inscribed, by means of the language and rhythm of the liturgy of the Church, in the solemnity of the Lord's Nativity.

Birth always speaks of a beginning, the beginning of what is born. *The Lord's Nativity speaks of an extraordinary beginning.* In the first place it speaks of that beginning which precedes any time, of the origin that is God himself, without a beginning. In the last few days we have been, in a special way, witnesses of the earthly birth of his Son. Being born in Bethlehem of the Virgin Mary as Man, Word-God, he accepts time. He enters history. *He submits to the law of human flow.* He closes the past: with him there ends the time of expectation, that is, the Old Covenant. He opens the future: the New Covenant of Grace and reconciliation with God.

He is the new 'Beginning' of the New Time. Every new year is a share in this Beginning. From the very beginning you are the measure of the new time, inscribed in the mystery of the birth of God!

Rome 1.1.79

Peace be with you.

(Luke 24:36)

These were the first words that Jesus spoke to his Apostles after his Resurrection. Today, I repeat these words to you, for they are words of life.

Jesus does not merely give us peace. He gives us *his* Peace accompanied by *his* Justice. *He is Peace and Justice. He becomes our Peace and our Justice.*

What does this mean? It means that Jesus Christ — the Son of God made man, the perfect man — perfects, restores and manifests in himself the unsurpassable dignity that God wishes to give to man from the beginning.

He is the one who realizes in himself what man has the vocation to be: the one who is fully reconciled with the Father, fully one in himself, devoted to others. *Jesus Christ is living Peace and living Justice.*

New York 2.10.79

INTERNATIONAL DESIRE FOR PEACE   January 3

Peace I bequeath to you, my own peace I give you.

(John 14.27)

Never before in the history of mankind has peace been so much talked about and so ardently desired as in our day. The growing interdependence of peoples and nations makes almost everyone subscribe — at least in principle — to the ideal of universal human brotherhood.

Great international institutions debate humanity's peaceful co-existence. Public opinion is growing in consciousness of the absurdity of war as a means to resolve differences. More and more, peace is seen as a necessary condition for fraternal relations among nations, and among peoples. *Peace is more and more clearly seen as the only way to justice;* peace is itself the work of justice.

And yet, again and again, one can see how peace is undermined and destroyed. Why is it then that our convictions do not always match our behaviour and our attitudes? Why is it that we do not seem to be able to banish all conflicts from our lives?

Drogheda 29.9.79

VIOLENCE IS A LIE January 4

The devil was a murderer from the start; he was never grounded in the truth; there is no truth in him.

(John 8:44)

To work for peace is the concern of all individuals and of all peoples. And because everyone is endowed with a heart and with reason and has been made in the image of God, he or she is capable of the effort of truth and sincerity which strengthens peace.

I invite all Christians to bring to the common task the specific contribution of the Gospel which leads to the ultimate source of truth, to the Incarnate Word of God.

The Gospel places in striking relief the bond between falsehood and murderous violence, in the words of Christ: 'You want to kill me when I tell you the truth . . . the devil is your father, and you prefer to do what your father wants. He was a murderer from the start; he was never grounded in the truth.'

This is why I was able to say with such conviction at Drogheda in Ireland and why I now repeat: 'Violence is a lie, for it goes against the truth of our faith, the truth of our humanity . . . *do not believe in violence: do not support violence.* It is not the Christian way. Believe in peace and forgiveness and love.'

Rome 8.12.79

TRUTH, THE POWER OF PEACE January 5

You will learn the truth and the truth will make you free.

(John 8:32)

Truth, the power of peace! Let us join together to strengthen peace through the resources of peace itself. The foremost resource is truth, for *it is pre-eminently truth, radiating its light without restriction, that is the serene and powerful driving force of peace.*

It is a fact, and no one doubts it, that truth serves the cause of peace;

15

it is also beyond discussion that non-truth in all its forms and at all levels (lies, partial or slanted information, sectarian propaganda, manipulation of the media, and so on) goes hand in hand with the cause of war.

Is there any need here to list all the different forms that non-truth takes? Let it suffice to give just a few examples. For, although there is justifiable disquiet at the increase of violence in national and international society and at open threats to peace, public opinion is often less sensitive to the various forms of non-truth that underlie violence and that create a fertile soil for it.

Rome 8.12.79

THE EPIPHANY January 6

Going into the house they saw the child with his mother Mary, and falling to their knees they did him homage.

(Matt. 2:11)

Today we turn to those characters who, according to tradition, were three in number: the Magi. St. Matthew's concise text renders very well what is part of the very substance of man's meeting with God: 'they fell down and worshipped him.' *Man meets God in the act of veneration, or worship*, of cult.

It is useful to note that the word 'cult' (cultus) is closely related to the term 'culture'. Admiration, veneration for what is divine, for what raises man on high, belongs to the very substance of human culture, of the various cultures.

A second element of man's meeting with God, highlighted by the Gospel, is contained in the words: 'opening their treasures, they offered him gifts . . .' In these words, St. Matthew indicates a factor that deeply characterizes the very substance of religion, understood both as knowledge and meeting. A merely abstract concept of God does not constitute, does not begin to form this substance.

Man gets to know God by meeting him, and vice versa he meets him in the act of getting to know him. He meets God when he opens up to him with the interior gift of his human 'ego', to accept God's Gift and make his own gift in return.

Rome 24.1.79

Jesus said, 'Put your sword back, for all who draw the sword will die by the sword.'

(Matt. 26:53)

Underlying all these forms of non-truth, and fostering and feeding upon them, is a mistaken ideal of man and of the driving forces within him.

The first lie, the basic falsehood, is to refuse to believe in man, with all his capacity for greatness but at the same time with his need to be redeemed from the evil and sin within him.

Encouraged by differing and often contradictory ideologies, the idea is spreading that the individual, and humanity as a whole, achieve progress principally through violent struggle. It has been thought that this could be demonstrated historically.

It has become more and more the custom to analyse everything in social and international life exclusively in terms of relationships of power and to organize accordingly in order to impose one's own interests.

Rome 8.12.79

THE PROPER NAMES FOR VIOLENCE   January 8

Pride is their chain of honour, violence the garment that covers them.

(Ps. 73:6)

Building up peace by works of peace is difficult. It demands that truth be restored, in order to keep individuals, groups and nations from losing confidence in peace and from consenting to new forms of violence.

Restoring peace means *in the first place calling by their proper names acts of violence in all their forms.* Murder must be called by its proper name: murder is murder; political or ideological motives do not change its nature, but are on the contrary degraded by it.

The massacre of men and women, whatever their race, age or position, must be called by its proper name.

Torture must be called by its proper name: and, with the appropriate qualifications, so must all forms of oppression and exploitation of man by man, of man by the State, of one people by another people.

The purpose of doing so is not to give oneself a clear conscience by means of loud all-embracing denunciations – this would no longer be calling things by their proper names – nor to brand and condemn individuals and peoples, but *to help to change people's behaviour and attitudes, and in order to give peace a chance again.*

Rome 8.12.79

THE PROMOTION OF PEACE   January 9

Malice must be banished from your tongue, deceitful conversation from your lips; seek peace, pursue it.

(Ps. 34:14)

To promote truth as the power of peace means that we ourselves must make a constant effort not to use the weapons of falsehood, even for a good purpose. *Falsehood can cunningly creep in anywhere.*

If sincerity – truth with ourselves – is to be securely maintained, we must make a patient and courageous effort to seek and find the higher and universal truth about man, in the light of which we shall be able to evaluate different situations, and in the light of which we will first judge ourselves and our own sincerity.

It is impossible to take up an attitude of doubt, suspicion and sceptical relativism without very quickly slipping into insincerity and falsehood. *Peace is threatened when uncertainty, doubt and suspicion reign,* and violence makes good use of this.

Do we really want peace? Then we must dig deep within ourselves and, going beyond the divisions we find within us and between us, we must find the areas in which we can strengthen our conviction that man's basic driving forces and the recognition of his real nature carry him towards openness to others, mutual respect, brotherhood and peace.

Rome 8.12.79

THE MAN OF PEACE   January 10

When the Spirit of truth comes, he will lead you to the complete truth.

(John 16:13)

The desire for peace does not cause the man of peace to shut his eyes to the tension, injustice and strife that are part of our world. He looks at them squarely. He calls them by their proper name, out of respect for truth.

And since he is closely attuned to the things of peace, he is necessarily all the more sensitive to whatever is inconsistent with peace. This impels him to push courageously ahead and investigate the real causes of evil and injustice, in order to look for appropriate remedies.

Truth is a force for peace, because it sees the factors of truth that the other has — factors that share the nature of truth — and tries to link up with them.

Rome 8.12.79

DENOUNCING THE ERROR NOT THE MAN   January 11

Anyone who can bring back a sinner from the wrong way that he has taken will be saving a soul from death.

(James 5:20)

Truth does not allow us to despair of our opponents. *The man of peace inspired by truth does not equate his opponent with the error into which he sees him fall.* Instead he reduces the error to its real proportions and appeals from it to man's reason, heart and conscience, in order to help him to recognize and accept truth.

This gives the denunciation of injustice a specific tone: such denunciation cannot always prevent those responsible for injustice from stubbornly disregarding the obvious truth, but at least it does not set out to provoke such stubbornness, the cost of which is often paid by the victims of the injustice.

One of the big lies that poison relations between individuals and groups consists in ignoring all aspects of an opponent's action, even the good and just ones, for the sake of condemning him more completely.

Truth follows a different path; that is why *truth does not throw away any of the chances for peace.*

Rome 8.12.79

Happy those who hunger and thirst for what is right: they shall be satisfied.
(Matt. 5:6)

Above all, truth gives us all the more reason not to despair of the victims of injustice. It does not allow us to drive them to the despair of resignation or violence. It encourages us to count on the forces for peace that suffering individuals or peoples have deep within them.

It believes that by confirming them in awareness of their dignity and inalienable rights, it gives them the strength to exercise upon the forces of oppression effective pressure for transformation, pressure more effective than acts of violence, which generally lack any future prospect — except one of greater suffering.

It is because I am convinced of this that I keep proclaiming the dignity and the rights of the person.

Rome 8.12.79

HUMANITY ON THE MARCH January 13

We have no power to resist the truth; only to further it.

(2 Cor. 13:9)

Promoting truth also means having the courage to foresee the future: to take into account the new aspirations, compatible with what is good, that individuals and peoples begin to experience as culture progresses, in order to adjust national and international institutions to *the reality of humanity on the march.*

Statesmen and international institutions therefore have an immense field for building a new and more just world order, based on *the truth about man and established upon a just distribution not only of wealth but also of power and responsibility.*

Yes, I am convinced of this: truth gives strength to peace within, and an atmosphere of greater sincerity makes it possible to mobilize human energies for the one cause that is worthy of them: *full respect for the truth about man's nature and destiny,* the source of true peace in justice and friendship.

Rome 8.12.79

CHRIST'S GOSPEL OF PEACE January 14

Happy the peacemakers: they shall be called Sons of God.

(Matt. 5:9)

The Gospel of Christ is a Gospel of peace. And *the driving force of evangelical peace is truth.*

Jesus revealed to man the full truth about man; he restores man to the truth about himself by reconciling him with himself and by reconciling him with others. *Truth is the driving power of peace because it reveals and brings about the unity of man with God, with himself and with others.*

Forgiveness and reconciliation are constitutive elements of the truth which strengthens peace and which builds up peace. To refuse forgiveness and reconciliation is for us to lie and to enter into the murderous logic of falsehood.

Rome 8.12.79

PERSONAL ACTION FOR PEACE January 15

You will learn the truth and the truth will make you free.

(John 8:32)

I know that all men and women of good will can understand all this from personal experience, when they listen to the profound voice of their hearts.

For this reason I invite you all, all of you who wish to strengthen peace by putting back into it its content of truth which dispels all falsehoods: join in the effort of reflection and of action by examining your own readiness to forgive and be reconciled, *and by making gestures of forgiveness and reconciliation in the domain of your own family, social and political responsibilities.* You will be doing the truth and the truth will make you free.

The truth will release unsuspected light and energy and give a new opportunity for peace in the world.

Rome 8.12.79

Only faith can guarantee the blessings that we hope for.

(Heb. 11:1)

The author of the Letter to the Hebrews speaks these words to us.

Faith, which makes man pass from the world of visible things to the invisible reality of God and eternal life, resembles that way to which Abraham was called by God (and therefore described as 'the father of all who believe'). Further on we read in the Letter to the Hebrews: 'By faith Abraham obeyed the call to set out for a country that was the inheritance given to him.'

Yes, it is so. *Faith is the spiritual pilgrimage on which man goes on his way, following the Word of the Living God*, to arrive at the land of promised peace and happiness, to union with God 'face to face', to that union which will fill, in man's heart, the deepest hunger and thirst: the hunger for truth and the thirst for love.

Castel Gandolfo 10.8.80

THE NEED FOR A PERSONAL FAITH January 17

This is the victory over the world — our faith.

(1 John 5:4)

Today, in fact, an enlightened, deep, logically personalized faith is necessary, and this can only be achieved by means of reflection, in order not to let it be disturbed and swept away by the impetuous fury of current opinions, morals and mentality.

Continue, therefore, to meditate from time to time on the supreme truths revealed by Jesus and taught by the Church, which illuminate our destiny in a unique and determinant way: commit yourselves to being more and more men convinced about the truth of faith!

This is what the times require; this is what the Lord demands of us, each in his profession, in his work.

Rome 27.3.80

THE GREAT TASK

How good, how delightful it is for all to live together like brothers.

(Ps. 133:1)

The work for the unity of Christians, is, in my opinion, *one of the greatest and finest tasks of the Church for our age.*

You would like to know if I am expecting unity and how I view it? I see it as a special call of the Holy Spirit. As regards its implementation, the different stages of this can be found — set out as fundamental principles — in the teaching of the Vatican Council. They must be put into practice, and their concrete applications must be sought. Above all it is necessary to pray always, with fervour, constancy and humility.

The union of Christians cannot be realized otherwise than *through deep maturation in the truth, and a constant conversion of hearts.* We must do all that in accordance with our human capacities, taking up again all the 'historical processes' that have lasted for centuries.

But finally this union, for which we must spare no efforts or work, will be *Christ's gift to his Church.* Just as it is already one of his gifts that we have already entered upon the way to unity.

Rome 16.6.80

PRAYER FOR CHRISTIAN UNITY

May they all be one. Father, may they be one in us, as you are in me and I am in you.

(John 18:21)

A privileged instrument for participation in the pursuit of Christian Unity is prayer. Jesus Christ himself left us his extreme desire for unity through a prayer to the Father: 'May they all be one.'

As the soul is to the body, so prayer gives life, consistency, spirit, and finality to the ecumenical movement.

Prayer puts us, first and foremost, before the Lord, purifies us in intentions, sentiments, in our heart, and produces that 'interior conversion', without which there is no real ecumenism.

Prayer, furthermore, reminds us that unity, ultimately, is a gift of God, a gift for which we must ask and for which we must prepare in order that we may be granted it. Thus also unity, like every gift, like every grace, depends 'upon God's mercy' (Rom. 9:16). Since the reconciliation of all Christians transcends human powers and gifts, continual and fervent prayer expresses our hope, which does not play us false, and our confidence in the Lord who will make everything new (Rom. 5:5).

Rome 17.1.79

EXISTING UNITY BETWEEN CHRISTIANS   January 20

There is one Lord, one faith, one baptism, and one God who is Father of all.

(Eph. 4:5)

All of us realize the great value that prayer has in accomplishing what is humanly difficult or even impossible. Jesus himself has told us: 'Things that are impossible for men are possible for God' (Luke 18:27). We know how important it is to turn humbly to God, day after day, asking him for the gift of constant conversion of life, which is so closely linked to the question of Christian unity.

At the same time, as we pursue our efforts towards the goal of perfect unity, we give thanks for the great bonds that already unite us in faith in the divinity of Christ. *We praise God for our common faith in Baptism* as an incorporation into the death and Resurrection of the Lord. *We praise him for the common love and esteem that we have for the Holy Scriptures*, which speak to us of Christ and his Church. And by the grace of God we are already in a position to confess together that 'Jesus is the Son of God' (1 John 4:15) and that 'there is only one mediator between God and mankind, himself a man, Christ Jesus' (1 Tim. 2:5).

Because we believe in Christ and in 'the infinite treasure of Christ', we feel led by the Spirit to do everything possible to remove the divisions in faith that impair our perfect common witness to the Lord and his Kingdom. Then we may better serve our neighbour and more effectively bring the Good News of salvation to the world that continues to see in us a divided Christ. And yet we know that *Christ has prayed for unity, and that the Father listens to his prayer.* Christ's prayer is the reason for our hope.

Rome 2.6.80

The Kingdom of God means righteousness and peace and joy brought by the Holy Spirit.

(Rom. 14:17)

How can we pass over in silence the fact that, in this modern age of ours, human rights are violated? *In various countries terrorism is growing, anxiety and fear are increasing.* Well, it is in these concrete situations that the coming of the Kingdom must be proclaimed, in order to change them not only into places of peaceful co-existence, but even more into places of communion of life in mutual respect and service of one another.

The Kingdom of God, St. Paul wrote to the first Christians of the city of Rome, 'is righteousness and peace and joy in the Holy Spirit'.

The division between Christians is contrary to the requirements of the Kingdom of God, opposed to the very nature of the Church which is the beginning and instrument of this Kingdom. Furthermore, *division dims the proclamation of the Kingdom of God*, it hinders its efficacy, making its witness weaker.

Whenever we recite the 'Our Father' we ask: 'Thy kingdom come.' As the coming of the Kingdom is closely connected, as I said, with the cause of the union of Christians, then the daily and repeated recitation of the 'Our Father' can become an intention of prayer for unity.

We must daily ask the Lord for unity until all Christians, having overcome their divergences and reached full unity of faith, will be able to celebrate and take part together in the one Eucharist of the Lord, the sacrament of the coming of God's Kingdom.

Rome 23.1.80

HUMANITY'S EXPECTATION   January 22

I saw another angel, flying high overhead, sent to announce the Good News of eternity to all who live on the earth.

(Rev. 14:6)

When we pray for Christian unity, then we pray for a matter of great concern for all humanity. That part of humanity which is outside the Church and outside Christianity is watching us, believe me.

Maybe it does not say so out loud, but in some way it sub-consciously expects this from us, from us Christians. And this is a return towards the Gospel, it is gradual, step-by-step, but it is a profound recognition of the truth revealed in the Gospel.

Cracow 25.1.63

THE UNITY OF ALL MEN   January 23

Men help one another, they say to each other, Take heart!

(Is. 41:6)

Christian unity is not just an internal matter for us, not just an internal matter for the Church, not even just an internal matter for all Christianity, for all denominations and all Churches. My dear friends, it is a great question for all mankind.

If we Christians can manage to meet in peace, to unite, if we can manage to become really united, then *this will be an enormous lesson of great optimism for all mankind* on what man can do, a lesson that human life, the life of humanity, must not be based on conflict and hatred and hostilities, that human life can base itself on peace, on unity, on understanding, on love, and can find a common denominator.

Cracow 25.1.63

THE WITNESS OF UNITY   January 24

The Father and I are one.

(John 10:30)

Here, we are dealing with the revelation of God himself; so Christ put the matter.

When he prayed for the unity of his disciples, he said: 'Father, may they all be one, as you are in Me and I am in you.' This is a revelation of the unity of God, the highest unity, the unity of the Holy Trinity.

We, through our unity, through the unity of Christians, have to give expression to, have to bear witness here on earth, before all people, before all consciences, before all hearts, we have to bear witness to the supernatural unity which is in God himself, in the Holy Trinity.

Cracow 25.1.64

STRAINING AHEAD TOWARDS UNITY January 25

All I can say is that I forget the past and I strain ahead for what is still to come.

(Phil. 3:13)

A movement does not stop, should not stop before reaching its goal. We have not reached it, even though we have to thank God for the road we have covered since the Vatican Council.

After these years of many-sided efforts, animated by immense good will and untiring generosity, nourished by so many prayers and sacrifices, it is good to survey the ground so as to assess the results obtained and make out the best routes for further progress. For it is this we are concerned with. As the Apostle tells us, we should be 'straining ahead for what is still to come' with a faith which knows no fear because it knows what it believes in and who it counts on.

But our haste to get there, the eagerness to put an end to the intolerable scandal of Christian divisions, means that we must avoid all superficiality, all rash enthusiasms which might hinder the progress towards unity.

Rome 18.11.78

CONSEQUENCES OF NUCLEAR WAR January 26

You will hear of wars and rumours of wars.

(Matt. 24:5)

I have recently received from some scientists a concise forecast of the immediate and terrible consequences of a nuclear war. Here are the principal ones:

— Death, by direct or delayed action of the explosions, of a population that might range from 50 to 200 million persons;

— A drastic reduction of food resources, caused by residual radio-activity over a wide extent of arable land;

— Dangerous genetic mutations, occurring in human beings, fauna and flora;

— Considerable changes in the ozone layer in the atmosphere, which would expose man to major risks, harmful for his life;

— In a city stricken by a nuclear explosion the destruction of all urban services and the terror caused by the disaster would make it impossible to offer the inhabitants the slightest aid, creating a nightmarish apocalypse.

Just two hundred of the fifty thousand nuclear bombs which it is estimated already exist, would be enough to destroy most of the large cities in the world. It is urgent, those scientists say, that the peoples should not close their eyes to what an atomic war can represent for mankind.

Rome 1.1.80

THE NEED FOR MUTUAL TRUST   January 27

Never yield to evil, practise good, seek peace, pursue it.

(Ps. 34:14)

The Pope discusses the subject of the danger of war and the necessity of saving peace with many men and on various occasions. The way to safeguard peace lies through bilateral or multilateral negotiations. However, at their basis we must find again and reconstruct a principal factor, without which they will not yield fruit in themselves and will not ensure peace.

We must find again and reconstruct mutual trust! And this is a difficult problem. Trust cannot be acquired by means of force. Nor can it be obtained with declarations alone. *Trust must be won with concrete acts and facts.*

'Peace to men of goodwill!' These words once uttered, at the moment of Christ's birth, continue to be the key to the great cause of peace in the world. Those in particular on whom peace depends most, must remember them.

Rome 1.1.80

THE STATE OF THE WORLD   January 28

Since they refused to see it was rational to acknowledge God, God has left them to their own irrational ideas.

(Rom. 1:28)

Clearly this is a picture of ancient Rome, one we are familiar with from other descriptions, such as the one in *Quo Vadis* by Sienkiewicz. But doesn't it bear some resemblance to the picture of our own times? Much has been written describing the present state of mankind, about the environment and about society, from the standpoint of the so-called 'three worlds' into which humanity is divided.

The picture of *human life under the totalitarian regimes is a terrible one*; for there man is deprived of his essential raison d'être, his freedom of decision and action.

There is no lack of literature bearing sad witness to our 'century of progress' which has become the age of a new enslavement, the age of the concentration camp and the oven. Even under the liberal regimes, where *men have grown sick from too much prosperity and too much freedom*, human life presents a saddening picture of all kinds of abuses and frustrating situations. Isn't this borne out by the phenomena of drug-addiction, terrorism and kidnappings of innocent people?

Added to all that there is an ever-widening gap between the prosperous societies and the Third World, where millions endure hunger and live in conditions of dire poverty.

S. of C.

MODERN MAN'S FEARS January 29

Do not be afraid of those who kill the body and after that can do no more.
(Luke 12:4)

The modern generation of men is in the grips of fear. They feel it in a marked way. Perhaps it is felt most deeply by those who are more aware of the whole situation of man and who *at the same time have accepted the death of God in the human world.*

This fear does not appear on the surface of human life. On the surface it is compensated by the various means of civilization and modern technology, which enable man to liberate himself, from the depth of his spirit, and to live in the dimension of *homo oeconomicus*, *homo technicus*, *homo politicus*, and, to a certain extent, also in the dimension of *homo ludens*.

Man, in his planetary dimension, has never been so much aware of all the forces that he is capable of utilizing and harnessing in his own service, and he has never used them to such an extent. From this point of view and in this dimension, the conviction about the progress of humanity is fully justified.

In countries and environments where technical progress and material prosperity are greatest, this conviction is accompanied by an attitude which is generally described as that of the consumer society.

It bears witness, however, that the conviction about man's progress is only partly justified. It bears witness, in fact, that *this trend of progress can kill in man what is most deeply and most essentially human.*

Turin 13.4.80

THE CONSUMER APPROACH TO LIFE January 30

How happy are the poor in Spirit; theirs is the kingdom of heaven.

(Matt. 5:2)

If Mother Teresa of Calcutta — one of those women who are not afraid to descend, following Christ, to all the dimensions of humanity, to all the situations of man in the modern world — were present here, she would tell us that along the streets of Calcutta and other cities in the world, men are dying of hunger.

The consumer approach to life does not take into consideration the whole truth about man — not the historical truth, nor the social, interior and metaphysical truth. It is rather a flight from this truth. It does not take into consideration the whole truth about man.

Man is created for happiness. Yes, but man's happiness is not to be identified with pleasure! The consumer-orientated man loses, in this pursuit of pleasure, the full dimension of his humanity and loses awareness of the deepest meaning of life. Such orientation of progress kills in man, therefore, what is most deeply and most essentially human.

Turin 13.4.80

MODERN MAN FEARS DEATH January 31

We believe that having died with Christ we shall return to life with him.

(Rom. 6:8)

Man is afraid of death.
Man defends himself from death.
Progress, which has been constructed by generations of men with so much difficulty, with the waste of so much energy and at such a cost, contains, however, in its complexity, a powerful factor of death. *It even conceals within it a gigantic potential for death.* Is it necessary to prove this in a society that is aware of what possibilities of destruction there are in modern military and nuclear arsenals?

30

Modern man, therefore, is afraid. The superpowers, who have those arsenals at their disposal, are afraid – and the others: continents, nations, cities – are afraid.

This fear is justified. Not only do there exist possibilities of destruction and slaughter unknown before, but today already men are killing other men in large numbers! They are killing in homes, in offices, in universities. Men armed with modern weapons are killing defenceless and innocent men. Incidents of this kind have always occurred, but today this has become a system.

If men affirm that it is necessary to kill other men in order to change and improve man and society, then we must ask whether, together with this gigantic material progress, in which our age participates, we have not arrived at the point of wiping out man, himself, a value so fundamental and elementary!

Have we not already arrived at the denial of that fundamental and elementary principle, which the ancient Christian thinker, Irenaeus, expressed in the sentence: 'Man must live'?

Turin 13.4.80

February

IN THE LIKENESS OF GOD

They are the ones he chose and intended to become true images of his Son.

(Rom. 8:29)

Why is man afraid?

We live in an age of gigantic material progress, which is also the age of a denial of God, on a scale previously unknown. Perhaps, man is afraid because, as a consequence of his denial of God, in the last analysis, he remains alone — interiorly alone. Or perhaps he is afraid because man, who makes God die, will not find a decisive curb not to kill man too.

This decisive curb is in God. *The ultimate reason why man should live, respect and protect man's life, is in God.* The ultimate foundation of man's value and dignity, of the meaning of life, is the fact that he is the image and likeness of God.

Turin 13.4.80

MAN CAUGHT BETWEEN GOOD AND EVIL

I cannot understand my own behaviour. I fail to carry out the things I want to do, and I find myself doing the very things I hate.

(Rom. 7:15)

Did not Ovid, the ancient Roman poet, a pagan, say explicitly: '*I see and approve what is better, but I follow what is worse.*' His words are not so different from those written later by St. Paul. Man himself, after original sin, is between 'good and evil'.

The reality of man, the deepest 'reality of man', seems to be unfolded continuously between that which from the beginning was defined as the 'tree of life' and that which has been defined as 'the tree of the knowledge of good and evil.'

This expression may sound like an archaic legend. But the more we get to know 'the reality of man', as we can understand it from his history — and as our human inner experience and our conscience speak of it to each of us — the more we feel we cannot remain indifferent, shrugging our shoulders before these primitive biblical images. *How charged they are with the real truth about man!* A truth that each of us feels as his own.

Rome 20.12.78

CHRIST'S AUTHORITY   February 3

All authority in heaven and on earth has been given to me.

(Matt. 28:18)

Modern man has greatly increased his power over the earth, he is even thinking of his expansion beyond our planet.

It can be said at the same time that man's power over the other man is becoming heavier and heavier. Abandoning the covenant with eternal wisdom, he is less and less able to govern himself, nor is he able to govern others.

How pressing the question of fundamental human rights has become! What a threatening face totalitarianism and imperialism reveal! In them man ceases to be the subject, which is tantamount to saying that he ceases to count as a man. *He counts only as a unit and an object!*

Let us listen once more to what Christ said through these words: 'All authority in heaven and on earth has been given to me,' and let us meditate on the whole truth of these words.

Le Bourget 1.6.80

THE NARROW GATE   February 4

It is a narrow gate and a hard road that leads to life.

(Matt. 7:14)

Man must grow and develop as a man. Man must grow and develop on the basis of the divine foundation of his humanity, that is, as the image and likeness of God himself. *He must grow and develop as a son of divine adoption.*

As a son of divine adoption, man must grow and develop through everything that contributes to the development and progress of the world in which he lives. Through all the works of his hands and his genius. Through the success of contemporary science and the application of modern technology. Through everything he knows about the macrocosm and microcosm, thanks to more and more perfected equipment.

How does it come about that, for some time now, man has discovered in all this gigantic progress a source of menace for himself? How and by what ways have we reached the point that, at the very heart of modern science and technology, there has appeared the possibility of the gigantic self-destruction of man; that daily life offers so many proofs of the use, against man, of what should be for man and should serve man?

How have we reached this point? *Has not man on his way to progress taken only one way, the easier one, and has he not neglected the alliance with eternal wisdom?* Has he not taken the 'wide' way, neglecting the 'narrow' way?

Le Bourget 1.6.80

MAN COMPARED TO A TREE February 5

He is like a tree that is planted by water streams, yielding its fruit in season.

(Ps. 1:3)

So says the Psalmist. And the prophet Jeremiah, who uses the same comparison, adds that this tree 'does not fear when the heat comes, its foliage stays green' (Jer. 17:8).

Man is compared to a tree. And it is right. Man, too, grows, develops, keeps his health and strength, or loses them. However, the comparison of Holy Scripture refers to man particularly in the spiritual sense. It speaks, in fact, of the spiritual fruits of his works, which are manifested in the fact that this man 'never follows the advice of the wicked or loiters on the way that sinners take' (Ps. 1:1).

The source of this conduct, that is, of these good fruits of man, is 'his pleasure in the law of the Lord'.

Rome 17.2.80

Will not God see justice done to his chosen who cry to him day and night.
(Luke 18:7)

Be men of prayer!

The Christian, to be able to call himself such authentically, must be 'practising', that is, he must live in the 'grace' of God, observing all the Commandments and carry out the commandment of charity concretely and continually.

Only by means of the commitment of trusting and persevering prayer is it possible to lead a life in grace and charity. *The world is going through a crisis, also because people do not pray, or pray little and badly.*

Rome 27.3.80

THE MEANING OF LIFE   February 7

You will reveal the path of life to me, give me unbounded joy in your presence.

(Ps. 16:11)

Yours is the age of the supreme question: *what is the meaning of life?* And consequently, what is the meaning of man's history?

This is certainly the most dramatic and also the most noble of questions, and it really stamps man as a person with intelligence and free will. *Man, in fact, cannot confine himself within the limits of time, the circle of matter, the knot of a permanently indwelling and self-sufficient existence.*

He can try to do so, and he can affirm in words and acts that his homeland is merely time and his dwelling merely the body. But actually the supreme question agitates him, goads him, and torments him. It is a question that cannot be eliminated.

Unfortunately, we know how a great part of modern, atheistic, agnostic, secularized thought insists on affirming and teaching that this supreme question is an illness of man, a put-up affair of a psychological and sentimental kind, from which it is necessary to be cured by facing up courageously to the ultimate absurdity of life and death.

It is a subtly dangerous philosophy, above all, because a young person, still immature in thought, shaken by the painful events of past and present history, by the instability and uncertainty of the future, sometimes betrayed in his deepest affections, dispossessed, misunderstood, unemployed, may feel driven by it to seek escape in drugs, violence or in despair.

Rome 1.3.79

GENESIS; THE KEY TO MEANING February 8

The Lord God fashioned men of dust from the soil.

(Gen. 2:7)

A non-Catholic philosopher once said to me: 'You know – I just can't stop myself reading and re-reading and thinking over the first three chapters of Genesis.'

And indeed it seems to me that unless one does so reflect upon that fundamental ensemble of facts and situations it becomes extremely difficult – if not impossible – to understand man and the world. It may sound a trifle strange, but I think it is true, that today one cannot understand either Sartre or Marx without having first read and pondered very deeply the first three chapters of Genesis.

These are the key to understanding the world of today, both its roots and its extremely radical – and therefore dramatic – affirmations and denials.

S. of C.

THE CREATION OF MAN February 9

The Lord God breathed into his nostrils a breath of life, and thus man became a living being.

(Gen. 2:7)

Certainly the text of Genesis is among the most ancient ones: according to biblical scholars, it was written about the ninth century BC. That text contains the fundamental truth of our faith, the first article of the 'Apostles' Creed'.

The part of the text which presents *the creation of man is stupendous in its simplicity and at the same time in its depth*. The affirmation it contains corresponds to our experience and to our knowledge of man.

It is clear to everyone, regardless of ideologies about the conception of the world, that man, though belonging to the visible world, to nature, is in some way differentiated from this same nature. In fact, the visible world exists 'for him' and he 'has dominion' over it: although, in various ways, he is 'conditioned' by nature, he 'dominates' it.

He dominates it by the strength of what he is, of his capacities and faculties of the spiritual order, which differentiate him from the natural world. It is these very faculties that constitute man.

On this point the book of Genesis is extraordinarily precise. Defining man as 'God's image', it shows clearly the reason why man is man; the reason why he is a being distinct from all the other creatures of the visible world.

Rome 6.12.78

THE QUESTION OF EVOLUTION   February 10

You too are gods, sons of the most High, all of you.

(Ps. 82:6)

Science has made — and continues to make — a great many attempts in the various fields, to prove man's ties with the natural world and his dependence on it, in order to integrate him in the history of the evolution of the various species. While respecting these researches, we cannot limit ourselves to them.

If we analyse man in the depth of his being, we see that he differs more from the world of nature than he resembles it. Anthropology and philosophy are going in this same direction, when they set out to analyse and understand man's intelligence, freedom, conscience and spirituality.

The book of Genesis seems to meet all these experiences of science, and, speaking of man as 'God's image', lets it be understood that the answer to the mystery of his humanity is not to be found along the path of similarity with the world of nature. *Man resembles God more than nature.* Psalm 82:6 says so: 'You are gods', the words that Jesus will take up again subsequently (cf. John 10:34).

Rome 6.12.78

NATURE AS A SISTER

God saw all he had made, and indeed it was very good.

(Gen. 1:31)

I am very attached to the first chapter of Genesis. *Original sin has by no means totally altered for the worse the primal goodness.* Human knowledge of the world is a means of participating in the science of the Creator.

It thus constitutes a first degree of resemblance of man with God, an act of respect towards God, since everything which we discover pays homage to the primal truth.

The universe has a harmony in all its parts and every ecological disequilibrium entails harm to man. The scientist will not therefore treat nature as a slave but, drawing his inspiration, perhaps, from the Canticle of Creation of St. Francis of Assisi, he will consider it rather as *a sister called to co-operate with him in opening up new ways to human progress.*

Rome 9.4.79

THE BENEFITS OF SCIENCE

Be masters of the fish of the sea, the birds of heaven and all living animals on the earth.

(Gen. 1:28)

There is no doubt that in many respects the technical progress which has been born out of scientific discoveries is helping man to solve such serious problems as food, energy and the struggle against certain diseases which are more than ever wide-spread in the countries of the Third World.

But it is also true that man, today, is the victim of a great fear, as if he were menaced by that which he creates, by the results of his work and the use which he makes of them.

To ensure that science and technology do not become the slaves of tyrannical 'will to power', political as well as economic, and to give science and technology a positive direction towards the benefit of man, it needs, as one is accustomed to say, more of the soul, a new breath of the spirit, a fidelity to the moral standards which govern the life of man.

So long as scientists proceed with humility in their research into the secrets of nature, the hand of God will lead them towards the peaks of the spirit.

Rome 9.4.79

RELIGION IS FOR MEN   February 13

There was one of the Pharisees called Nicodemus, a leading Jew, who came to Jesus by night.

(John 3:1)

There is a traditional view that religion is a kind of feminine affair, feminine rather than masculine, and somewhat embarrassing for a man.

Men have always tended to feel like Nicodemus, to adopt the religious outlook of Nicodemus. Nicodemus, you remember, was the man, a member of the Sanhedrin, who acknowledged Christ secretly — I wouldn't go so far as to say that he believed in him — he acknowledged him and came to him by night. When no one could see him.

We men are inclined to adopt the religious outlook of Nicodemus. An outlook which, maybe, is characterized only by discretion but very often is characterized by concealment.

It is difficult to get us involved, just like the young man who would be only too willing to take everything that Christ had to offer, but when it came to actually getting involved, drew back.

Cracow 14.4.62

LOVE CONSTRUCTS THIS WORLD   February 14

God is love and anyone who lives in love lives in God and God lives in him.
(1 John 4:16)

Only love constructs this world. *It constructs it with difficulty.* It must struggle to give it shape: it must struggle against the forces of evil, sin, hatred, against the lust of the flesh, against the lust of the eyes and against the pride of life.

40

This struggle is an incessant one. It is as old as the history of man. In our time, this struggle to give shape to our world seems to be greater than ever. More than once we wonder, trembling, if hatred will not get the better of love, war of peace, destruction of construction.

How extraordinary the eloquence of Christ's question to Simon Peter by the lake of Galilee, 'Do you love me?' It is fundamental for one and all of us. It is fundamental for the individual and for society, for the nation and for the State. 'Do you love?'

Only love lasts for ever. Alone, it constructs the shape of eternity in the earthly and short-lived dimensions of the history of man on the earth.

Paris 30.5.80

RESPONDING TO GOD'S LOVE   February 15

Anybody who loves me will be loved by my Father, and I shall love him and show myself to him.

(John 14:21)

There is no one who cannot discover and find a place for himself in God's love. From it flows our Christian optimism, which means hope, hope in relation to man.

There exists no one so bad, so brought down, so broken down, that he cannot find his place in that love, the love of the Father who feeds him, the love of the Son sacrificed for him, the love of the Spirit who enlightens him. *There is no one who cannot find his place in that love.* It is the source of our Christianity, our hope.

But on the other hand, when someone, even someone who cannot comprehend it, receives that love – he receives it because love wants him to receive it. First and foremost, when someone receives this love there must at once be born in him some need to respond. *No one can receive this love unresponsively.* God does not ask that man should match this love – he wants him to receive it, he wants him to receive it with humility, 'Lord, I am not worthy . . .' but God wants man to try to reply to this love, try to respond to the utmost of his human ability.

Cracow 24.3.64

His son said: 'Father, I have sinned against heaven and against you. I no longer deserve to be called your son.'

(Luke 15:21)

God forgives. God wants to forgive. The next question is: what road leads to forgiveness? First and foremost, what road leads to forgiveness by the Lord God himself?

It is obvious that forgiveness is always an act of free will, it is always a manifestation of love. When a child says: 'I'm sorry', to its father, and the father says: 'I forgive you!' and kisses the child on the forehead, this is an expression of love, an expression of free will, the spontaneity of forgiveness which is so natural to love.

But we know quite well that true and meaningful forgiveness, being such an act of love and likewise an act of mercy, must also be in harmony with justice. In a certain sense, it is impossible to forgive 'free of charge', it is impossible to forgive without some down-payment, to absolve without some down-payment. There must be the down-payment. And in the forgiveness which God offers us the down-payment is made by God himself. His love and mercy.

Cracow 22.3.64

CHRISTIAN MORALITY   February 17

If you love me you will keep my commandments.

(John 14:15)

We are fully aware that the Passion of Christ, his Gethsemane, his scourging, his Calvary is an accomplished fact. We cannot now change history, so that Christ would not have to go through his Passion in a factual sense, but we can try to do so in a moral sense. *In the moral sense, we must try to live so that Christ would not have to go to the Cross.*

And at the same time to live so that from the fact that Christ did, indeed, go to the Cross comes everything that is good. Namely, that good ordained by God, undertaken by the Saviour.

And this is our Christian vocation. Such is our relationship to Christ. From this is born our morality. Our Christian morality is not a collection of statutes, formulae, isolated prescriptions, based possibly on some human sanctions. Our morality lives with a more profound life, it lives in our relationship with God-made-Man, with that extra-ordinary Man, whom no one can replace in our consciousness, who is rooted in our consciousness, and who grows there by the strength of our faith. *Our morality lives by our relationship with Christ.* With the Crucified Christ. And this is its special force.

Cracow 22.3.64

THE VOICE OF CONSCIENCE   February 18

I do my best to keep a clear conscience at all times before God and man.
(Acts 24:16)

Every one of us bears it within himself. It is our deepest, most intimate possession − conscience. It gives us total mastery over the world of good and evil. But it also bears with it total servitude.

For conscience is not only a master, it is also a servant. It is the master of our actions, but the servant of the moral order. This moral law, this moral order, has an extremely objective character. And to this order conscience is a servant.

And one must acknowledge that the more it is a master, the more it is a servant. The better it governs the actions of man − and not only of the individual, but of the whole of society − the more keenly it hears, the more profoundly it understands, the moral order.

The more it penetrates into the law of God, the law of nature, the keener is its knowledge of that law and that order, the better and more effectively it governs the actions of man, both on the individual scale and on that of Society.

Cracow 22.3.64

FREEDOM OF CONSCIENCE   February 19

They can call a witness, that is, their own conscience − they have accusation and defence, that is their own inner mental dialogue.
(Rom. 2:15)

What is freedom of conscience? First and foremost, it means that man in society should be able to form a true and trustworthy conscience for himself and proceed according to this conscience.

43

A true and trustworthy conscience is obviously an internal function of every one of us but it also depends on other people. It depends on the whole atmosphere reigning in society, which can warp the conscience. Different environments can influence this warping of the conscience.

It is a great task, and also a fundamental condition of social morality, to produce a true and trustworthy conscience. Every warping of the conscience, every indirect or direct pressure on the conscience, every alienation of the right to act according to one's true, rightful and trustworthy conscience, all this is the most profound outrage against the human person.

This is the fundamental condition of freedom, that the conscience should be true and trustworthy (I am able to direct my actions) and that no one should interfere with me. It is obviously a task for every one of us, every individual, every person, but it is also a task for society.

Cracow 22.3.64

THE QUESTION OF TOLERANCE   February 20

Jesus said to him, 'You must not stop him: anyone who is not against you is for you.'

(Luke 9:50)

There exists also the problem of tolerance. This is also a problem of conscience. For we know that a person can sometimes fall into errors in his beliefs and in his conscience, while being quite convinced that he is in the right.

This is a very profound problem of man's inner life. A problem which the Church respects. From the very beginning, from the writings of the Apostles, we come across clear traces of respect for the conscience which is in error but is at the same time convinced that it is in the right. And in this lies the problem of tolerance.

Cracow 22.3.64

Have mercy on me, O God, in your goodness . . . purify me from my sin.
(Ps. 51:1)

Sin destroys. Sin destroys, first and foremost, one fundamental good: an immanent good, which is part of the fibre of every one of us. *Sin destroys the good which is in men.* The good which is me.

I am not my own property, I did not give myself existence and, in the last analysis, not even my parents gave me existence. God has a fundamental right to me. I am a created being.

As a created being I am in some way penetrated by the ideas of God who creates, who enlarges. And if I cause damage and destruction around myself and to myself, then I am involved in a conflict of ideas with God. I acknowledge ideas different from his.

Cracow 9.4.62

THE CROSS OF MORALITY February 22

Anyone who does not carry his Cross and come after me cannot be my disciple.
(Luke 14:27)

The Christian is a person who takes upon himself the whole burden of morality. For *morality is a burden*. It is also a lever as well as a burden.

The person who wants to stand beside Christ must take upon himself the whole burden of morality. This burden will be his lever. *If we try to get rid of this burden, we are in conflict with Christ.* For then we try to rid ourselves of a Cross, for morality is a Cross.

All that has ever been written about it in all the treatises and essays, in all the novels and plays cannot match the concept that morality is a Cross. Christian morality, morality in general, is a Cross. And man can try to rid himself of his Cross. Man can; but Christ bore his to the end. Therefore sin is a conflict with Christ.

Cracow 10.4.62

Do not be thoughtless but recognise what is the will of the Lord.

(Eph. 5:17)

It is obvious, moreover, that sin involves a conflict of wills. For ideas act through reason. But reason goes hand-in-hand with will.

Since I possess reason, since I am a reasoning being, I possess moral standards, moral principles: 'Do this! Shun that!' Furthermore, God himself defined these principles and moral standards: He said: 'Thou shalt not have strange gods before me, honour thy father and thy mother, thou shalt not kill, thou shalt not commit adultery, thou shalt not steal . . .'

And therefore, I know, I am aware, what is his will. So it is not just a conflict of ideas but a clash of his will and mine. 'I want something different from you!'

Cracow 10.4.62

REPENTANCE   February 24

Have mercy on me, O God, in your goodness, in your tenderness wipe away my faults; wash me clean of my guilt, purify me from my sin.

(Ps. 51(50) 1—2)

So many generations have passed and yet these words have lost nothing of their authenticity and power.

The man who endeavours to live in truth, accepts them as his own. He utters them as if they were his own.

The man who is not able to identify himself with the truth of these words, is a wretch. If he does not scrutinize his conscience in the light of these words — they judge him by themselves. Without him.

Conversion to God is the eternal way to man's liberation. It is the way to find oneself again in the full truth of one's own life and one's own works.

Rome 20.2.80

My hope is in the God who will save me.

(Mic. 7:7)

Lent, as the forty-day period of preparation for Easter, has its precise history in the Church, through which it is inscribed in the history of hearts and human consciences.

As you know, the origin of Lent seems to go back to the fourth century; but already in the second and third centuries – before the fixed period of forty days was established – the faithful prepared for Easter with special fasting and prayers. In this period, public penitents prepared for reconciliation, and catechumens for Baptism.

Lent is a period of repentance, conversion and change of heart, which springs from various reasons, but above all from meditation on the Passion and death of Jesus Christ. Precisely from this meditation there begins that turning of one's glance to the Lord, that 'waiting for the God of salvation', of which the prophet Micah speaks: 'For my part, I look to the Lord, my hope is in the God who will save me; my God will hear me.'

Rome 20.3.80

THE CROSS, SIGN OF REJECTION   February 26

Pilate said, 'Here is the man.' When they saw him the chief priests and the guards shouted, 'Crucify him! crucify him.'

(John 19:6)

The Cross is a visible sign of the rejection of God by man. The living God came amongst his people through Jesus Christ, his eternal Son, who became man: the son of Mary of Nazareth. But 'his own people received him not' (John 1:11).

They held that he must die as one who was leading the people astray. Before Pilate's praetorium they raised the hateful cry: 'Crucify him, crucify him.'

The Cross became the sign of the rejection of the Son of God by his chosen people; the sign of the rejection of God by the world. But at the same time that very Cross became the sign of the acceptance of God by man, by the whole people of God, by the world.

Everyone who accepts God in Christ accepts him through the Cross. The person who has accepted God in Christ expresses it through this sign: he signs himself with the sign of the Cross on the forehead, shoulders and breast, to show and to profess that in the Cross he finds anew his whole self: body and soul, to show and to profess that in this sign he welcomes and embraces Christ and his kingdom.

The Cross became the sign of the rejection of man in Christ. In an extraordinary way the rejection of God and the rejection of man go hand in hand. When it cried 'Crucify him', the crowd in Jerusalem pronounced the death sentence on all this truth about man which was revealed to us by Christ, the Son of God.

And therefore the truth about man's origin and about the goal of his earthly pilgrimage was rejected. The truth about his dignity and about his highest vocation was rejected. The truth about love, which so ennobles and unites people, and about the mercy which raises them up even from the greatest falls was rejected.

Rome 4.4.79

THE LIGHT OF CHRIST February 27

I am the light of the world; anyone who follows me will not be walking in the dark; he will have the light of life.

(John 8:12)

Lent is the time of a special meeting with Christ, who does not cease to speak about himself as 'the light of the world'.

Lent is that blessed time in which each one of us can, in a particular way, pass through the area of light. A powerful light, an intense light comes from the Upper Room, from Gethsemane, from Calvary, and finally from the Sunday of the Resurrection.

It is necessary to cross this area of light so as to find life in oneself again.

Is the light in me? Is life in me? This life that Christ grafted?

Together with the light of faith, Christ grafted in each of us the life of Grace. Is the life of Grace in me? Or has sin, perhaps, prevailed in me?

In the paschal light, *in the light of the Passion and the Cross, sin stands out more clearly.* In the paschal light, in the light of the Resurrection, the way to overcome sin and arrive at expiation, repentance and remission, opens up more clearly. 'Anyone who follows me will have the light of life.'

Rome 20.3.80

48

CONVERSION

'Return to me, and I will return to you,' says the Lord.

(Mal. 3:7)

Let us open ourselves to God, who wishes to open himself to us.

Conversion is not a one-way process. It is an expression of mutual action. We return to God, who is waiting for us. He is waiting to turn, to 'return' to us.

To be converted means to believe in God who loved us first, who loved us eternally in his Son, and who, through his Son, gives us Grace and truth in the Holy Spirit. Therefore that Son was crucified to speak to us with his arms open wide as God is open to us. How incessantly through the Cross of his Son, is God 'converted' to us!

In this way our conversion is not at all a one-sided aspiration. It is not just an effort of man's will, intellect and heart. It is not just the commitment to direct upwards our humanity, which has a heavy downward tendency.

Conversion is above all acceptance. It is the effort to accept God in all the riches of his 'conversion' to man. This conversion is a Grace. The effort of the intellect, of the heart and the will is also indispensable for the acceptance of the Grace. It is indispensable not to lose the divine dimension of life in the human dimension; to persevere in it.

Let us walk towards God, who wishes to come to meet us.

Rome 9.3.79

THE SUMMONS OF LENT

May he give you the power through his Spirit for your hidden self to grow strong.

(Eph. 3:16)

If we feel we are in that unity with Christ, which the very name 'Christian' suggests, we must acknowledge this by making Lent special in our lives.

For this purpose a more abundant measure of prayer than usual is necessary, as well as meditation on the Passion of the Redeemer, and finally commitment in the multiple works of love of one's neighbour, to which our age offers so many opportunities. An age in which millions of adults and children literally die of hunger, while at the same time the cult of luxuries and a surfeit of materialism prevail in other countries and environments.

Let us recall that the Christ of Lent is above all the Christ who is waiting for us in every suffering man, he who stimulates us to love and judges according to what we have done to one of the least of these brothers of ours.

Lent is not only a reminder, but a continual summons. To enter this period and live it in the spirit handed down to us by the most ancient and living tradition of the Church, means: to open one's own conscience. To let Christ himself open it with the word of his Gospel, but above all with the eloquence of his Cross.

Lent is, therefore, an exceptional opportunity to save in each of us 'the inner man' (Eph. 3:16), so often forgotten, who, thanks to the Passion and the Resurrection of Christ, is created 'in true righteousness and holiness' (Eph. 4:24).

Rome 14.3.79

March

THE TOOLS OF LENT

Sell your possessions and give alms. Get yourselves purses that do not wear out, treasure that will not fail you.

(Luke 12:33)

Prayer, almsdeeds and fasting need to be understood more deeply if we want to integrate them thoroughly into our lives and not to consider them just as passing practices which only demand something momentary from us or only momentarily deprive us of something. With this way of thinking we would not arrive at the real meaning and the real power that prayer, fasting and almsdeeds have in the process of conversion to God and spiritual development.

One keeps pace with the other: *we mature spiritually by being converted to God*. Conversion takes place by means of prayer, as also by means of fasting and almsdeeds, adequately understood.

It should perhaps be said at once that it is not momentary 'practices', but constant attitudes that give our conversion to God a lasting form. Lent lasts only forty days a year: but we must always strain towards God: this means that it is necessary to be continually converted.

Lent must leave a strong and lasting mark on our lives. It must renew in us an awareness of our union with Jesus Christ, who makes us see the necessity of conversion and shows us the ways to reach it. And these ways are prayer, fasting and almsdeeds.

Rome 14.3.79

Jesus went out into the hills to pray; and he spent the whole night in prayer to God.

(Luke 6:12)

First, then, the way of prayer. I say 'first' because I wish to speak of it before fasting and almsdeeds. But saying 'first' I want to add today that in the complete work of our conversion, that is, of our spiritual development, prayer is not isolated from the other two ways which the Church defines with the evangelical term of 'fasting and almsdeeds'.

The way of prayer is perhaps more familiar to us. We understand more easily, perhaps, that without it it is impossible to be converted to God, to remain in union with him, in that communion which makes us spiritually mature. There are certainly a great many among you now listening to me who have their own experience of prayer, who know its various aspects, and can make others share it. *We learn to pray, in fact, by praying.*

The Lord Jesus first taught us to pray by his own example: 'he spent the whole night in prayer'; another day, as St. Matthew writes, 'he went up into hills by himself to pray. When evening came, he was there alone' (Matt. 14:23). Before his Passion and death he went to the Mount of Olives and encouraged the Apostles to pray, and he himself knelt down and prayed. During his agony, he prayed more intensely. Only once, when requested by the disciples: 'Lord, teach us to pray' (Luke 11:1), did he give them the simplest and the deepest content of his prayer: the 'Our Father'.

Rome 14.3.79

PRAYER, THROUGH AND IN CHRIST   March 3

We will continue to devote ourselves to prayer and to the service of the word.
(Acts 6:3)

All of us, when we pray are disciples of Christ, not because we repeat the words that he once taught us — sublime words and the complete content of prayer though they are — we are disciples of Christ even when we do not use these words. *We are his disciples only because we pray*; 'Listen to the Master praying; learn to pray. He prayed, in fact, to teach people to pray,' St. Augustine affirms.

And a modern author writes: 'Since the end of the way of prayer is lost in God, and no one knows the way but the One who comes from God, Jesus Christ, it is necessary to fix our eyes on him alone. He is the way, the truth and the life. Only he has travelled along the way in both directions. We must put our hand in his and start out' (Y. Raguin).

To pray means speaking to God. I would venture to say even more: *to pray means finding oneself again in that one eternal Word through which the Father speaks, and which speaks to the Father*. This Word became flesh, so that it would be easier for us to find ourselves again in him, even with our human words of prayer.

Our word may sometimes be very imperfect, sometimes we may even have none at all, but this incapacity of our human words is continually completed in the Word that became flesh in order to speak to the Father with the fullness of that mystical union which all those who pray form with him. In this particular union with the Word lies the greatness of prayer, its dignity and, in some way, its definition.

Rome 14.3.79

THE 'OUR FATHER' March 4

One of his disciples said, 'Lord, teach us to pray.'

(Luke 11:1)

When the disciples asked the Lord Jesus: 'Teach us to pray', he replied with the words of the prayer 'Our Father', thus creating a model that is concrete and at the same time universal.

In fact, all that can and must be said to the Father is contained in those seven requests, which we all know by heart. There is such a simplicity in them that even a child can learn them, and also such a depth that a whole life can be spent meditating on the meaning of each of them. Is this not so? Does not each of them speak to us, one after the other, of what is essential of our existence, directed completely to God, to the Father? Does it not speak to us of our 'daily bread', of 'forgiveness of our trespasses as we also forgive them', and at the same time of 'preservation from temptation' and 'deliverance from evil'.

When, in answer to the request of the disciples, 'Teach us to pray', Christ utters the words of his prayer, he teaches not only the words, but he teaches that in our talk with the Father there must be complete sincerity and full openness.

ALL – EMBRACING PRAYER   March 5

Through him, let us offer God an unending sacrifice of praise.
(Heb. 13:15)

Prayer must embrace everything that is part of our life. It cannot be something additional or marginal. *Everything must find in it its true voice.* Even things that burden us; things of which we are ashamed; things that by their very nature separate us from God. This above all: it is prayer that always, first of all and essentially, demolishes the barrier which sin and evil may have raised between us and God.

Through prayer the whole world must find its proper direction: that is, an orientation towards God: my interior world and also the objective world, the world in which we live, and the world of our experience.

If we are converted to God, everything in us is directed to him. Prayer is the expression of this being directed to God; and it is, at the same time, the source of our continual conversion.

Prayer is the way of the Word which embraces everything. It is the way of the eternal Word which goes to the depths of so many hearts; which brings back to the Father everything that has its origin to him.

Prayer is the sacrifice of our lips. It is, as St. Ignatius of Antioch writes, 'spring water that murmurs within us and says: "Come to the Father."'

Rome 14.3.79

SOLIDARITY WITH CHRIST   March 6

When you fast, put oil on your head and wash your face, so that no one will know you are fasting.
(Matt. 6:16)

Why fasting in Lent? At this moment, there perhaps come into our minds the words with which Jesus answered the disciples of John the

Baptist when they asked him: 'Why do your disciples not fast?' Jesus answered: 'Can the wedding guests mourn as long as the bridegroom is with them? The day will come when the bridegroom is taken away from them, and then they will fast' (Matt. 9:15).

In fact the time of Lent reminds us that the bridegroom has been taken away from us. Taken away, arrested, imprisoned, slapped, scourged, crowned with thorns, crucified . . . *Fasting in the time of Lent is the expression of our solidarity with Christ.* Such was the meaning of Lent throughout the centuries and such it remains today.

'My love has been crucified and there is no longer in me the flame that desires material things,' as the Bishop of Antioch, Ignatius, writes in his letter to the Romans.

Rome 21.3.79

FASTING VERSUS THE CONSUMER ATTITUDE   March 7

The time will come for the bridegroom to be taken away from them, and then they will fast.

(Matt. 9:15)

Why fasting?

It is necessary to give this question a wider and deeper answer, in order to clarify the relationship between fasting and 'metanoia' that is, between fasting and a spiritual change bringing man closer to God. We will try therefore to concentrate not only on the practice of abstention from food or from drink — which is the meaning of 'fasting' in the usual sense — but on the deeper meaning of this practice which, moreover, can and must sometimes be 'replaced' by another one.

Food and drink are indispensable for man: he uses them and must use them, but he may not abuse them in any way. *The tradition of abstention from food and drink is intended to introduce into man's existence not only the necessary balance, but also detachment from what might be defined as a 'consumer attitude'.* The consumer attitude! In our times this attitude has become one of the characteristics of civilization and in particular of Western civilization.

Rome 21.3.79

I turned my face to the Lord God begging for time to pray and to plead with fasting.

(Dan 9:3)

It is now easier for us to understand why Christ the Lord and the Church unite the call to fasting with a call to repentance, that is, with conversion.

To be converted to God it is necessary to discover in ourselves what it is that makes us sensitive to what belongs to God; therefore, *we must explore the spiritual layers of our personality*, and the superior values which speak to our intellect, to our conscience, to our 'heart' (in biblical language). And to open up to our spirituality, to these values, it is necessary to detach oneself from things that only serve the satisfaction of the senses, the consumer spirit.

So in the opening of our human personality to God, fasting — understood both in the traditional way and in the modern way — must go hand in hand with prayer because it is addressed directly to him.

Furthermore, *man discovers that fasting, that is, the mortification of the senses and the mastery of the body, confer on prayer a greater efficacy*. He discovers, in fact, that he is 'different', that he is more 'master of himself', that he has become interiorly free. And he realizes this in as much as conversion and the meeting with God, through prayer, bear fruit in him.

It is clear from these reflections that fasting is not only a vestige of a religious practice of past centuries, but that it is also indispensable for the man of today, for Christians of our time.

Rome 21.3.79

ALMSDEEDS – A THING OF THE PAST?   March 9

To share your bread with the hungry, and shelter the homeless poor, to clothe the man you see to be naked . . . then will your light shine like the dawn.

(Is. 58:7)

Today we do not like to listen to the word 'alms'. We feel that there is something humiliating about it. The word seems to presuppose a social system in which there is injustice and an unequal distribution of goods, a system which should be changed by adequate reforms. And if these reforms were not carried out, the need for radical changes, especially in the sphere of social relations, would then loom up on the horizon.

We find the same conviction in the texts of the Prophets of the Old Testament, on which the liturgy often draws during ,Lent. The Prophets consider this problem at the religious level: there is no true conversion to God, there can be no real religion, without putting right offences and injustices in relations among men, in social life.

Yet .in this context *the Prophets also exhort us to almsdeeds*. They do not even use the word 'alms' which, moreover, is *sedaqah* in Hebrew which means 'justice'. They ask for help for those who are victims of injustice and for the needy: not so much by virtue of mercy, but rather by virtue of the duty of active charity.

Rome 28.3.79

WHAT ARE ALMSDEEDS? March 10

Go and sell everything you own and give the money to the poor, and you will have treasure in heaven.

(Mark 10:21)

The Greek word *eleemosyne* is found in the late books of the Bible and the practice of almsdeeds is a verification of an authentic religious spirit. *Jesus makes almsdeeds a condition of access to his kingdom*, and of real perfection.

What does the word 'alms' mean?

The Greek word *eleemosyne* comes from *éleos*, which means compassion and mercy. *Originally it indicated the attitude of the merciful man and, later, all works of charity for the needy*. This word, transformed, has remained in nearly all European languages; in French: *aimône*; Spanish: *limosna*; Portuguese: *esmola*; German: *almosen*; English: *alms*. Even the Polish expression *jalmuzna* is a transformation of the Greek word.

We must differentiate here the objective meaning of the word from the meaning we give it in our social conscience. As can be seen from what we have already said, we often attribute in our social conscience, a negative meaning to the word. Various circumstances have contributed to this and continue to contribute to it today. But on the contrary, *'alms' in itself, as help for those who need it, as 'letting others share in one's own goods'*, absolutely does not give rise to such negative associations.

57

We may not agree with the person who gives alms, because of the way in which he does it. We may also not be in agreement with the person who stretches out his hand asking for alms, in that he does not try to earn his own living. We may disapprove of the society, the social system, in which almsdeeds are necessary. However, the actual fact of giving help to those who need it, the fact of sharing one's own goods with others, must inspire respect.

Rome 28.3.79

HELP FOR THE NEEDY   March 11

You have the poor with you always, you will not always have me.

(John 12:8)

When the Lord Jesus speaks of alms, when he asks for almsdeeds to be practised, he always does so in the sense of bringing help to those who need it and sharing one's own goods with the needy. This does not permit us to doubt the value of the act we call 'almsdeeds', but, on the contrary, urges us to approve it as a good act, as an expression of love for one's neighbours and as a salvific act.

Moreover, at a moment of particular importance, Christ utters these significant words: 'You have the poor with you always.' He does not mean by these words that changes in social and economic structures are not important and that we should not try to eliminate injustice, humiliation, want and hunger. He merely means that man will always have needs which cannot be satisfied except by help for the needy and by sharing one's own goods with others.

Rome 28.3.79

DECISIVE FOR CONVERSION   March 12

For I was hungry and you gave me food; I was thirsty and you gave me drink.

(Matt. 25:35)

'Alms' understood in this way has a meaning which is, in a certain sense, decisive for this conversion. To convince ourselves of this, is it enough to recall the image of the Last Judgement that Christ gave us:
'For I was hungry and you gave me food. I was thirsty and you gave

me drink. I was a stranger and you made me welcome, naked and you clothed me, sick and you visited me, in prison and you came to me. Then the virtuous will say to him: "Lord, when did we see you hungry and feed you, or thirsty and give you drink? When did we see you a stranger and make you welcome, naked and clothe you? Sick or in prison and visit you?" And the king will answer them: "I tell you solemnly in so far as you did it to one of the least of these my brethren, you did it to me"' (Matt. 25:35–40).

And the Fathers of the Church will then say with St. Peter Chrysologus: 'The poor man's hand is the treasury of Christ, since Christ received everything that the poor man receives,' and with St. Gregory of Nazianzus: 'The Lord of all things wants mercy, not sacrifice; and we give it through the poor.'

Therefore, in this opening to others, which is expressed by 'help', by sharing food, a glass of water, a good word, consolation, a visit, etc., in this interior gift offered to others, we are opening ourselves to Christ and to God. It is a direct meeting with him. It is conversion.

Rome 28.3.79

OPENING TOWARDS OTHERS   March 13

Give alms from what you have and then indeed everything will be clean for you.

(Luke 11:41)

We are touching the heart of the problem here. In Holy Scripture and according to evangelical categories, *'alms' means in the first place an interior gift*. It means the attitude of opening 'to the other'. Along with prayer and fasting, this attitude is an indispensable element of 'metanoia', that is, of conversion. ·

St. Augustine expressed this very well. 'How quickly the prayers of those who do good are granted! And this is man's justice in the present life: fasting, alms, prayer', prayer, as opening to God; fasting, as an expression of self-mastery through depriving oneself of something, by saying 'no' to oneself: and finally *alms, as opening 'towards others'*.

The Gospel draws this picture clearly when it speaks to us of repentance, of 'metanoia'. Only with a total attitude in his relationship with God, with himself and with his neighbour — does man reach conversion and remain in the state of conversion.

Rome 28.3.79

I tell you truly, this poor widow has put in more than any of them; . . . she has put in all she had to live on.

(Luke 21:3–4)

What sort of help are we speaking about? What do we mean exactly by sharing? Is it a question of 'alms', understood in the form of money, of material aid?

Certainly, Christ does not remove alms from our field of vision. He also thinks of pecuniary, material alms, but in his own way. The most eloquent expression of this is the example of the poor widow, who put a few small coins into the treasury of the temple: from the material point of view, an offering that could hardly be compared with the offerings given by others. Yet Christ said: 'This poor widow has put in . . . all she had to live on.' *So it is, above all, the interior value of the gift that counts: the readiness to share everything, the readiness to give oneself.*

Let us here recall St. Paul: 'If I give away all I have . . . but have not love, I gain nothing' (1 Cor. 13:3). St. Augustine, too, writes well in this connection: 'If you stretch out your hand to give, but have not mercy in your heart, you have not done anything; but if you have mercy in your heart, even when you have nothing to give with your hand, God accepts your alms.'

Rome 28.3.79

ALMS – GIVING THE MEASURE OF PERFECTION   March 15

Sell your possessions and give alms.

(Luke 12:33)

We can find many texts in the Gospel and in the whole of Scripture, that confirm this. 'Alms', understood according to the Gospel, according to the teaching of Christ, has a definitive, decisive meaning in our conversion to God. *If alms are lacking, our life does not yet converge fully towards God.*

Before concluding, let us dwell for another moment on the real meaning of 'alms'. It is very easy, in fact, to misunderstand the idea, as we noted at the beginning. Jesus also gave a warning about the danger of almsdeeds becoming a purely exterior attitude. This problem is still a living one. If we realize the essential significance that 'alms' has for our conversion to God in the whole of the Christian life, we must avoid, at all costs, all that falsifies the meaning of alms, mercy and words of charity, all that may distort their image in ourselves.

So it is very important to cultivate an awareness of the real needs of our neighbour, in order to know how we can help him, how to act in order not to wound him, and how to behave in order that what we give, what we bring to his life, may be a real gift, a gift not dimmed by the usual negative meaning of the word 'alms'.

We see, therefore, what a field of work — wide and at the same time deep — opens before us, if we want to put into practice the call, 'Sell your possessions and give alms.' It is a task not only for Lent, but for every day. For the whole of one's life.

Rome 28.3.79

THE PARABLE OF THE PRODIGAL SON – THE GOING AWAY
March 16

The younger son got together everything he had and left for a distant country.

(Luke 15:13)

By means of the parable of the Prodigal Son, the Lord Jesus wished to impress deeply this splendid and very rich truth not only upon our intellect, and our imagination but also in our heart and in our conscience. How many men in the course of the centuries, and how many of our time, *can find in this parable the fundamental features of their own personal history.*

There are three key phases in the story of the Prodigal Son. The first phase: going away. We go away from God, as that son went away from his father, when we begin to behave with regard to every good that is in us in the same way as he did with the goods he had received as his inheritance. We forget that good is given to us by God as a task, as an evangelical talent. Operating with it, we must multiply our inheritance, and, in this way, render glory to him from whom we received it.

Unfortunately, we sometimes behave as if that good which is in us, the good of the soul and of the body, capacities, faculties, strength, were exclusively our property, which we can use and abuse in any way, wasting and dissipating it.

Sin, in fact, is always a squandering of our humanity, a squandering of

61

our most precious values. Such is the actual reality, even if it may sometimes seem that sin enables us to obtain success. Going away from the Father always brings with it great destruction.

Rome 16.3.80

THE PRODIGAL SON – RETURN TO REASON   March 17

Then he came to his senses and said, . . . I will leave this place and go to my father.

(Luke 15: 17–18)

The second phase in our parable is that of the return to sound reason and the process of conversion. *Man must discover painfully what he has lost*, what he has deprived himself of by committing sin, living in sin, in order that the decisive step may mature in him: 'I will go to my father.'

He must see again the face of that Father, upon whom he had turned his back and with whom he had broken off relations in order to be able to sin 'freely', to be able to waste 'freely' the goods he had received. *He must come face to face with the Father*, realizing, like the young man in the parable, that he has lost the dignity of a son, that he does not deserve a welcome in his father's house.

At the same time he must long to return. The certainty of the goodness and love that belong to the essence of God's fatherhood, must outweigh in him awareness of his guilt and his own unworthiness. In fact, this certainty must appear as the only way out, to be undertaken with courage and confidence.

Rome 16.3.80

THE PRODIGAL SON – THE RETURN HOME   March 18

Father, I have sinned against heaven and against you. I no longer deserve to be called your son.

(Luke 15:21)

Finally the third phase: return. The return will take place as Christ describes in the parable. The Father of the Prodigal Son, is waiting and forgets all the wrongs committed by his son, and no longer considers all the waste of which his son is guilty.

For the Father only one thing is important: that his son has been found again; that he has not completely lost his humanity; that, in spite of everything, he has the firm resolve to live again as a son, precisely because of his awareness of his unworthiness and sin. 'Father, I have sinned, I no longer deserve to be called your Son.'

Our reconciliation with God, the return to the Father's house, is carried out by means of Christ. His Passion and death on the Cross are set between every human conscience, every human sin, and the infinite Love of the Father. *This love — ready to raise and forgive, is nothing but mercy.*

Each of us, in personal conversion, in the firm resolution to change our ways, agrees to carry out a personal spiritual labour, which is the prolongation and reflection on the saving work of our Redeemer. Here is what Paul, the Apostle of reconciliation, says: 'For our sake God made the sinless one into sin, so that in him we might become the goodness of God' (2 Cor. 5:21).

So let us undertake this effort of conversion and repentance of ours through him, with him and in him. If we do not undertake it, we are not worthy of Christ's name, we are not worthy of the inheritance of redemption.

Rome 16.3.80

THE INTERIOR DIGNITY OF MAN   March 19

Out of his infinite glory, may he give you the power through his Spirit for your hidden self to grow strong.

(Eph. 3: 16)

The first and principal meaning of penitence is interior, spiritual. The principal effort of penitence consists 'in entering oneself', one's deepest being, entering this dimension of one's own humanity in which, in a certain sense, God is waiting for us.

The exterior man must, I think, yield, in each of us, to the interior man and, somehow, 'make way for him'. *These days, man does not live enough on the interior plane.* Jesus Christ clearly indicates that even acts of devotion and penitence (such as fasting, charity, prayer) which because of their religious purpose are mainly interior, may yield to the current exteriorism, and can therefore be falsified.

Penitence, on the contrary, as turning to God, requires above all that man should reject appearances, succeed in freeing himself from falsehood, and find himself again in all his interior truth. *Even a rapid, summary look into the divine splendour of man's interior truth is an achievement in itself.*

It is necessary, however, to consolidate this success skilfully by means of systematic work on oneself. This work is called 'ascesis' (a name given by the Greeks about the time of the beginning of Christianity). Ascesis means an interior effort not to let oneself be swept along and pushed by the different exterior currents, in such a way as to remain always oneself and keep the dignity of one's own humanity.

Rome 28.2.79

PREPARING FOR EASTER JOY   March 20

Your endurance will win you your lives.

(Luke 21:19)

The main current of Lent must flow through the interior man, through hearts and consciences. The essential effort of repentance consists in this. In this effort the human determination to be converted to God is invested with the predisposing grace of conversion and, at the same time, of forgiveness and of spiritual liberation.

Penance is not just an effort, a weight, but it is also a joy. Sometimes it is a great joy of the human spirit, a delight that other sources cannot bring forth.

Contemporary man seems to have lost, to some extent, the flavour of this joy. He has also lost the deep sense of that spiritual effort which makes it possible to find oneself again in the whole truth of one's interior being. Many causes and circumstances, contribute to this. Our civilization — especially in the West — closely connected as it is with the development of science and technology, catches a glimpse of the need for intellectual and physical effort. But it has lost to a considerable extent the sense of the effort of the spirit, the fruit of which is man seen in his inner self.

The whole period of Lent is — since it is a preparation for Easter — a systematic call to this joy that comes from the effort of patiently finding oneself again. Let no one be afraid to undertake this effort.

Rome 28.2.79

You cannot belong to Christ Jesus unless you crucify all self-indulgent passions and desires.

(Gal. 5:24)

The temperate person we say is one who does not abuse food, drinks, pleasures, who does not drink alcohol to excess, who does not deprive himself of consciousness by the use of drugs, etc. This reference to elements external to man has its basis, however, within man.

It is as if there existed in each of us a 'higher self' and a 'lower self'. In our 'lower self', our body and everything that belongs to it is expressed: its needs, its desires, its passions of a sensual nature particularly. The virtue of temperance guarantees every man mastery of the 'lower self' by the 'higher self'.

Is this a humiliation of our body? Or a disability? On the contrary, this mastery gives higher value to the body. It is as a result of the virtue of temperance that our whole body and our senses can properly serve our human condition.

A temperate man is one who is master of himself, one in whom passions do not prevail over reason, will, and even the heart. A man who can control himself. If this is so, we can easily realize how fundamental the virtue of temperance is. If a man is to be fully a man it is downright indispensable.

Look at someone who is carried away by his passions and becomes a victim of them, for example, an alcoholic, a drug addict; of his own accord he gives up the use of reason. *'To be a man' means respecting one's own dignity*, and therefore, among other things, letting oneself be guided by the virtue of temperance.

Rome 22.11.78

TRUE BEAUTY COMES FROM WITHIN   March 22

You who are like whitewashed tombs that look handsome on the outside, but inside are full of dead men's bones.

(Matt. 23:27)

I think, too, that the virtue of temperance demands from each of us a specific humility with regard to the gifts that God has put in our human nature. I would distinguish between the humility of the body and that of the heart. This humility is a necessary condition for man's interior harmony: for man's interior beauty.

Let everyone think it over carefully; and in particular young men, and even more young women, at the age when one is so anxious to be handsome or beautiful in order to please others! *Let us remember that it is the interior man who must above all be beautiful.* Without this beauty, all efforts aimed at the body alone will not make — either him or her — a really beautiful person.

Isn't it more than just the body that often undergoes considerable damage to health, if man lacks the virtue of temperance, of sobriety? In this connection, the statistics and files of hospitals all over the world could say a great deal.

Doctors who work on the advisory bureaux to which married and engaged couples, and young people apply have great experience of this. It is true that we cannot judge virtue on the exclusive basis of the criterion of psychophysical health; there are many proofs, however, that the lack of the virtue of temperance or sobriety damages health.

Rome 22.11.78

MEETING GOD IN THE TRUTH

March 23

True worshippers will worship the Father in spirit and truth.

(John 4:23)

Man meets God through the truth. The true worshippers of God are those who worship him in spirit and truth, as the Lord Jesus said to the Samaritan woman. Like any other period of the year, Lent presents before the eyes of our spirit the magnitude and importance of these words of Christ.

At this time, therefore, we contemplate in a special way the fact that the Son of God, by his Passion and death, confirmed the truth of his words.

Man meets God through the truth and turns away from him through untruth. We call untruth a lie when it is expressed in words; we call it deceit when it goes still deeper into man's inner life. 'The Father of lies' is the name which Holy Writ gives to the evil spirit who constantly turns away from God and does not know how to meet him in truth. And from the beginning, this spirit has tried to influence man in the same direction.

But man can meet with God 'in spirit and truth'. *On truth, too, rests man's true freedom*. Hence the Lord Jesus said: 'You will learn the truth and the truth will make you free' (John 8:32). Only the man who follows the truth is truly free.

Cracow 24.2.70

THE LIGHT OF CONSCIENCE March 24

If your eye is sound, your whole body will be filled with light.
(Matt. 6:22)

The words of the Lord Jesus Christ guide man to God, by means of his own conscience. *Conscience in man is like an inner source of light* and an organ of sight. The Lord Jesus compares it to the sense of sight, saying: 'If your eye is diseased, your whole body will be in darkness.'

According to Christ's words, we must be very attentive to the promptings of our conscience, for on this depends the inner truth of every man. *Conscience first and foremost determines whether or not man lives in truth*. Conscience like man's intellect is also fallible; it can sometimes make a mistake without knowing that it has done so. A man who is guided by such a conscience does not commit a sin.

Cracow 24.2.70

ERROR OF CONSCIENCE March 25

If the light inside you is darkness, what darkness that will be.
(Matt. 6:23)

An error of conscience is one thing and negligence of the truth is quite another. In this area we must be very strict with ourselves. For on occasion we take for the voice of conscience a temporary mood of the state of our feelings.

We consider that something is in accordance with our conscience if it matches up with those feelings. We do not take into account that moods, feelings and passions may in fact be blocking the voice of conscience, preventing it from getting through to our souls. We lose detachment from our own actions and allow something evil to occur, saying, 'This is the dictate of my conscience.' But this is not true. The voice of conscience could not make itself heard.

Cracow 24.2.70

THE STRENGTH OF CONSCIENCE   March 26

All the truth about us will be brought out in the law court of Christ.
(2 Cor. 5:10)

The season of Lent is meant to allow conscience to make its voice heard more effectively in each of us. *Jesus Christ stands beside every one in whom conscience begins to make itself heard*, he desires and intends to help him regardless of how far the voice of conscience will accuse him. For he is the true Saviour of souls. He has the power to put man right with God. Conscience, however, must do its work, for *man can meet God only and exclusively through the truth.*

Cracow 24.2.70

THE SCOURGING OF CHRIST   March 27

He ordered Jesus to be first scourged and then handed over to be crucified.
(Matt. 27:26)

Historians and biblical scholars have tried to reconstruct the detail of this appalling laceration of body and spirit, from other sources. The scourging is the subject of much devotion in Poland, where many hymns written around it are sung in the course of the special Lenten liturgy of compassion for the Lord, known in Polish as 'The repentance of grief'.

'0, my Jesus, how cruelly you were bound to the pillar; scourged for our great faults . . .' And then in the second part: 'For my wickedness the Lord's back is being scourged. Come, you sinners, see — for you is being prepared in the blood of Jesus, a spring of living water to quench the heart's thirst.'

Then in the third part of the liturgy, as though it were a lamentation by Our Lady of Sorrows, Polish devotion has her say: 'Ah, I see my son, stripped naked against the pillar, scourged with whips . . .' The simple words and the gentle melodies, both dating from the eighteenth century, express very poignantly the sentiments in the hearts of the faithful.

The dominant feature of this devotion is its awareness of the close link between that atrocious torture inflicted on Christ's body and mankind's sins of the flesh. The potency of the mystery of the scourging seen in that light is truly remarkable. For many people the scourging of the Lord became the decisive reason for their determination to break the bonds of sin, the reason for mortifying the concupiscence of the flesh, for turning their desires towards the noble and the holy.

'I treat my body hard and make it obey me' (1 Cor. 9: 27) wrote St. Paul, and many others have said the same thing and stressed it by their behaviour.

S. of C.

PILATE'S VERDICT   March 28

Pilate said: 'Take him yourselves and crucify him; I can find no case against him.'

(John 19:6)

Pilate's verdict was pronounced under pressure from the priests and the crowd. The sentence of death by crucifixion was meant to calm their fury and meet their clamorous demand of 'Crucify him! Crucify him!' The Roman procurator thought he could dissociate himself from the sentence by washing his hands, just as he had evaded what had been said by Christ — who identified his kingdom with the truth, with witness to the truth (John 18:37).

In both instances, Pilate was trying to preserve his own independence, to remain somehow 'not involved'. So it may have seemed to him, on the surface. But the Cross to which Jesus of Nazareth was condemned, like the truth he told about his kingdom, was to strike deep into the Roman procurator's soul. All this was a reality in the face of which one cannot remain uninvolved, on the side-lines.

When Jesus, the Son of God, was interrogated about his kingdom and, because of his kingdom, was judged guilty by men and condemned to death, his final testimony began: he was about to demonstrate that 'God loved the world so much . . . .'. We have this testimony before us, and we know that we are not allowed to wash our hands of it.

S. of C.

They then took charge of Jesus, and carrying his own cross he went out of the city.

(John 19:17)

The execution, the implementation of the sentence, is beginning. Christ condemned to death must be burdened with the Cross just like two other men who are to undergo the same punishment: 'he was numbered among the malefactors' (Is. 53: 12).

Christ draws near to the Cross, his body atrociously bruised and lacerated, blood trickling down his face from his head crowned with thorns. *Ecce homo!* In him there is all the truth foretold by the prophets about the Son of man, the truth predicted by Isaiah about the servant of Yahweh: 'He was pierced through for our faults . . . through his wounds we are healed' (Is. 53:5).

And in him there is also an amazing sequel: here is what man has done to his God. Pilate says *'Ecce homo!'* 'Look what you have done to this man!' But there seems to be another voice speaking as well, a voice that seems to be saying: 'Look what you have done, in this man, to your God!'

It is very moving, this voice we can hear from centuries away in the background of what comes to us through knowledge of the faith. *Ecce homo!* Jesus 'called the Messiah' takes the Cross on his shoulders. The execution has begun.

S. of C.

CHRIST ACCEPTED INSULTS   March 30

Do you think that I cannot appeal to my Father who would promptly send more than twelve legions of angels?

(Matt. 26:53)

Jesus falls under the weight of the Cross. He falls to the ground. *He does not resort to superhuman force*, nor does he resort to the power of the angels. He does not ask for that. Having accepted the cup from his Father's hands, he is resolved to drink it to the end. He wills it no other way. And so he has no thoughts of any superhuman force, although such forces are at his disposal.

People who have seen him when he exercised power over human infirmities, crippling diseases and even death may well, in their grief, be wondering 'What now? Is he repudiating all that?' 'We had hoped', the Emmaus disciples were to say a few days later (cf Luke 24:21); 'If you are the Son of God . . .' the members of the Sanhedrin were to fling to him; 'He saved others but he cannot save himself' the crowd was to yell.

And he accepts these provocations, which seem to undermine the whole meaning of his mission, his teaching, his miracles. He accepts them all, for he is determined not to combat them. *To be insulted is what he wills*. To stagger and fall under the weight of the Cross is what he wills. He wills it all. To the end, down to the very last detail, he is true to his undertaking: 'Not my will but yours be done.'

S. of C.

MARY UNITED WITH HER SON   March 31

Simeon blessed them and said to Mary . . . a sword will pierce your own soul.

(Luke 2:35)

Mary greets her son along the way of the Cross. His Cross becomes her cross, his humiliation is her humiliation, the public scorn is on her shoulders. This is the way of the world. This is how it must seem to the people around, and this is how her heart reacts: 'A sword will pierce your own soul.' The words spoken when Jesus was forty days old are now coming true. They are reaching complete fulfilment.

And so, pierced by that invisible sword, Mary moves towards her son's Calvary, her own Calvary. Christian devotion sees her with this sword through her heart, and depicts and sculptures her thus. Mother of sorrows!

'You who shared his suffering!' say the faithful, with an inner awareness that the mystery of this suffering can be expressed in no other way. Although the pain is proper to her, striking deep into her maternal heart, the full truth of this suffering can be expressed only in terms of shared suffering – 'com-passion'. That word is part of the mystery; it expressed unity with the suffering of the Son.

S. of C.

April

SIMON CARRIES THE CROSS

They seized on a man, Simon from Cyrene, and made him shoulder the Cross.

(Luke 23:26)

Simon of Cyrene, called upon to carry the Cross, doubtless had no wish to do so. He was forced to. He made his way alongside Christ, bearing the weight himself. When the condemned man's shoulders became too weak, he lent him his.

He moved along very close to Jesus, closer than Mary, closer than John who – though he too was a man – was not called upon to help. They called on him, Simon of Cyrene, father of Alexander and Rufus. They summoned him, they compelled him.

How long did he go on resenting being forced into this? How long did he go on walking beside this condemned man yet making it clear that he had nothing in common with him, nothing to do with his crime, nothing to do with his punishment? How long did he go on like that, divided within himself, a barrier of indifference getting between him and the man who was suffering? 'I was naked, I was thirsty, I was in prison' (Cf Matt. 25, 35–36). I have carried the Cross . . . and: Did you carry it with me? . . . Did you really carry it with me right to the end?

We do not know. St. Mark simply records the names of the Cyrenian's sons, and tradition has it that they were members of the Christian community close to St. Peter (cf Rom. 16:13).

S. of C.

73

Here am I, now more worm than man, scorn of mankind, jest of the people.
(Ps. 22:6)

The words of the Psalmist-prophet come wholly true in these steep, narrow little streets of Jerusalem in the last hours before the Passover. And we know that those hours before the feast are unnerving, with the streets teeming with people.

This is the context in which the words of the Psalmist are coming true, even though nobody gives this a thought. Certainly it passes unnoticed by those who are displaying their scorn, people for whom this Jesus of Nazareth has become a laughing-stock.

And he wills all this, he wills fulfilment of the prophecy. So he falls, exhausted by all the effort. He falls in accordance with the will of the Father, a will expressed in the words of the prophet. He falls in accordance with his own will, so that the Scriptures may be fulfilled. 'I am a worm, not a man.' So, not even '*Ecce homo*' but something much less, much worse.

A worm creeps and crawls along the ground whereas man, the king among creatures, strides high above it. A worm will gnaw even at wood: like a worm, remorse for sin gnaws at the human conscience.

S. of C.

THE WOMEN WEEP FOR JESUS April 3

Daughters of Jerusalem, do not weep for me; weep rather for yourselves and for your children.

(Luke 23:28)

Here is the call to repentance, true repentance, sorrow, in the truth of the evil that has been committed. One cannot merely scrape away at the surface of evil; one has to get down to its roots, its causes, the inner truth of the conscience.

This is the meaning of the Jesus who carried the Cross, who always 'knew what is in man' and always does know. This is why he must always be for us the nearest onlooker of all, the one who sees all our actions and is aware of all the verdicts passed on them by our consciences.

Perhaps he even makes us understand that these verdicts have to be carefully thought out, reasonable, objective (for he says: 'Do not weep') but at the same time bound up with all that this truth contains; he warns us of this because he is the one who carries the Cross.

Lord, let me know how to live and walk in the truth!

S. of C.

THE TRADITIONAL STORY OF VERONICA   April 4

I tell you solemnly, in so far as you did this to one of the least of these brothers of mine, you did it to me.

(Matt. 26:40)

Tradition has bequeathed us Veronica. Perhaps she is a counterpart to the story of the man from Cyrene. For although, being a woman, she could not physically carry the Cross or be called upon to do so, there is no doubt that she did in fact carry the Cross with Jesus: she carried it in the only way open to her at the time, in obedience to the dictates of her heart: she wiped his face.

Tradition has it that an imprint of Christ's features remained on the handkerchief she used. This detail seems fairly easily explainable: because the handkerchief was impregnated with blood and sweat, traces and outlines of this remain.

Yet a different significance can be attributed to this detail if it is considered in the light of Christ's eschatological discourse. There will undoubtedly be many who will ask: 'Lord, when did we ever do these things for you?' And Jesus will reply: 'Whatever you did for the least of these brothers of mine, you did for me.' In fact *the Saviour leaves his imprint on every single act of charity*, as on Veronica's handkerchief.

S. of C.

CHRIST IS STRIPPED ON CALVARY   April 5

They shared out his clothing, casting lots to decide what each should get.

(Mark 15:24)

When Jesus is stripped of his clothes at Golgotha our thoughts turn once again to his mother: they go back in time to the first days of this body which now, even before the crucifixion, is one mass of wounds. The mystery of the Incarnation: the Son of God derives his body from

75

the Virgin's womb. The Son of God speaks to the Father in the words of the Psalmist: 'You wanted neither sacrifices nor burnt offerings . . . but you have shaped a body for me' (Ps. 40).

The man's body expressed his soul. Christ's body expressed his love for the Father: 'Then I said: See, I come . . . to do your will, O God' (Ps. 40). With every wound, every spasm of pain, every wrenched muscle, every trickle of blood, with all the exhaustion in its arms, all the bruises and lacerations on its back and shoulders, this unclothed body is carrying out the will of both Father and Son.

It carries out the Father's will when it is stripped naked and subjected to torture, when it takes unto itself the immeasurable pain of humanity defiled and profaned. Men's bodies are defiled and profaned in a number of ways.

At this point we must think of the Mother of Christ, because in her womb, before her eyes and at her hands the body of the Son of God was adored to the full.

S. of C.

JESUS IS NAILED TO THE CROSS   April 6

They tie me hand and foot . . . I can count every one of my bones.
(Ps. 22:16)

'I can count . . .' how prophetic those words turned out to be! And yet we know that this body is a ransom. The whole of this body, hands, feet and every bone, is a priceless ransom. The whole of this man is in a state of utmost tension: bones, muscles, nerves, every organ, every cell is stretched and strained to breaking-point.

'When I am lifted up from the earth, I will draw all men to myself' (John 12:32). Therein lies the full reality of the crucifixion. And part of this reality is the terrible tension driving its way into hands, feet and every bone: driving its way into his entire body which, nailed like a mere thing to the beams of the Cross, is about to be utterly 'voided' in the convulsive agony of death. And the whole of the world which Jesus wills to draw to himself comes into the reality of the Cross. The world is dependent on the gravitation of this body, which inertia is causing to sink lower and lower.

The Passion of Christ crucified resides in this gravitation. 'You are from below, I am from above' (John 8:23).

S. of C.

They found that the stone had been rolled away from the tomb, but on entering discovered that the body of the Lord Jesus was not there.

(Luke 24:2)

So they returned to the Upper Room, waiting for the further development of events. If the evangelist John, who took part actively in all this, writes that they were there while the doors were closed for fear of the Jews, this means that fear, in the course of that day, was stronger in them than other feelings.

They did not expect anything good from the fact that the tomb was empty; rather they expected more trouble, vexations, from the representatives of the Jewish authorities. This was a mere human fear, caused by the immediate threat.

However, underlying this immediate fear for their own sake, there was a deeper fear, brought about by the events in the preceding days. This fear, which started on Thursday night, had reached its climax in the course of Good Friday, and, after the Deposition of Jesus, it continued to exist, paralysing all initiatives. It was the fear that sprang from Christ's death.

In fact, once when they were questioned by him: 'Who do people say the Son of Man is?' (Matt. 16:13), they had reported various rumours and opinions about Christ; and then, when questioned directly: 'But who do you say I am?' they had heard and accepted in silence, as their own, the words of Simon Peter: 'You are the Christ, the Son of the living God.'

The Son of the living God, therefore, had died on the Cross. The fear that had taken possession of the hearts of the Apostles, had its deepest roots in this death: *it was the fear born, so to speak from the death of God.*

Turin 13.4.80

THE EMPTY TOMB   April 8

When Mary of Magdala came to the tomb, she saw that the stone had been moved away from the tomb.

(John 20:1)

Beneath the weight of the stone at the tomb, behind its massive barrier, in the silence of the tomb, the process of death takes place:

that is to say, the human being taken from the dust of the earth slowly turns to dust.

The stone, put there on the evening of Good Friday, before the tomb of Jesus, had become, like all tombstones, the silent witness to the death of the Man, the Son of Man.

To what does this stone bear witness on the day after the sabbath, during the first hours of daybreak? What does it say? What does the stone taken away from the tomb proclaim?

In the Gospel there is no ready human answer which is adequate. It does not appear on the lips of Mary of Magdala. When the woman, frightened by the absence of Jesus' body in the tomb, runs to tell Simon Peter and the other disciple, the one whom Jesus loved, her human language finds only these words to explain what has happened:

'They have taken the Lord out of the tomb, and we do not know where they have laid him.'

Simon Peter and the other disciple also hastened to the tomb, and Peter, entering it, saw the cloths lying on the ground, and the piece of cloth that had been put on Jesus' head set in a place by itself.

Then the other disciple entered too, and he saw and believed; 'for as yet they did not understand the Scripture, that he must rise from the dead' (John 20:9). They saw and they realized that men had not been able to conquer Jesus with the tombstone, sealing it with the seal of death.

Rome 6.4.80

THE JOY OF THE RESURRECTION   April 9

The disciples were filled with joy, when they saw the Lord.

(John 20:20)

So he is alive! The empty tomb had no other meaning but that he had risen again, as he had foretold.

He is alive – in his own body. After greeting them, in fact, 'he showed them his hands and his side.' Why? Certainly because there had remained the signs of the crucifixion. It is, therefore, the same Christ that was crucified and died on the Cross – and now he is alive. It is the Risen Christ.

'The disciples were filled with joy.' It does not speak directly of the depth and the power of the joy in which the witnesses of the Risen Christ have become participants — but it lets us divine it. If their fear had its deepest roots in the fact of the death of the Son of God — then the joy of the meeting with the Risen Christ must have been in proportion to that fear. It must have been greater than fear. *This joy was all the greater, the more difficult it was to accept, on the human plane.* How difficult it was, is testified by the subsequent behaviour of Thomas, who 'was not with them when Jesus came' (John 20:24).

It is hard to describe this joy. And it is hard to measure it with the yardstick of human psychology. It is simple, with all the simplicity of the Gospel — and, at the same time, it is deep with its whole depth.

Turin 13.4.80

RESURRECTION; A NEW LIFE   April 10

God proved this by raising this man from the dead.

(Acts 17:31)

Does this mean that he returned to that life which he had had before?

We know that the one who rose from the dead was the same one. It was not difficult for the holy women, the Apostles, the disciples to identify him. Even doubting Thomas was finally convinced when he had seen, when he had touched him. *The one who rose from the dead was the same one.* But he was not just the same.

Resurrection means a new life, a new body. Resurrection means, as it were, a new creation, a new birth. Christ, who went to his death as our Brother — Christ spoke, the closer he was to death, about the prospect of being glorified. 'Now has the Son of Man been glorified' (John 13:31).

Resurrection is not just a return to life, to life as it was before, which belonged to the past. Resurrection is the future, the beginning of the future, a new life, a new body, a new creation, and, above all, being glorified.

Cracow 26.3.78

Come, you whom my Father has blessed, take for your heritage the kingdom prepared for you.

(Matt. 26:34)

Nine hundred years have passed since the death of St. Stanislaus at the hands of King Boleslaw the Bold at Skalka. The death of the bishop who proclaimed to everyone – not excluding the king – the truth of the faith and of Christian morality is significant as a special witness to the Gospel and to Christ himself.

Because of the way he died, Church tradition has included Stanislaus of Szczepanow among the martyrs. The martyr Bishop of the second century of Christianity in Poland, blood of the blood and bone of the bone of the nation, is linked in our early history with another martyr bishop, one who belonged to the first missionary generation and the time of the nation's baptism – St. Wojciech (Adalbert), who was of Czech origin. I mention him because, in the memory of the People of God on Polish soil, these two figures are linked together and surrounded by a special veneration and devotion.

Stanislaus of Szczepanow was bishop of Cracow and a member of the Polish episcopate at the time of his death, and therefore the present Polish episcopate has particular reasons for surrounding this figure with special veneration, especially at the anniversary of his martyrdom.

As Bishop and pastor of the See of Cracow, St. Stanislaus was one of the pillars of that hierarchical order which was established in the lands of the Piasts from the year 1000, instituted during the Congress of Gniezno upon the solid foundations of the apostolic mission of St. Wojciech and his martyrdom.

Rome 5.6.79

GOD RAISES MAN UP   April 12

He was humbler yet, even to accepting death, death on a cross. But God raised him high.

(Phil. 2:9)

There is no other exaltation for man but in God, and *only through God can man be exalted*. Through his work, through his toil, man becomes, as it were, constrained to the reality which is the earth, which is matter; to this reality man becomes subjected. He bows his back, he tenses his shoulders, he bears that toil, the toil of work. If that were all there were for him, life would be completely degraded.

And precisely for that reason, the Son of God, the man, Jesus Christ, became obedient unto death, even unto the death of the Cross so that man might be exalted in God, so that man might bear his exaltation in God with him everywhere.

Even in the great factories, he will bear his exaltation where sweat must flow from his brow, where he is degraded by the toil of that work, and the resistance of matter, where he is sometimes battered down, exhausted to his last gasp. So man, wherever he bears the toil of his degradation, may also carry the imprint of his exaltation in God, for he is a son of God.

Cracow 17.9.76

GLORY, MAN'S DESTINY   April 13

Now has the Son of Man been glorified, and in him God has been glorified.
(John 13:31)

God, who is the Creator of the world, the Creator of life, is at the same time the Father of eternal glory. And he, existing in the fullness of glory, *desires that glory for his creation*, which he called into being in his own image and likeness . . .

But the man who dies is always an unfinished being. That which lies deepest in him, the striving for truth, the striving for good, the need for love, the restless heart, the sense of beauty, the horizon of the Absolute, all this in man is here while he lives. But when he dies, all this is cut off. Therefore, he is an unfinished being.

Cracow 26.3.78

GLORY, THE FULFILMENT OF MAN   April 14

God will in turn glorify him in himself, and will glorify him very soon.
(John 13:32)

The Resurrection of Jesus Christ means the beginning of a new life. The beginning of that future which thrust death down to the abyss, to the past.

81

The Resurrection means the beginning of that life in glory to which man was called, since he has within himself *a hunger for truth and glory flows from truth*. He has within himself *a hunger for the good* and *glory flows from the good*. He has within himself *a hunger for love* and *glory is the fulfilment of love*.

The Resurrection is the beginning of all this. It is the confirmation of the sense of our existence on earth. It is the confirmation of the sense of our humanity.

Cracow 26.3.78

THE NEW DAY OF THE LORD April 15

This is the day which the Lord has made; let us rejoice and be glad in it.
(Ps. 118:24)

Once upon a time, God the Creator created the world from nothingness, placed life in it and started time. He also created man in his image and likeness; male and female he created them, so that they might have dominion over the visible world.

This world, owing to man, has undergone the corruption of sin; it has been subjected to death; and time has become the yardstick of life, which measures hours, days, and years, from man's conception to his death.

The Resurrection inserts in this world, subjected to sin and death, the New Day; the day which the Lord has made. *This Day is the leaven of the New Life*, which must grow in man, going beyond the limit of death in him, towards eternity in God himself.

This Day is the beginning of the definitive (eschatological) future of man and of the world, to which the Church professes and to which she leads man by means of faith, 'the communion of the saints, forgiveness of sins, the resurrection of the flesh and eternal life'.

The foundation of this faith is Christ, who 'suffered under Pontius Pilate, was crucified, died, was buried and on the third day rose from the dead'.

Rome 9.4.80

82

Jesus said to them, 'Peace be with you,' and showed them his hands and his side.

(John 20:20)

These are the first words of his Easter message.

How great is the peace he gives us, a peace the world cannot give. How closely it is linked with his coming and his mission!

How necessary for the world is his presence, the victory of his Spirit, the order coming from his commandment of love, if men and women, families, nations and continents are to enjoy peace.

Peace! The fruit of fundamental order; the expression of respect for every human being's right to life, truth, freedom, justice and love.

Peace of consciences and peace of hearts. This peace cannot be had unless each one of us does everything in his or her power so that a life worthy of the children of God will be ensured for all men and women from the first moment of their existence: they are brothers and sisters of Christ, loved by him to death.

Rome 15.4.79

CAUSE FOR REJOICING   April 17

Let us thank God for giving us the victory through our Our Lord Jesus Christ.

(1 Cor. 15:57)

His triumph expresses the fullness of the redemptive goodness of God.

How could we fail to rejoice? *Through his triumph man has been called to the highest dignity.*

How can we fail to rejoice at the victory of him who was so unjustly condemned to the most terrible Passion and death on the Cross; at the victory of him who was first scourged, buffeted and spat upon with inhuman cruelty?

How can we fail to rejoice at the revelation of the power of God and at the victory of this power over sin and human blindness?

How can we fail to rejoice at the victory won once and for all by good over evil?

This is the day that the Lord has made! This is the day of universal hope.

Rome 15.4.79

THE GIFT OF THE HOLY SPIRIT April 18

He breathed on them and said: 'Receive the Holy Spirit.'

(John 20:22)

How significant are these first words of Jesus after his Resurrection! The message of the Risen Christ is contained in them.

When he says: 'Receive the Holy Spirit', there comes into our minds the same Upper Room in which Jesus delivered this farewell address. Then he uttered the words that revealed the mystery in his heart: 'It is for your own good that I am going because unless I go, the Advocate will not come to you; but if I do go, I will send him to you' (John 16:7): he said this thinking of the Holy Spirit.

So after having made this sacrifice, his 'departure' through the Cross, he returns to the Upper Room to bring them the One he has promised. The Gospel says: 'He breathed on them, and said to them, "Receive the Holy Spirit."'

This is the full meaning of his Passover. He brings them the Gift of the Passion and the Fruit of the Resurrection. With this gift he models them anew.

Rome 18.4.79

WITNESSES TO CHRIST April 19

As the Father sent me, so am I sending you.

(John 20:21)

To accept the Risen Christ means accepting this as those who were gathered at that moment in the Upper Room accepted it.

84

To believe in the Risen Christ means taking part in the same mission of salvation which he carried out with the paschal mystery. Faith is a conviction of the intellect and of the heart.

This conviction takes on its full meaning when participation in the mission which Christ accepted from the Father springs from it.

Among the Apostles, Thomas was absent when the Risen Christ came for the first time to the Upper Room. This Thomas, who declared aloud to his brothers, 'Unless I see . . . I refuse to believe', was convinced by the next coming of the Risen Christ. Then, as we know, all his reservations vanished and he professed his faith with these words: 'My Lord and my God' (John 20:28).

Together with the experience of the paschal mystery, he confirmed his participation in Christ's mission. It was as if, eight days afterwards, these words of Christ: 'As the Father sent me, so am I sending you', had reached him, too. *Thomas then became a mature witness to Christ.*

Rome 18.4.79

THE GOOD SHEPHERD April 20

I am the good shepherd: the good shepherd is one who lays down his life for his sheep.

(John 10:11)

The first words of this allegory explain its paschal significance. We know that these words were confirmed during his Passion. Christ laid down his life on the Cross. And he did so with love.

Above all, he wished to respond to the love of the Father, who 'loved the world so much that he gave his only Son, so that everyone who believes in him may not be lost but may have eternal life' (John 3:16).

Carrying out this charge received from his Father and revealing that love, Jesus, too, felt, in a particular way, the Father's own love. *The Sacrifice on Calvary is, above all, the giving of himself*; it is the gift of his life, which, remaining in the power of the Father, is restored to the Son in a splendid new form. In this way *the Resurrection is the same gift of life restored to the Son in return for his sacrifice.*

Rome 9.5.79

The Lord God says, I am going to look after my flock myself, and keep all of it in view.

(Ez. 34:11)

Jesus is the Good Shepherd because of the fact that he gives his life to the Father in this way: in giving it back in sacrifice, he lays it down for the sheep.

Here we are introduced to a splendid and fascinating simile, already so dear to the Old Testament prophets. Taking up this image again, Jesus revealed an aspect of the Good Shepherd's love that the Old Testament had not yet divined: *the laying down of one's life for one's sheep.*

As we know, Jesus often used parables in his teaching to make the divine truth which he proclaimed comprehensible to men who were generally simple and accustomed to think by means of images. The image of the Pastor and his fold was familiar to the experience of his listeners, as it still is to the mind of modern man. Even if civilization and technology are progressing by leaps and bounds, we can still understand the meaning of this image.

The shepherds take the sheep to the pastures (as, for example, on the Polish mountains where I come from) and remain there with them during the summer. They accompany them from one pasture to another. They watch them so that they do not go astray, and in particular they defend them from wild animals; just as we hear in the Gospel account: 'the wolf attacks and scatters the sheep.'

Rome 9.5.79

THE SACRIFICE OF THE SHEPHERD   April 22

No one takes it from me; I lay it down of my own free will.

(John 10:18)

The Good Shepherd, according to Christ's words, is he who, 'seeing the wolf come', does not flee, but is ready to risk his own life, struggling with the beast of prey so that none of the sheep will be lost. If he were not ready to do so, he would not be worthy of the name of Good Shepherd. He would be a hireling, but not a shepherd.

This is Jesus' allegorical discourse. Its essential meaning lies in this, that 'the good shepherd is the one who lays down his life for his sheep':

and this, in the context of the events of Holy Week, means that *Jesus, dying on the Cross, laid down his life for each one of us and for all mankind.*

By means of the paschal sacrifice, all men became his fold — because he has ensured to each one that divine and supernatural life which had been lost, because of original sin, since man's fall. He alone was able to restore it to man.

Rome 9.5.79

THE FOLD OF THE CHURCH April 23

Other sheep I have that are not of this fold, and these I have to lead as well.
(John 10:16)

The allegory of the Good Shepherd and, in it, the image of the fold, are of fundamental importance in understanding what the Church is and what her role is in history. *Not only must the Church be a 'fold', but she must make real the mystery of the Good Shepherd that Christ has accomplished*: the laying down of one's life for one's sheep.

The Church, which is the People of God, is, at the same time, a historical and social reality, in which this mystery is continually renewed and realized in different ways. And different men have their part to play in this concern for the salvation of the world and for the sanctification of one's neighbour, which is and will always be the concern characteristic of the crucified and risen Christ.

Such is certainly, for example, the concern of parents for their children. What is more, *it is the concern of every Christian, without discrimination, for his neighbours, the brothers and sisters that God puts on his way.*

Rome 9.5.79

SHEPHERD TO THE EARLY CHRISTIANS April 24

I have come so that they may have life and have it to the full.
(John 10:10)

For us who feel the constant solicitude of Christ for man, for the salvation of souls, for the dignity of the human person, and for the uprightness and goodness of earthly human ways, the image of the Good Shepherd is as eloquent as it was for the early Christians.

They expressed the same faith, the same love and the same gratitude in the paintings in the catacombs representing Christ as the Good Shepherd. And they expressed them in periods of persecution, when for avowing Christ they were threatened with death, and when they were obliged to look for underground cemeteries to pray together and to take part in the Holy Mysteries.

The catacombs of Rome and of the other cities of the ancient Empire continue to be an eloquent testimony to man's right publicly to profess faith in Christ. They also continue to be *a testimony to that spiritual power which springs from the Good Shepherd.* He proved to be more powerful than the ancient Empire, and the secret of this strength was truth and love, for which man is always hungry.

Rome 16.5.79

THE NEED TO BE KNOWN   April 25

I know my own . . . just as the Father knows me and I know the Father.
(John 10:15)

How marvellous this knowledge is! What knowledge! It includes eternal Truth and Love, which is what we are talking about when we say 'Father'. *It is the source of complete trust*; and it is reciprocal: 'I know . . . and they know.'

This knowledge is not abstract, the sort of purely intellectual certainty expressed in the sentence, 'I know everything about you.' Such knowledge, in fact, arouses fear, it induces one to withdraw into oneself, do not touch my secrets, leave me alone.

Christ says, on the contrary: 'I know my own', and he is talking about a liberating knowledge which brings forth trust. For, although man defends access to his secrets; although he wants to keep them for himself, he has a still greater need, 'he is hungry and thirsty', *for Someone to whom he can open up, to whom he can reveal himself.*

Rome 16.5.79

A SHEPHERD TO TRUST

I am the good shepherd; I know my own and my own know me.

(John 10:14)

Man is a person; the need for secrecy and the need to reveal belong to a person's nature. These needs are closely united. Together they indicate *the need for Someone before whom man can reveal himself.*

Even more, man needs Someone who can help him to understand his own mystery. That Someone must, moreover, win absolute trust; he must, in revealing himself, show that he is worthy of this trust. *He must confirm and reveal that he is the Lord and, at the same time, the Servant of man's spiritual mystery.*

This is precisely how Christ revealed himself. His words, 'I know my own and my own know me', are clearly confirmed by the words that follow, 'I lay down my life for the sheep.'

That is the spiritual character of the Good Shepherd.

Rome 16.5.79

FOLLOWING THE GOOD SHEPHERD

The sheep that belong to me listen to my voice; I know them and they follow me.

(John 10:27)

Let us look towards Calvary, on which the Cross has been raised. Christ died on that Cross, and was then laid in the tomb.

God, who had created man, restored that man, after his sin – every man and all men – in a particular way to his Son. When the Son was raised on the Cross, when he offered his sacrifice, he accepted at the same time man, entrusted to him by God, Creator and Father. *He accepted and embraced man with his sacrifice and his love: every man and all men.*

In the unity of the Divinity in union with his Father, this Son, himself become a man, restored one and all of us to the Father.

To the One who created us in his image and likeness and who predestined us, in the image and likeness of this eternal Son of his, 'to be his sons through Jesus Christ' (Eph. 1:5).

For this adoption by means of grace, for this inheritance of divine life, for this pledge of eternal life, Christ 'our paschal lamb' struggled to the end, in the mystery of his Passion, his Sacrifice and his Death.

The Resurrection became the confirmation of his victory; the victory of the love of the Good Shepherd who says: 'they follow me.'

Rome 27.4.80

IN THE HANDS OF THE SHEPHERD April 28

I give them eternal life; they will never be lost and no one will ever steal them from me.

(John 10:28)

Christ is the Good Shepherd because he knows man: one and all. *He knows him with this unique paschal knowledge.* He knows us, because he has redeemed us. He knows us, because 'he has paid for us': we are redeemed at a high price.

He knows us with the most 'interior' knowledge, with the same knowledge with which he, the Son, knows and embraces the Father and, in the Father, embraces infinite Truth and Love. *By means of participation in this Truth and in this Love, he makes us, in himself, once more sons of his Eternal Father.*

He obtains, once and for all, the salvation of man: of each man and of all, of those that no one shall snatch out of his hand . . . *Who, in fact, could snatch them?*

Rome 27.4.80

REDEEMED BY THE SHEPHERD April 29

The Father who gave them to me is greater than anyone and no one can steal from the Father.

(John 10:29)

Who can cancel the work of God himself, which the Son has carried out in union with the Father? Who can change the fact that we are redeemed? A fact as powerful and as fundamental as creation itself?

In spite of all the instability of human destiny and the weakness of the human will and heart, the Church orders us today to contemplate the might, the irreversible power of the Redemption, which lives in the heart and hands and feet of the Good Shepherd.

Of him who knows us . . .

We belong once more to the Father because of this Love, which did not draw back before the ignominy of the Cross, in order to be able to assure all men: 'no one shall snatch you out of my hand.'

Rome 27.4.80

PRAYING FOR 'OTHER SHEEP'   April 30

There are other sheep I have . . . they too will listen to my voice, and there will be only one flock, and one shepherd.

(John 10:16)

It can easily be guessed that Jesus Christ, speaking directly to the children of Israel, was indicating the necessity of the spread of the Gospel and of the Church and, through this, the extension of the solicitude of the Good Shepherd beyond the limits of the People of the Old Covenant.

We know that this process had already begun to be realized in apostolic times; that it was constantly realized later and that it continues to be realized.

Therefore, concluding this meditation of ours on the Good Shepherd, let us pray with special ardour for all those 'other sheep' that Christ has still to lead to the unity of the fold.

Perhaps they are those who do not yet know the Gospel. Or perhaps those who, for some reason, have abandoned it; perhaps, in fact, even those who have become its fiercest adversaries, the persecutors.

Let Christ take on his shoulders and press to him those who are not capable of returning alone. The Good Shepherd lays down his life for the sheep. For them all.

Rome 16.5.79

THE GIFT OF LOVE   MAUNDY THURSDAY

Until the Lord comes, therefore, every time you eat this bread and drink this cup you are proclaiming his death.

(1 Cor. 12:26)

How often in our lives have we seen separated two persons who love each other. During the severe and ugly war in my youth, I saw fathers torn away from their homes, without hope of return, without knowing whether they would meet their dear ones again one day. At the moment of departure, a gesture, a photo, an object; which passes from one hand to the other to prolong, somehow, presence in absence. And nothing more. *Human love is capable only of these symbols.*

As a testimony and as a lesson of love, at the moment of separation, 'Jesus knew that the hour had come for him to pass, from this world to the Father. He had always loved those who were his in the world, but now he showed how perfect his love was' (John 13:1). And thus, on the eve of that last Passover spent in this world with his friends, Jesus 'took some bread, and thanked God for it and broke it, and he said, "This is my body, which is for you; do this as a memorial of me"' (1 Cor. 12:23).

In this way, the Lord Jesus Christ, perfect God and perfect man, departing from his friends, leaves them not a symbol, but the reality of himself. He returns to the Father, but he remains among us men. He does not leave a mere object to conjure up his memory. Under the species of bread and wine it is he, really present with his Body, his Blood, his Soul, and his Divinity.

Fortaleza 9.7.80

CHRIST DIES IN UNION WITH THE
FATHER   GOOD FRIDAY

Jesus cried out in a loud voice: 'Eloi, Eloi, lama sabachthani?' – 'My God, my God, why have you deserted me?'

(Mark 15:34)

Nailed to the Cross, pinned immobile in that terrible position, Jesus invokes the Father. All his invocations bear witness that he is one with the Father. 'The Father and I are one' (John 10:30); 'Anyone who has seen me has seen the Father' (John 14:9).

Here we have the finest, the most sublime work of the Son in the union with the Father. Yes: in union, in the most perfect union possible, precisely at the moment when he cries: 'Eloi, Eloi, lama sabachthani' – 'My God, my God, why have you deserted me?'

This work finds expression in the vertical position of the body stretched against the perpendicular beam of the Cross and in the horizontal outreach of the arms, stretched along the transverse timber. To see those arms one would think that in the effort they expend they embrace all humanity and all the world. They do indeed embrace.

Here is the man. Here is God himself. 'In him we live and move and exist' (Acts 17:18). In him: in those arms outstretched along the transverse beam of the Cross.

The mystery of redemption.

S. of C.

THE CORNERSTONE IS RISEN   EASTER SUNDAY

The angel of the Lord, descending from heaven, came and rolled away the stone and sat on it.

(Matt. 28:2)

Many times the builders of the world, for whom Christ was willing to die, have sought to put a final stone before his tomb. But the stone is always removed from his tomb; the stone, the witness to his death, has become the witness to the Resurrection.

Let this world which, today, unfortunately, in various ways seems to desire the 'death of God', listen to the message of the Resurrection.

All of you who proclaim 'the death of God', who seek to drive God out of the human world, stop and think that 'the death of God' can fatally carry within itself 'the death of Man' too!

Christ rose again so that man could find the true meaning of existence, so that man could live his own life fully; so that man, who comes from God, could live in God.

Christ has risen. He is the cornerstone. Already at that time they tried to reject him and defeat him with the sealed and guarded tombstone. But that stone was rolled away. Christ is risen.

Let no man or woman refuse him, for each one is responsible for his or her destiny, and is the builder or destroyer of his or her own existence.

Christ rose even before the Angel had rolled away the tombstone. And then he revealed himself as the cornerstone, upon which is built the history of the whole of humanity and the history of each one of us.

Rome 6.4.80

May

WORK: A PARTNERSHIP WITH GOD

May 1

God blessed them, saying to them, Be fruitful, multiply, fill the earth and conquer it.

(Gen. 1:28)

Work is not a curse, it is a blessing from God who calls man to rule the earth and transform it, so that the divine work of creation may continue with man's intelligence and effort. I want to tell you with all my soul and with all my might that I suffer because of the lack of work, and because of the ideologies of hate and of violence that are far removed from the Gospel and that cause so many wounds in mankind today.

It is not enough for the Christian to denounce injustices; he who works has rights that he must defend legally, but he also has duties which he must carry out generously. *As Christians you are called to be architects of justice and of real freedom* as well as promoters of social charity.

Modern technology creates a whole set of new problems and sometimes produces unemployment. But it also opens great possibilities that require the worker to be increasingly well qualified, and to contribute more of his human capacities and his creative imagination.

For this reason, *work must not be a mere necessity, but it must be considered a real vocation*, a call from God to build a new world in which justice and brotherhood dwell, a foretaste of the Kingdom of God, in which there will certainly not be shortcomings or limitations.

Work must be the means by which the whole of creation will be made subject to the dignity of the human being and son of God. Work offers the opportunity to dedicate oneself to the whole community without resentment, without bitterness, without hatred, but with the universal love of Christ that excludes no one and embraces everyone.

Guadalajara 30.1.79

You should carry each other's troubles and fulfil the law of Christ.

(Gal. 6:2)

As you know, I, too, have been a worker: for a short period of my life, during the last world conflict I, too, had direct experience of factory work. I know, therefore, what the commitment of daily toil in the employment of others means. I know how heavy and monotonous it is; I know the needs of the workers and their just demands and legitimate aspirations. And I know how necessary it is that work should never be alienating and frustrating, but should always correspond to man's superior spiritual dignity.

In the first place, it is *my earnest wish that work may be a real right for every human person.* Today the national and international situation is so difficult and complicated, that it is not possible to oversimplify. But, since, we know that work is life, serenity, commitment, interest, meaning, we must wish everyone to have it.

He who has a job, feels he is useful, sound, engaged in something which gives his life value. To be without a job is psychologically negative and dangerous, particularly for the young and for those who have a family to support.

Therefore, while we must thank the Lord if we have work, *we must also feel the grief and distress of the unemployed*, and as far as is in our power endeavour to meet these painful situations. Words are not enough! It is necessary to help concretely, in a Christian way! While I appeal to those responsible for society, I also address each of you directly: commit yourselves, you, too, in order that everyone may find work!

Rome 9.12.78

PRAYER OVERCOMES THE FATIGUE OF WORK   May 3

Accursed be the soil because of you. With suffering shall you get your food from it.

(Gen. 3:17)

Work must help man to be more of a man. Work, despite its elements of fatigue, monotony and constraint was given to man by God, before sin, precisely as an instrument for the elevation and perfection of the universe, for the completion of his personality, and as a means for collaborating in God's work of creation.

The fatigue connected with it, associates man with the value of Christ's redeeming Cross; and, in the overall view of the Gospel, it becomes an instrument for co-operation between brothers: In a word, it becomes the expression of charity, in the one love of Christ, which must drive us to seek one another's good, to bear one another's burdens.

Therefore, *let work never be to the detriment of man!* It is now recognized in so many quarters that technical progress has not always been accompanied by adequate respect for man. Technology, marvellous though it is in its continual conquests, has often impoverished man in his humanity, depriving him of his interior and spiritual dimension, stifling in him the sense of true, superior values. *Primacy must be restored to the spiritual!*

May the famous motto of the Benedictines, 'Ora et labora' (Pray and work) be for you, an inseparable source of true wisdom, certain balance, human perfection. May prayer give wings to work, purify intentions, defend it from the dangers of obtuseness and carelessness.

Let work cause us to discover again, after toil, the bracing power of the meeting with God, in which man finds again his true, great stature. 'Ora et labora.' Yes, pray and work!

Turin 13.4.80

SUPPORTING FAMILIES BY WORK   May 4

We do urge you to go on making even greater progress and to make a point of living quietly, attending to your own business and earning your living.

(1 Thess. 4:11)

In the course of my life, I had the good fortune, the divine grace, to be able to discover these fundamental truths about human work, thanks to my personal experience of manual work. I shall remember as long as I live the men with whom I was linked in the same workyard, whether in the stone quarries or in the factory.

I shall not forget the human kindness that my fellow workers showed towards me. I shall not forget the discussions we had, in free moments, on the fundamental problems of existence and of the life of workers. I know what value their home, the future of their children,

97

the respect due to their wives, to their mothers, had for these men, who were at the same time fathers of families.

From this experience over a period of some years, I drew the conviction and the certainty that man expressed himself in work as a subject capable of loving, oriented towards fundamental human values, ready for solidarity with every man.

Paris 31.5.80

THE DIGNITY AND MEANING OF WORK May 5

My Father goes on working, and so do I.

(John 5:17)

There exists a close and particular connection between man's work and the fundamental environment of human love which bears the name of the family.

Man has been working from the beginning to subdue the earth and dominate it. We take this definition of work from the first chapters of the Book of Genesis.

Man works to earn his living and that of his family. We take this definition of work from the Gospel, from the life of Jesus, Mary and Joseph, and also from everyday experience.

These are the fundamental definitions of human work. They are both authentic, that is, fully humanistic, and the second one contains a particular fullness of the Gospel content.

These fundamental contents must be followed to ensure man an adequate place in the economic order as a whole. It is easy, in fact, to lose this place. It is lost when work is envisaged, above all, as one of the elements of production, as a 'merchandise' or an 'instrument'.

The name of the systems on which this position is based is not important: if man is subordinated to production, if he becomes merely its instrument, then work, human work, is deprived of its dignity and its specific meaning.

We are happy to remember here Cardinal Cardijn's famous words: 'A young worker is worth more than all the gold in the world.'

Paris 31.5.80

It is always my greatest joy to hear that my children are living according to the truth.

(3 John 4)

It is wise to be alert to the growing influence which the mass media, and especially television, are exercising on the developing minds of the young, particularly as regards their vision of man, of the world and of relationships with others; for the vision furnished them by the media often differs profoundly from that which the family would wish to transmit to them.

Parents, in many cases, do not show sufficient concern about this. Generally they pay vigilant attention to the type of friends with whom their children associate, but do not exercise a similar vigilance regarding the ideas which the radio, the television, records, papers and comics carry into the 'protected' and 'safe' intimacy of their homes.

And so the mass media often enter the lives of the youngest members of the family with no possibility of the necessary explanations or corrections from parents which could neutralize any harmful elements. Equally, the many valuable aspects of television, and the other media, could be used to assist in the process by which children are gradually transformed into well-adjusted men and women.

Rome 19.5.80

FAMILY PRAYER   May 7

The faithful met in their houses for the breaking of bread . . . they praised God and were looked up to by everyone.

(Acts 2:46)

Every effort to make society sensitive to the importance of the family is a great service to humanity. When the full dignity of parents and children is realized and is expressed in prayer, a new power for good is unleashed throughout the Church and the world.

John Paul I expressed this eloquently when he said: 'The holiness of the Christian family is indeed a most apt means for producing the serene renewal of the Church which the Council so eagerly desired.

Through family prayer, the *ecclesia domestica* — the church of the home — becomes an effective reality and leads to the transformation of the world.'

Rome 7.5.80

OUR RESPONSIBILITY TO CHILDREN May 8

Jesus said: Let the little children alone, and do not stop them coming to me.
(Matt. 19:14)

He spoke these words, we will recall, to the Apostles who, considering the tiredness of the Master, wanted to prevent the children from coming to Christ. They wanted to send them away, perhaps, because they did not want the children to be wasting the Master's time. Christ, however, seeing things from a different perspective, insisted on seeing the children.

The second phrase which comes to my mind sounds very severe. In fact, it defends the child from those who would corrupt him: 'Anyone who is an obsctacle to bring down one of these little ones who have faith in me, would be better drowned in the depths of the sea' (Mark 18:6). This admonition is very stern, but *the corruption of any innocent being is a great evil.* It results in great damage to the young soul, sowing evil where there should develop grace and truth, confidence and love. Only he who personally loved the innocent soul of children so much could express himself in this way on such corruption. Only he could threaten, with such powerful words, those responsible for it.

Rome 29.8.79

LETTING GO TO FULLER MATURITY May 9

Jesus replied, Anyone who does the will of my Father in heaven, he is my brother, and sister and mother.
(Matt. 12:50)

It is perfectly normal for children, whether adolescents or adults, to leave home and set out in the direction of their own choice of life. Obviously, then, the thirty-year-old son of Mary setting off from home will go in the one and only direction for which he came into the world.

And it is also perfectly normal and right for those children, even if they do go away, to keep always in their hearts a great love for their mothers. It is a love quite different from that of the young child, although it is fundamentally the same. As the personality develops the love becomes more mature and at the same time deeper.

But if this love is to mature in the child's mind, it is essential that the mother should not seek to hold him back for herself but should follow him in spirit. Such mothers respect the inner secrets of their children, who have been brought up, so to speak, under their wings and who at a given moment want to fly off relying on their own wing-power.

The great messianic wings of the will of the Father, on which the son of Mary relies when he flies off from Nazareth, can be discerned in the reply — at first sight a little puzzling — which he gave when he was told: 'Your mother and your brothers are outside and would like to speak to you.' His reply was: 'Who is my mother, and who are my brothers? . . . Anyone who does the will of my Father in heaven, he is my brother and sister and mother.'

S. of C.

THE WEDDING AT CANA May 10

The mother of Jesus was there, and Jesus and his disciples had also been invited.

(John 2:1)

Humanly speaking, Mary could not have been surprised that her son left home. It was something perfectly normal. Once they reach a certain age, children do leave their parents. They go out into the world to take up their calling, as is commonly said. So Jesus too left the family circle, once when he was twelve and then, for good, when he was about thirty.

At the time when Jesus leaves to take up his public ministry we find him with his mother — but already with disciples as well — attending the wedding feast at Cana in Galilee. St. John has given us in his Gospel a detailed description of all that happened here.

This was the occasion of Jesus's first miracle, in which Mary had a part to play. Let us recall it carefully. Let us remember the words, heavy with meaning, exchanged by mother and son: the mother's request: 'They have no wine'; Jesus's reply: 'Woman, why turn to me?

My hour has not come yet.' It is a highly significant reply. Mary must have heard in it an echo of what she had earlier heard from the lips of the twelve-year-old.

It again faces her with that hidden Father: 'I always do what pleases him' (John 8:29). But this time the Gospel-writer does not add: 'But they did not understand what he meant.' Quite the reverse! Mary turns to the servants and says: 'Do whatever he tells you.'

From this it is possible to conclude that Mary knew what the Father willed. And that she also knew, without any doubt, that her son would not reject her request. Mary's request, and the Father's will coincided.

S. of C.

THE MOTHERHOOD OF MARY   May 11

Near the cross of Jesus stood his mother.

(John 19:25)

Mother means the one who gives birth, and giving birth implies training for life.

She trains her children by intuition; she trains them from her heart. These are tremendous means of training a child. She trains her child, and not only her child, she trains, first and foremost a human being. That is the fundamental thing. She trains a human being.

It is not without significance that Christ, the Son of God, God himself, entrusted himself to the care of a woman, a mother. This is not without significance for us. That woman, united with Christ, reigns in her motherhood.

Cracow 12.4.62

JESUS HONOURED HIS MOTHER   May 12

For God said: Do your duty to your father and mother.

(Matt. 15:4)

His indebtedness to his mother is apparent in him every day of his life; it shows itself in his kindness of heart, in his human sensitivity to the beauties of nature.

When little children are brought to him he blesses them, laying his hands on them; and when he rebukes the disciples, saying: 'Let the little children come to me; do not stop them' (Mark 10:14), his mother too is, in a way, present in those words. And they are words in which he pays her tribute, for they recall his own childhood spent in the home she made at Nazareth where he thrived in the climate created by her love and motherly protection.

Jesus Christ was the living expression of his all-important duty — the duty he owed to the Father — which was deeply engraved in his whole being both human and divine; but he also respected the rights of his mother: 'Honour your father and your mother.' These two orders of duty owed were woven together in the depth of his personal being.

S. of C.

THE ROLE OF MARY   May 13

When the appointed time came, God sent his Son, born of a woman . . . to enable us to be adopted as sons.

(Gal. 4:4)

It was because she received the Word of God both in her heart and in her body that the Blessed Virgin has a unique role in the mystery of the Word incarnate and in that of the Mystical Body. She is closely united with the Church, for which she is the model of faith, charity and perfect union with Christ.

In this way, in answer to our devotion and our prayer, Mary, who in a way gathers and reflects in herself the highest aspirations of faith, calls the faithful to her Son and to his sacrifice, as well as to the love of the Father.

With the Virgin, the Church started her way through the history of this world two thousand years ago, in the Upper Room at Pentecost. Since then, the Church has traversed every stage of this way with her, the luminous sign of hope and comfort for the people of God.

Rome 31.1.80

All generations will call me blessed, for the Almighty has done great things for me.

(Luke 1:48)

People of all climates, races and languages have echoed down the ages, 'Of all women you are the most blessed' (Luke 1:42). Some have been more enlightened than others, but the Christian faithful do not cease to have recourse to Our Lady, the Holy Mother of God; in moments of joy calling her 'the Cause of our happiness'; in moments of sadness, invoking her as 'the Consoler of the afflicted'; in moments of dismay, imploring her as 'the Refuge of sinners'.

These expressions of a search for God, rooted in the way of life and culture of every people and, not infrequently, in emotional states of mind, will not always appear solidly based on an adherence to the faith. It may even happen that they are not duly separated from elements foreign to religion. But they are a reality worthy of consideration, and often truly rich in genuine values.

Popular piety, normally connected with devotion to Our Lady, certainly needs to be enlightened, guided, and purified. But as it is — as my predecessor Paul VI wished to call it — a devotion 'of the simple and poor', it generally expresses a certain 'thirst for God'. And then it is not necessarily a vague sentiment, or an inferior form of religious expression. In fact it often contains a deep sense of God and his attributes, such as fatherhood, providence, loving presence, and mercy.

Belem 8.7.80

THE FAITH OF MOTHERS   May 15

Blessed is she who believed that the promise made her by the Lord would be fulfilled.

(Luke 1:45)

Let us do honour to motherhood, because faith in man is expressed in it. The act of faith in man is the fact that his parents give him life. The mother bears him in her womb, and she is ready to suffer all the pains of childbirth; thereby, with all her feminine and maternal self, she proclaims her faith in man. She bears witness to the value which is in her and transcends her at the same time.

The value constituted by the one who, still unknown, fully hidden in his mother's womb, must be born and be manifested to the world as a child of his parents, as a confirmation of their humanity, as a fruit of their love, as a future of the family: of the closest family, and at the same time of the whole human family.

This child might be born weak or maladjusted. It sometimes happens this way. Motherhood is always pain — the love for which one pays with one's suffering — and it happens that this love may have to be even greater than the pain of childbirth itself. This pain may be extended to the whole life of the child. The value of humanity is confirmed also by these children and by these people in which it is retarded and sometimes undergoes a painful degradation.

This is a further reason for affirming that it is not enough to define man according to all the bio-physiological criteria, and that it is necessary to believe in man, from the beginning.

Paris 31.5.80

THE MYSTERY OF MAN   May 16

You see this child: he is destined for the fall and for the rising of many.
(Luke 2:34)

Blessed are you, Mary, you who believed! The one you bear in your heart, as the fruit of your womb, will come into the world in the night of Bethlehem. He will then proclaim the Gospel to men, and he will be raised on the Cross. It was for that purpose, in fact, that he came into the world, to bear witness to the truth.

In him there will be manifested to the end the truth about man, the mystery of man, his ultimate and highest vocation: the vocation of every man, even of the man whose humanity will not, perhaps, reach a complete and normal development. The vocation of every man without exception, not stopping at any consideration of qualification or degrees of intelligence, sensitiveness or physical performance, but by virtue of his very humanity, owing to the fact that he is a man. Because thanks to that, *thanks to his humanity itself, he is the image and likeness of the infinite God.*

Paris 31.5.80

Jesus said to his mother: 'Woman, this is your Son.' Then to the disciple he said: 'This is your Mother.'

(John 19:27)

We are witnesses to the death of Christ on the Cross: we hear his last bequest, in which we find the word 'Mother'.

Jesus, who by his whole life, by his mission, the Gospel, revealed to man and to mankind the great love of God, in this, his last bequest, pronounced the word 'Mother', as if he wished to link the great eternal love of the Father, which transcends man, though it is so close to him, with something closer, more visible and perceptible. Therefore, he said from the Cross: 'This is your mother!'

He spoke to one man, but in him he spoke at the same time, to all mankind, to all nations, to all generations of mankind and nations. Therefore today, hearing his words, pronounced from on high on the Cross, we understand and feel that this is our mother.

In Christ's last bequest, we feel again and again, generation after generation, ever more maturely, the eternal love of the Father.

Cracow 31.6.68

THE HUNGER OF MODERN MAN   May 18

The hungry he has filled with good things, the rich sent empty away.

(Luke 1:53)

These words of Mary's Magnificat are uttered in the finest outburst of gratitude to God, who – as Mary proclaims – has done great things in her. *They say that the world, willed by God, cannot be a world in which some, few in number, accumulate excessive goods in their hands, and the others – who are clearly greater in number – suffer from want, poverty and die of hunger.*

Who are the former? And who are the others? Is it a question of only two social classes opposed to each other? Here we must not confine ourselves to too narrow an outline. It is a question today, in fact, of whole societies, of whole areas of the world, which have been defined in different ways. We talk, for example, of developed societies and underdeveloped societies.

We must also speak of consumer societies, and of those in which men are literally dying of starvation. Today it is necessary to have a very wide, universal view of the problem as a whole.

These needs exist, however, not only in the field of economy, and the distribution of material goods. There exist other real human needs. There exist also other human rights which are subject to violence. And not only the rights of man, but also the rights of the family and the rights of nations. 'Man does not live on bread alone' (Matt. 4:4).

He is not only hungry for bread, he is hungry, perhaps even more, for truth. He is hungry for freedom, when some of his fundamental rights are violated, such as the right to freedom, of conscience and to religious freedom, the right to the education of his children in conformity with the faith and convictions of parents and families, the right to instruction according to capacities and not, for example, according to a political situation or a conception of the world imposed by force.

Paris 31.5.80

THE HUMAN CONCEPT OF LOVE   May 19

Jesus replied: 'Surely the bridegroom's attendants would never think of mourning as long as the bridegroom is still with them?'

(Matt. 9:15)

In love, as people commonly understand it, as they write and sing about it, subjectivism and selfishness frequently raise their voices. We give the name love to what is our momentary experience, and we give it that name for just as long as the experience lasts. The moment it passes we stop talking about love.

So often love comes to an end in our human life, when boy and girl cease to be a source of revelation to each other, and even, after marriage, when husbands and wives cease to be a source of revelation to each other.

I think that the reason for this is that our concept of love is too shallow. Spouses do not pay enough attention to the fact that they are also 'friends of the Bridegroom', and they do not fulfil, conscientiously and sufficiently, those duties which they owe to the heavenly Bridegroom regarding their spouses.

Cracow 15.1.78

The love of God has been poured into our hearts by the Holy Spirit which has been given us.

(Rom. 5:5)

For someone who has read and given some thought to the Gospel, not only 'God is love' but also 'Love is from God'.

How? There are indeed the paths of grace without which no human love, however subjectively absorbing and reciprocated, can plumb the depths nor unite to the end. This is a most practical matter, though it is also a matter of belief, or, let us say, a matter of living faith and the whole life-style which flows from it.

What can be more essential for a Christian life-style than the education of love, or *the overcoming of the various forms of egoism.* If it is beyond doubt that the education of love is an indispensable condition of marriage, then we must add that a quite adequate view of the sacrament of marriage is simply what follows from the truth 'God is love' and the other truth 'Love is from God'.

Cracow 15.1.78

THE EDUCATION OF LOVE   May 21

This has taught us love — that he gave up his life for us.

(1 John 3:16)

The education of love, in the view of those who believe in God, must mean, on top of everything else, co-operation with grace.

If the principle of co-operation with thought can seem somewhat pallid, all the more so will the principle of co-operation with grace be something abstract and elusive. If it is assumed that the whole course of love can be reduced simply to some emotional-biological reactions and experiences which spontaneously tend towards their own gratification.

Such an assumption is unacceptable, however, since it does not accord with truth, and moreover, rules out the very possibility of educating love. This possibility does not exist where no effort is made to 'educate' love — an 'education' which takes place first and foremost in practice, not in theory.

Cracow 15.1.78

The Father, from whom every family, whether spiritual or natural, takes its name.

(Eph. 3:14)

In a world in which the supporting function of many institutions seems to be failing, the family can and must become a place of real serenity and harmonious growth; not, indeed, in order to isolate itself in forms of proud self-sufficiency, but to offer the world a luminous testimony that the recuperation and complete advancement of man is possible if the latter has as its starting point and frame of reference the healthy vitality of the primary cell of the civil and ecclesial fabric.

The Christian family, therefore, must change more and more —
— into a community of love, such as to make it possible to overcome, in faithfulness and harmony, the inevitable difficulties of everyday life;
— into a community of life, in order to give rise to, and cultivate joyfully, precious new existences in the image of God;
— into a community of grace, which will constantly make the Lord Jesus Christ its own centre of gravity and focal point, in such a way as to make the commitment of each one fruitful and to draw ever new vigour in daily progress.

Rome 5.5.79

THE GREATNESS OF PARENTHOOD   May 23

Your kinswoman Elizabeth has, in her old age, herself conceived a Son.
(Luke 1:36)

The greatness of motherhood, fatherhood, parenthood lies in the fact that in giving life the parents also hand on humanity — *they teach the child to be a human being.* And the most powerful means of teaching someone to be a human being is mature humanity, the example of humanity. This never falls short.

All children's homes, which must be esteemed for their great humanitarian significance are nevertheless at the same time only substitutes and proofs of the sad reality that the family alone is not strong enough.

Therefore *we must do everything to ensure that the family is strong*, strong as a medium for bringing up children. This is the greatest task of the nation, society, the state, and the Church.

Cracow 31.6.68

THE SMILE OF DAWN   May 24

All I want is to know Christ and the power of his resurrection.

(Phil. 3:11)

Live your life in Easter awareness! The Christian, in fact, must be distinguished precisely by this paschal sense of life and history. And what does it mean?

It means being convinced that the Resurrection of Jesus is the decisive and determinant event of the whole of human history, and therefore of our existence, since it guarantees it a transcendent and eternal meaning.

It is difficult sometimes to see light beyond the darkness! And yet *the Christian is he who, at night, waits trustfully for the smile of dawn*: he who, beyond the darkness and anguish of Good Friday, sees the joy and the glory of Easter Sunday! Christ has risen again, and therefore his word is divine: God loves us, man is saved, history is redeemed!

Bring to your life and your environment, to your family, and your work, in moments of serenity and in places of suffering, this paschal sense of salvation and true hope; this is what the modern world expects and desires from the Christian!

Rome 12.4.80

FRIENDSHIP OF MARY AND ELIZABETH   May 25

Mary went to Zechariah's house and greeted Elizabeth.

(Luke 1:40)

The visitation of the mother of God to St. Elizabeth teaches us the great values of friendship as a medium of education. Mary meets Elizabeth, her kinswoman, in a spirit of friendship.

This friendship of the mothers becomes, as it were, a magnificent setting for the later friendship of their sons, John the Baptist and Jesus Christ.

We know what significance that friendship had in the events of our salvation. How much was accomplished through it on the threshold of the Old and New Testaments.

Cracow 31.6.68

MATURING INFLUENCE OF FRIENDSHIP May 26

Meanwhile the child grew up and his spirit matured.

(Luke 1:80)

In modern programmes for bringing up children, it is essential that great significance should be given to friendship. *Friendship finds its beginnings in the family.*

The first friendship is the friendship of parents as spouses, spouses as parents; the next is the friendship of parents and children, children and parents. This friendship evolves, passes through various stages.

We know how easy it is for a father, and still more a mother, to be on friendly terms with a small child, and how hard it is to be on friendly terms with an adolescent son or daughter. But it is just at this time that the friendship of father, mother, or teacher is all the more necessary.

Cracow 31.6.68

FEAR AND THE DEATH OF GOD May 27

The doors were closed in the room where the disciples were for fear of the Jews.

(John 20:19)

The Apostles, gathered in the Upper Room in Jerusalem, were overcome by fear: 'the doors were closed . . . for fear.' The Son of God had died on the Cross.

Is not the fear, that besets modern men, also due, in its deepest root, to the 'death of God'? Not to the death on the Cross, which became the beginning of Resurrection and the source of the glorification of the Son of God and at the same time the foundation of human hope and the sign of salvation — not to that death.

But to the death with which man causes God to die in himself and particularly in the course of the latest stages of his history, in his thought, in his conscience, in his actions. This is, as it were, a

111

common denominator of many initiatives of human thought and will.

Man, therefore, 'makes God die' in himself and in others. Whole philosophical systems, social, economic, and political programmes, serve this purpose. *We live, therefore, in an age of gigantic material progress, which is also the age of a denial of God previously unknown.*

Such is the image of our civilization. But why is man afraid? Perhaps because, as a consequence of this denial in the last analysis, he remains alone: metaphysically alone . . . interiorly alone.

Or perhaps? . . . perhaps precisely because man, who makes God die, will not find a decisive curb not to kill man too. This decisive curb is in God. *The ultimate reason why man should live, respect and protect man's life, is in God.* The ultimate foundation of man's value and dignity, of the meaning of his life, is the fact that he is the image and likeness of God!

Turin 13.4.80

THE HOLY SPIRIT PRAYING IN US   May 28

When we cannot choose words in order to pray properly, the Spirit himself expresses our plea.

(Rom. 8:26)

Prayer is indispensable for persevering in pursuit of the good, indispensable for overcoming the trials life brings to man owing to his weakness. *Prayer is a strength for the weak and weakness for the strong!* This is what the Apostle is saying, 'the Spirit expresses our plea in a way that could never be put into words' (Rom. 8:26).

Prayer can be said to be a constitutive element of human existence in the world. Human existence is 'being directed towards God'. At the same time it is 'being within the dimensions of God', a humble but courageous entering into the depths of God's thought, the depths of his mystery and his plans. It is a kind of drawing on the source of divine power: will and grace.

It is also, as St. Paul says, the work of the Holy Spirit in us. And the Spirit, says the Apostle in another letter, 'reaches the depths of everything, even the depths of God' (1 Cor. 2:10).

S. of C.

You will receive power when the Holy Spirit comes on you and then you will be my witnesses.

(Acts 1:8)

Those whom the Lord Jesus sends — those who after the ten days following the Ascension will emerge from the Upper Room at Pentecost, and all the generations after, until our time — bring with them a testimony which is the first source and the fundamental content of evangelization: 'You will receive power.' They are charged to *teach by bearing witness*. 'Modern man listens more willingly to witnesses than teachers, or if he listens he does so because they are witnesses' (the words of Paul VI).

When we re-read, both in the Acts of the Apostles and in the Letters, we see how perfectly the first executors of Christ's apostolic mandate incarnated this task in their lives. St. John Chrysostom says, 'If the leaven, mixed with the flour, does not transform the whole mass into the same quality, will it really have been a ferment? Do not say that you cannot sweep others along; in fact, if you are a true Christian, it is impossible that that should not happen.'

He who carries out the work of evangelization is not first and foremost a teacher. He is a messenger. *He behaves like a man to whom a great mystery has been entrusted.* And at the same time like one who has discovered personally the greatest treasure, 'hidden in a field', like the one in Matthew's parable.

The state of his soul is also marked by a readiness to share this with others. Even more than readiness, he feels an interior imperative, like those magnificent words of Paul 'the love of Christ overcomes us' (2 Cor. 5:14).

Rome 23.5.79

MARY, MOTHER OF ALL   May 30

May you be the joy of your father, the gladness of her who bore you.

(Prov. 23:25)

Is it not true that at occasional family meetings round their mother, all brothers and sisters feel more disposed to kindness, reconciliation, and unity? And then on similar occasions piety and filial love demand that the last word should be left to the mother. It is this time of family affection and good resolutions which soothes the mother's heart.

We have arrived at such a moment. *As a mother full of kindness, the Blessed Virgin does not cease to invite all her sons, members of the Mystical Body, to cultivate kindness, reconciliation, and unity among themselves.* Allow me this moment, as an elder brother to gather and interpret what is certainly in the hearts of all, and to place it in the Immaculate Heart of the Mother of Jesus and our mother. I invite you all to follow, in silent prayer, the prayer that I recite on behalf of all:

Mary, you said, under the inspiration of the Holy Spirit, that the generations would call you blessed. We take up again the song of past generations so that it will not be interrupted, and exalt in you the most radiant being that mankind has offered to God: the human creature in its perfection, created anew in justice and holiness in a peerless beauty which we call 'the Immacualte' or 'Full of Grace'.

Mother, we ask through your intercession, like the disciples in the upper room, for the continual assistance of the Holy Spirit and the docility to accept him in the Church; we ask this for those who seek God's truth and for those who must serve it and live it. May Christ always be the 'light of the world', and may the world recognize us as his disciples because we remain in his Word and know the truth that will make us free with the freedom of the Sons of God.
Amen!

Belem 8.6.80

THE VISITATION   May 31

Of all women, you are the most blessed, and blessed is the fruit of your womb.

(Luke 1:42)

A greeting which is addressed to a woman bearing in her womb a man: the fruit of life and the beginning of life. This woman comes from far away, from Nazareth, and now she is entering the house of her relatives, whom she has come to visit. From the threshold of the house, she hears: 'Blessed is she who believed that the promise made her by the Lord would be fulfilled' (Luke 1:45).

On the last day of the month of May the Church remembers this visit and these words: she greets Mary, the Mother of Jesus Christ. She does honour to her maternity, whereas the latter is still only a mystery in her womb and her heart.

I wish, in the first place, to do honour to maternity, and to the faith in men that it implies.

To do honour to maternity means accepting man in his full truth and full dignity, and that from the very beginning. Man's beginning is in his mother's womb.

The first measure of man's dignity, the first condition of respect for the inviolable rights of the human person, is the honour due to the mother. It is the cult of maternity. We cannot detach man from his human beginning.

Today when we have learned so much about the biological mechanisms which, in their respective fields, determine this beginning, we must, with keener awareness and all the more ardent conviction, proclaim the human – deeply human – beginning of every man as the fundamental value and the basis of all his rights. *The first right of man is the right to life.* We must defend this right and this value.

Paris 31.5.80

THE MISSIONARY CHURCH   ASCENSION DAY

Go, therefore, make disciples of all the nations; baptise them in the name of the Father and of the Son and of the Holy Spirit.

(Matt. 28:19)

Today ends the period of forty days which separates the moment of the Resurrection of Our Lord Jesus Christ from his Ascension. This is also the time of the Master's final separation from the Apostles and disciples. At this important moment, Christ entrusts to them the mission that he himself received from the Father and began on earth: as he said to them during the first meeting after the resurrection. 'As the Father sent me, so am I sending you' (John 20:21).

The words quoted above contain the so-called missionary mandate. *The duties that Christ hands down to the Apostles define at the same time the missionary nature of the Church.* The Church is always on her way, always in a state of mission. This condition reflects the interior forces of faith and hope that animate the Apostles, the disciples and the confessors of Christ the Lord during the centuries.

'In these places, a good many do not become Christians only because there is no one to make them Christians. It often comes into my mind to run and shout here and there in the academies of Europe . . . and to address those who show more doctrine than charity with the following words: "Oh, how great is the number of souls excluded from Heaven by your fault!" . . . Many of them should, on the contrary, practise listening to what the Lord says to them. Then they would exclaim warmly: "Here I am, Lord: what do you want me to do? Send me wherever you want"' (St. Francis Xavier).

Rome 23.5.79

THE BIRTH OF THE CHURCH   WHIT SUNDAY

You will receive power when the Holy Spirit comes to you, and then you will be my witnesses.

(Acts 1:8)

On the day of Pentecost, the prayer of the Apostles and the Mother of Christ culminates in a great event which fulfils the risen Lord's promise. *The external signs accompanying it are far less important than its inner meaning.* Even though the sudden gust of wind, and the tongues of flame above their heads, and the extraordinary ability of these simple men to speak different languages are certainly not lacking in significance, what matters far more is that the Spirit of Jesus Christ, the Spirit of the Father and the Son, comes down to the Upper room and, enters the human spirit, enters the hearts of men.

The Church came into the world simultaneously with that definitive change in the hearts of the Apostles. Only then did the Apostles whom Christ had chosen become his witnesses; only then did they start to testify to him before all Israel and before all who had come to Jerusalem to celebrate Pentecost. Their testimony is authentic, marked by 'power from on high'; it is highly effective in that it bears fruit in the souls of those who listen. Thus the Church is born: the People of God of the new covenant.

S. of C.

June

LOVE JESUS June 1

I shall not call you servants any more, I call you friends, because I have made known to you everything I have learnt from my Father.

(John 15:15)

Jesus is not an idea, a feeling, a memory! Jesus is a 'person', always alive and present with us!

Love Jesus present in the Eucharist. He is present in a sacrificial way in Holy Mass, which renews the Sacrifice of the Cross. To go to Mass means going to Calvary to meet him, our Redeemer.

He comes to us in Holy Communion and remains present in the tabernacles of our Church, for he is our friend, he is everyone's friend and wishes particularly to be the friend and support of your way through life: you need confidence and friendship so much.

Love Jesus present in the Church by means of his priests: present in the family by means of parents and those who love you.

Love Jesus especially in those who are suffering in any way: physically, morally, spiritually. Make a resolution to do all you can to love your neighbour, discovering Christ's face in him.

Rome 8.11.78

JESUS, THE MODEL OF LOVE June 2

There are three things that last, faith, hope and love; and the greatest of these is love.

(1 Cor. 13:13)

Jesus is the prophet of love — that love which St. Paul confesses and proclaims in the words, so simple and at the same time so profound, in the passage from the Letter to the Corinthians. *In order to know what true love is, what its characteristics and qualities are, we must look at Jesus,* at his life and his conduct. Words will never render the reality of love so well as its living model does. Even words, as perfect in their simplicity as those of the first Letter to the Corinthians, are only the image of this reality: the reality, that is, of which we find the complete model in the life and behaviour of Jesus Christ.

In the succession of generations, there have been and there are, men and women who have effectively imitated this perfect model. We are all called upon to do the same. *Jesus came above all to teach us love.* It constitutes the content of the greatest commandment he left to us. If we learn to put it into practice, we will reach our purpose: eternal life.

Love, in fact, as the Apostle teaches, 'does not come to an end'. While other charisms and also the essential virtues in the Christian's life end together with earthly life and pass away, love does not pass, it never ends. It is precisely the essential foundation and content of eternal life. And therefore 'the greatest of these is love'.

Rome 3.2.80

LOVE OPENS US TO OTHERS

June 3

Love is always patient and kind.

(1 Cor. 13:4)

Love is acquired in spiritual effort. Love grows in us and develops even among the contradictions, the resistances, that oppose it from within each of us, and at the same time from 'without' that is, among the many forces that are alien and even hostile to it.

For this reason St. Paul writes that 'love is patient'. Does it not so often come up against, in us, the resistance of our impatience, and even merely inadvertence? *To love, it is necessary to be able to 'see' the 'other',* it is necessary to be able to 'take him into account'. Sometimes it is necessary to put up with him. If we see only ourselves, and the 'other' does not exist for us, we are far from the lesson of love that Christ gave us.

'Love is kind', we read further on: not only does it 'see' the 'other', but it opens up to him, looks up to him, looks for him, goes to meet him. *Love gives lavishly and this is just what 'it is kind' means* (following the example of the love of God himself, which is expressed in grace) . . . But how often, nevertheless, we shut ourselves up in the shell of our self, we are not able, we do not want, we do not try to open up to the 'other', to give him something of our own self, going beyond the limits of our self-centred outlook, or even of selfishness, and endeavouring to become men and women 'for others', following the example of Christ.

Rome 3.2.80

THE FRIGHTENING ALTERNATIVE TO LOVE   June 4

You must want love more than anything else.

(1 Cor. 14:1)

Re-reading St. Paul's lesson on love, and meditating on the meaning of every word that the Apostle used to describe the characteristics of this love, we touch on the most important points of our life and our living together with others.

He touched not only on personal or family problems, the ones, that is, that have importance in the little circle of our interpersonal relations, but also on social problems of prime importance today.

Are not the times in which we live already a dangerous lesson on what society and humanity can become: when the evangelical truth about love is considered outdated, when it is eliminated from the way of looking at the world and life, from ideology, when it is excluded from education, the media of social communication, culture and politics? And may this lesson not become even more threatening as time goes on?

In this condition, are not the acts of terrorism, and the growing military tension in the world, already eloquent enough? *Every man — and the whole of mankind — lives between love and hatred. If he does not accept love, hatred will easily creep into his heart and begin to fill it more and more, yielding more and more poisonous fruits.*

Rome 3.2.80

BE HOLY JUST AS GOD IS HOLY   June 5

Happier those who hear the word of God and keep it.

(Luke 11:28)

To keep the word of God is synonymous with living the commandment of love: *love of oneself,* enlightened and orderly, a source of serenity: *love of one's brothers* in faith and of all men, an active love, a source of peace; *love of God* above all things, a source of joy.

Cultivate the truth, which he is, since obeying the truth you will sanctify your souls to practise sincere brotherly love: 'Have respect for everyone and love for our community; fear God' and honour the authorities (1 Pet. 2:17). Practise justice, that justice of the kingdom of God which has priority always and in everything. To do this, the Apostle John explains, is to remain in him, in Christ, and not to sin, since 'to live a holy life is to be holy just as he is holy' (1 John 3:7).

Yes, it is necessary to overcome evil with good, to put at one another's service, the gifts received, and continually to put on sentiments of mercy, goodness, humility, meekness, and patience, but 'over all these clothes, to keep them together and complete them, put on love' (Col. 3:14).

Fortaleza 9.7.80

THE SECRET OF TRUE HAPPINESS   June 6

God created man in the image of himself, in the image of God he created him.

(Gen. 1:27)

The ways of men are, not infrequently, very different from one another. Yet the ultimate goal towards which all alike are directed, is always the same; they all seek full personal happiness, in the context of a true communion of love. If you try to penetrate the depths of your desires and of those who pass at your side, you will discover that this is the common aspiration of all, this is the hope which, after failure, always springs up again in man's heart from the ashes of every disappointment.

Our heart seeks happiness and wishes to experience it in the context of true love. Well, the Christian knows that the true satisfaction of this aspiration can be found only in God, in whose image man was created.

'You made us for yourself and our heart is restless unless it rests in you.' When Augustine, back from a tortuous and useless pursuit of happiness in every kind of pleasure and vanity wrote these famous words on the first page of his *Confessions*, he did nothing but express the essential need that emerges from the depths of our being.

Fortaleza 9.7.80

Come to me, all you who labour and are overburdened, and I will give you rest.

(Matt. 11:28)

If man wishes to quench the thirst for happiness that burns in his heart, he must direct his steps towards Christ. Christ is not far from him.

Our life here on earth is, in fact, a continual succession of encounters with Christ: with Christ present in the Scriptures, as the Word of God; with Christ present in his ministers, as Teacher, Priest, and Shepherd; with Christ present in his neighbour, and especially in the poor, in the sick, in the underprivileged, who are his suffering limbs; with Christ present in the sacraments, which are the channels of his salvific action: with Christ the silent guest of our hearts, where he lives communicating his human life.

Every encounter with Christ leaves deep marks: they may be meetings at night, like that of Nicodemus; casual meetings, like that of the Samaritan woman; meetings sought like that of the sinful woman who had repented; meetings of supplication, like that of the blind man at the gates of Jericho; meetings out of curiosity, like that of Zacchaeus; or meetings of intimacy, such as that of the Apostles, called to follow him; dazzling meetings, such as that of Paul on the way to Damascus. But the deepest and most transforming encounter, to which all the others are subordinated, is the meeting at the table of the eucharistic mystery, that is, at the table of the bread of the Lord.

Here it is Christ in person who welcomes man, afflicted by the difficulties of the way, and comforts him with the warmth of his understanding and his love. It is in the Eucharist that those gentle words: 'Come to me, all you who labour and are overburdened' are fully verified.

Fortaleza 9.7.80

THE EUCHARIST IS A FAMILY EVENT   June 8

When the hour came he took his place at table, and the apostles with him.
(Luke 22:14)

A priest — whether he is the Pope, a bishop or a country parish priest — or a lay person participating fully in the Mass, cannot but be rapt in the marvels of this sacrament. There are so many dimensions in which it can be considered. It is Christ's sacrifice which is mysteriously renewed; it is the bread and wine transformed, transubstantiated into the Body and Blood of the Lord; it is Grace that is communicated by means of this spiritual food to the soul of the Christian.

On this occasion I wish to dwell on a no less significant aspect: *the Eucharist is a family meeting*, a meeting of the large family of Christians. The Lord Jesus willed to institute this great sacrament on the occasion of an important family meeting: the paschal Supper, and on that occasion his family was the Twelve who had been living with him for three years. For a long time, at the beginning of the Church, it was in the houses of families that other families met for the 'breaking of bread'.

Every altar will always be a table, round which there gathers a family of brothers, more or less numerous. The Eucharist gathers this family, manifests it in the eyes of everyone, and draws closer the ties that unite its members, all at the same time. St. Augustine was thinking of all this when he called the Eucharist: 'a sacrament of piety, a sign of unity, a bond of charity'.

Belo Horizonte 1.7.80

THE EUCHARIST SHAPES THE BODY OF CHRIST   June 9

Though there are many of us, we form a single body because we all have a share in this one loaf.

(1 Cor. 10:17)

It was not by chance that the Lord, wishing to give himself entirely to us, chose the setting of the family meal. Being gathered round a table means an interpersonal relationship and the possibility of mutual knowledge, mutual exchange, and enriching dialogue. In this way *the Eucharist becomes an expressive sign of communion, forgiveness, and love*.

Are not these the realities that our pilgrim heart feels it needs? True human happiness is unthinkable outside this context of meeting and sincere friendship. Well, not only does the Eucharist signify this reality, but it efficaciously causes it. In this connection, St. Paul makes it extremely clear 'we all have a share in this one loaf'. The eucharistic food, making us 'consanguineous' with Christ, makes us brothers and sisters to one another.

St. John Chrysostom vividly sums up the effects of participation in the Eucharist as follows: 'We are that same body. What is the bread actually? The Body of Christ. What do communicants become? The body of Christ. In fact, just as bread is the result of many grains, and although remaining themselves are not distinguished from one another because they are united, so we too are mutually united with Christ. We are not nourished, some from one body, others from another, but all from the same Body.'

Fortaleza 11.8.80

THE EUCHARIST UNITES ALL MEN June 10

There is no room for distinction between Greek and Jew . . . There is only Christ.

(Col. 3:11)

Eucharistic communion is therefore the sign of the meeting of all the faithful. A truly inspiring sign, because *at the holy table all differences of race or social class disappear*, leaving only the participation of all in the same holy food. This participation, identical in all, signifies and realizes the suppression of all that divides men, and brings about the meeting of all at a higher level, where all opposition is eliminated.

Thus the Eucharist becomes the great instrument of bringing men closer to one another. Whenever the faithful take part in it with a sincere heart, they receive a new impetus to establish a better relationship among themselves, leading to recognition of one another's rights and corresponding duties as well.

In this way the satisfaction of the requirements of justice is facilitated, precisely because of the particular climate of interpersonal relations that brotherly charity creates within the same community.

Fortaleza 11.8.80

EUCHARIST: SACRAMENT OF GOD'S CLOSENESS June 11

They told how they had recognised him at the breaking of bread.
(Luke 24:35)

It is possible to speak of the Eucharist in different ways. In the course of history all sorts of different things have been said about it. It is difficult to say something that has not been said already.

123

Yet at the same time, whatever we say, however we approach this Great Mystery of the faith and of the life of the Church, *we always discover something new*. This is not because our words reveal some new element: it lies in the Mystery itself. When we live with that Mystery in the spirit of faith, *it always brings with it new light, new amazement and new joy*.

The Eucharist brings us close to God in an extraordinary way. *It is the Sacrament of his closeness to man*. God wished to enter the history of man, and this is precisely what happens when he is present in the Eucharist. He wished to accept humanity; to actually become a man. The Sacrament of the Body and Blood reminds us continually of his Divine Humanity.

Rome 13.6.79

EUCHARIST: SACRAMENT OF GOD'S DESCENT   June 12

Every time you eat this bread and drink this cup, you are proclaiming his death.

(1 Cor. 11:26)

It is the Sacrament of God's descent to man, of his approach to everything that is human. As St. John Chrysostom put it, *it is the Sacrament of Divine 'condescension'*. By means of the Passion and death on the Cross, the entry of the divine into human reality reached its climax; the Son of God Incarnate became in a particularly radical way, the Son of Man, sharing in the human condition right to the end!

The Eucharist, the Sacrament of the Body and Blood, reminds us above all of the death that Christ suffered on the Cross. This is testified by the words with which Christ instituted *the Sacrament of his Body and his Blood*. It is the Sacrament of death, an expiatory sacrifice. The Sacrament of death, in which all the power of love was expressed. *The Sacrament of death, consisting in giving his life to win back fullness of life.*

By means of this Sacrament, the death that gives life is continually proclaimed in the history of man. It is continually realized in that very simple sign, which is the sign of the Bread and Wine. *In it God is present and close to man, with that penetrating closeness of his death on the Cross*, from which there sprang the power of resurrection. Man, by means of the Eucharist, becomes a participant in this power.

Rome 13.6.79

'Take it and eat,' he said . . . 'Drink all of you from this.'

(Matt. 26:26)

The Eucharist is the Sacrament of Communion. Christ gives himself to each of us who receive him under the eucharistic species. He gives himself to each of us who eats the eucharistic Food and drinks the eucharistic Drink.

This eating and drinking is a sign of communion. It is a sign of spiritual union, in which man receives Christ, is offered a participation in his Spirit, and renews in him his intimate relationship with the Father.

A great poet says:

I speak to you, who reign in heaven and at
the same time are a guest in the house of my spirit . . .
I speak to you! Words fail me for You;
Your thought listens to every thought of mine;
You reign far away and serve close at hand,
King in heaven and in my heart on the cross . . .

(Mickiewocz)

Rome 13.6.79

CHRIST RECEIVES US   June 14

Everyone is to recollect himself before eating this bread and drinking this cup.

(1 Cor. 11:28)

In the Eucharist, I receive Christ, but Jesus also receives me. And here I must answer: test myself, answer for myself: can he receive me as I am, receive, affirm, accept?

This is the old Christian tradition, and no other is ever possible. A person must test himself, must put the question to himself, must answer for himself: Can he accept me? Can he receive me?

Maybe sometimes this question is the start of the road to flight, to some withdrawal. Maybe sometimes the words 'I am not worthy' are misunderstood. This is not the Christian attitude. Christ, the Eucharist, Communion, while making ever increasing demands, also becomes ever more appealing. And the only true Christian attitude is that expressed in the words: 'I am trying, I am doing what I can. Lord, I am not worthy for you to enter' (Luke 7:6).

This is the attitude of those who receive Christ and are aware that, at the same time, Christ in some way receives them.

Cracow 14.4.62

EUCHARIST: A CALL TO CONVERSION June 15

For anyone who is in Christ, there is a new creation; the old creation has gone, and now the new one is here.

(2 Cor. 5:17)

The Eucharist is also a great call to conversion. We know that it is an invitation to the banquet; that, by nourishing ourselves on the Eucharist, we receive in it the body and the blood of Christ, under the appearances of bread and wine. Precisely because of this invitation, *the Eucharist is and remains the call to conversion.*

If we receive it as such a call, such an invitation, it brings forth in us its proper fruits. It transforms our lives. It makes us a 'new man', a 'new creation'. It helps us not to be 'overcome by evil, but to overcome evil by good' (Rom. 12:21). *The Eucharist helps love to triumph in us –* love over hatred, zeal over indifference.

Dublin 29.9.79

THE GENTLENESS OF CHRIST June 16

Learn from me, for I am gentle and humble in heart.

(Matt. 11:29)

This is, perhaps, the only occasion when the Lord Jesus referred to his own heart. And, when he did, he stressed this one feature; 'gentleness and humility'; as if he meant that it is only by this that he wishes to conquer man, that by means of 'gentleness and humility' he wishes to be the King of hearts. *The whole mystery of his reign was expressed in these words.*

Gentleness and humility include, in a certain sense, all the 'riches' of the Redeemer's heart, of which St. Paul wrote to the Ephesians. But also that 'gentleness and humility', reveal him fully, and enable us to get to know him and accept him; they make him the object of supreme admiration.

Rome 20.6.79

THE HEART OF CHRIST INVITES US June 17

I have been entrusted with this special grace, not only of proclaiming to the pagans the infinite treasure of Christ, but also of explaining how the mystery is to be dispensed.

(Eph. 3:8)

Many disciples, men and women, have understood this mystery particularly well. Paul of Tarsus, who was converted from being a persecutor and became an Apostle, was certainly prominent amongst them. He speaks as a man who has received a great grace.

The 'infinite treasure of Christ' and the 'mystery' are addressed by the Holy Spirit to the 'inner man', 'that Christ may live in your hearts through faith'. And when Christ, with the strength of the Holy Spirit, dwells through faith in our human hearts, then, with our human spirit (that is, with this heart), we will be able 'to grasp the breadth and the length, the height and the depth, knowing the love of Christ, which is beyond all knowledge' (Eph. 3:18–19).

It was so that the heart, every human heart, should have such knowledge, that the Divine Heart of the One who was condemned and crucified on Calvary was opened at the end of his earthly life.

This knowledge is different in different human hearts. Listening to Paul's words, let each of us ask how much of this knowledge our own heart has; for 'only by this can we be certain that we are children of the truth and be able to quieten our conscience in his presence' (1 John 3:19–20).

The Heart of the God-Man does not judge human hearts. The Heart calls. The Heart invites. That was why it was opened with the soldier's spear.

Rome 20.6.79

Knowing the love of Christ, which is beyond all knowledge, you are filled with the utter fullness of God.

(Eph. 3:19)

A book entitled *Who is Jesus Christ for me?* was published in Cracow in 1975. It contains the results of an investigation, in the form of a questionnaire, mounted by a Catholic weekly that for thirty years has concentrated on socio-cultural matters; as such it is almost unique in Poland. Hundreds of replies to the questionnaire were received. Reproduced in the book under various subject headings they provide a most impressive picture of many people's inner lives.

As a bishop and pastor I was greatly moved when I read the book, for every reply brought confirmation of the fundamental importance — for the Church and for Christianity — of the truth about the Person of Christ, alive in men, in their thoughts and in their hearts. Who is Jesus Christ for these people? All the replies received by the editors were anonymous, but nonetheless they all had the flavour of true confessions, because they disclosed deep spiritual problems arising out of the correspondent's own religious and moral experience.

Anonymity was of course a prerequisite for sincerity and honesty. And the sincerity and honesty of those replies showed me, as a bishop and pastor, how grace indeed abounds; and they showed me, too, the nature of the 'love of Christ which is beyond all knowledge'.

S. of C.

CHRIST IS SUPREME LOVE   June 19

I live now not with my own life but with the life of Christ who lives in me.
(Gal. 2:20)

Let me tell you a little more about the book *Who is Jesus Christ for me?* Among the writers are young and old alike, cultured people and simple people; but the cultured are more numerous and this affects the style of the book's comments. The vast majority are laity, and people facing difficulties of one kind or another. Most are believers; but some replies came from waverers or outright non-believers.

The list of headings is in itself informative. To the question: 'Who is Jesus Christ for you?', one young worker's reply can be summed up as: *'He was one of us'*, and that means a great deal. The young usually reply very briefly: 'He permeates my whole life', 'I know that he loves me', 'I see him in every human being', 'He has taught me how to love', 'My Christ is the one who listens and answers', 'I grow to understand him from what I find in other men', 'Christ is life – and these are not just fine words'.

Similar replies can be found throughout the book: 'Mystery', 'A perfect example of man', 'The most human of men', 'A Friend', 'The Christ of peace', 'He is now everything for me', 'The one who is waiting for me', 'The one who commands by the example he sets', 'The one who guides me', 'The one I trust', 'A guide and an authority', 'Presence', 'Meaning and purpose', 'Boundless mercy', 'Hope and mystery', 'A concrete reality', 'He is happiness', 'He just is'.

Here is one more: *'For me Christ is a supreme Love that awaits, forgives and embraces all men without exception'*, the writer was a man of twenty-eight, a university lecturer.

S. of C.

CHRIST NOT EASY TO ACCEPT   June 20

If anyone wants to be a follower of mine, let him renounce himself and take up his cross and follow me.

(Matt. 16:24)

In the book I have just referred to, a lawyer stressed the need for continually choosing in favour of Christ: 'I am infinitely grateful to my divine guide, my anchor of truth, who is so relevant to our times. I try always to have in mind the Master's words: "Nobody can serve two masters; for either he will despise the one and love the other, or he will become attached to the one and lose sight of the other." It is this firm statement that enables me to keep my self-respect, to be myself in my work, at home, among my friends and acquaintances. I continually thank the God-man for that; because it means that I am always free, at any time and in any place, to worship him unceasingly, regardless of whether the worship is public or private.'

Many correspondents admit quite frankly that for them Christ is not easy to accept. 'It is not enough to say just once in life: I will believe! One has to go on saying it again and again, whenever things get difficult. Difficulties do arise, times when one has to take up the Cross daily. And then *Christ is not easy to accept, but he is truer than ever* . . .

When I bow to this truth I feel myself a pupil of a really wonderful Master.'

S. of C.

ONLY IN AND THROUGH CHRIST June 21

Jesus said: 'I am the Way, the Truth and the Life, no one can come to the Father except through me.'

(John 14:6)

It is less possible than ever today to stop at a Christian faith that is superficial or which you have merely because everyone else does; times, as you well know, have changed. The increase in culture, the continual influence of the mass media, knowledge of past and present human events, increased sensitivity and a greater demand for certainty and clarity on fundamental truths, the massive presence in society and in culture of atheistic, agnostic, and even anti-Christian conceptions, call for a personal faith: *a faith, that is, sought with longing for the truth, and then put completely into practice in life.*

That is to say, it is necessary to arrive at the clear and certain conviction of the truth of one's Christian faith, namely, in the first place, the historicity and divinity of Christ and the mission of the Church willed and founded by him.

When one is really convinced that Jesus is the Word Incarnate and is still present in the Church, then one accepts his 'word' completely, because it is a divine word which does not deceive, which does not contradict itself, and which gives us the true and only meaning of life and eternity. *He alone, in fact, has words of eternal life! He alone is the way, the truth and the life!*

Rome 1.11.78

CERTAINTY IS JESUS June 22

Jesus said: 'I am the light of the world, anyone who follows me will not be walking in the dark.'

(John 8:12)

Jesus Christ alone is the adequate and ultimate answer to the supreme question about the meaning of life and history.

While respecting those who have other ideas, and well aware that faith in Christ has its times and its seasons and demands a personal development, bound up with God's grace, I tell you with confident frankness that, having passed the innocent age of childhood and the sentimental period of adolescence, and having arrived at youth, an exuberant and critical age, the most beautiful and stirring adventure that can happen to you is *the personal meeting with Jesus, who is the only one who gives real meaning to our life.*

It is not enough to just look: it is necessary to be looking for certainty. And certainty is Jesus who states, 'I am the way, the truth and the life' (John 14:6). 'I am the light of the world; anyone who follows me will not be walking in the dark.'

Rome 1.3.80

JESUS, THE MEANING OF OUR EXISTENCE   June 23

God gave his only Son, so that everyone who believes in him may have eternal life.

(John 3:16)

Only Jesus has convincing and consoling words; only he has the words of life, in fact of eternal life: 'For God sent his Son into the world so that through him the world might be saved.'

There is no solution for scepticism and despair except in faith in Christ. *Only Jesus reveals the meaning of our existence in the boundless mystery of the universe*, in the dark and unforeseeable turmoil of history.

The great and well-known French philosopher and mathematician, Blaise Pascal, when he finally arrived at the definitive and joyful meeting with Christ, wrote with unequalled lucidity in his *Pensées*:

'Not only do we know God only through Jesus Christ, but we know ourselves only through Jesus Christ. We do not know life and death, except through Jesus Christ. Outside Jesus Christ we do not know what our life is or our death, we do not know God or ourselves. For this reason, except for the Scriptures, the object of which is Jesus Christ alone, we know nothing and see nothing but darkness and confusion in the nature of God and in our own nature.'

Rome 1.3.80

For the foundation, nobody can lay any other than the one which has already been laid, that is Jesus Christ.

(1 Cor. 3:11)

In Christ you will discover the true greatness of your own humanity; he will make you understand your own dignity as human beings 'created to the image and likeness of God'.

Christ has the answers to your questions and the key to history; he has the power to uplift hearts. He keeps calling you, he keeps inviting you, he who is 'the way, and the truth, and the life'. Yes, Christ calls you, but he calls you in truth. *His call is demanding, because he invites you to let yourselves be captured by him completely*, so that your whole lives will be seen in a different light.

He is the Son of God, who reveals to you the loving face of the Father. He is the Teacher, the only one whose teaching does not pass away, the only one who teaches with authority. He is the friend who said to his disciples, 'I shall not call you servants any more, . . . I call you friends' (John 15:15). And he proved his friendship by laying down his life for you.

His call is demanding for he taught us what it means to be truly human. Without heeding the call of Jesus, it will not be possible to realize the fullness of your own humanity. You must build on the foundation which is Christ; only with him will your life be meaningful and worthwhile.

Galway 30.9.79

JESUS' ATTITUDE TO WOMEN   June 25

His disciples returned, and were surprised to find him speaking to a woman.
(John 4:27)

It is particularly moving to meditate on the attitude of Jesus to women. He showed himself to be bold and surprising by the standards of his day, when woman was considered in pagan culture to be merely an object of pleasure, of possession and of labour, and in Judaism, was subordinated and humiliated.

Jesus always showed the greatest esteem and the greatest respect for women, for every woman, and he was particularly sensitive to women's suffering. Breaking through the religious and social barriers of his time. *Jesus re-established woman in her full dignity as a human person before God and before men.*

How could we fail to recall his meetings with Martha and Mary, with the Samaritan woman, with the widow of Nain, with the adulterous woman, with the woman who suffered from a haemorrhage, with the sinner at the house of Simon the Pharisee.

And how could we fail to recall, above all, that Jesus wanted to associate some women with the twelve? They accompanied him and served him, and were of comfort to him during the painful way to the Cross. Then, after the Resurrection, Jesus appeared to the holy women and to Mary Magdalen, bidding her announce his Resurrection to the disciples.

Rome 29.4.79

SIMON PETER'S VOCATION   June 26

Jesus said to Simon Peter, 'Simon son of John, do you love me more than these others do?'

(John 21:15)

Christ asked this question three times and three times Peter answered — 'Yes, Lord, you know I love you.' *Peter committed himself with this answer, along the way that was to be his until the end of his life.* He was to be followed everywhere by the wonderful exchange in which he had also heard three times: 'Feed my sheep,' 'Feed my lambs.'

For ever, to the end of his life, Peter was to advance along the way, accompanied by this triple question: 'Do you love me?' *And he measured all his activities by the answer he had given then.* When he was called before the Sanhedrin. When he was put in prison in Jerusalem, a prison from which he should not have come out . . . and from which, nevertheless, he came out.

When he left Jerusalem towards the north, to Antioch, and then, even further, from Antioch to Rome. And when in Rome, he had persevered to the end of his days, he experienced the power of the words according to which 'Somebody else will take you where you would rather not go' (John 21:18).

He knew too that, thanks to the power of these words, the Church 'remained faithful to the teaching of the Apostles' and 'day by day the Lord added to their community those destined to be saved' (Acts 2:47).

Paris 30.5.80

A PEOPLE SET APART   June 27

He is the living stone, rejected by men but chosen by God.

(1 Peter 2:4)

Christ is the living stone. He is the cornerstone of this shape that the world, our human world, can take thanks to love.

Peter knew this, he whom Christ asked three times: 'Do you love me?' Peter knew, he who, when put to the test, denied his Master three times. His voice trembled when he answered: 'Yes, Lord; you know that I love you.' However, he did not answer: 'And yet, Lord, I disappointed you' — but: 'Lord, you know that I love you.'

Saying that, he knew already that Christ is the cornerstone, on which, in spite of all human weakness, this construction that will have the form of love can grow in him, Peter. Through all situations and through all trials. To the end. That is why he will write one day, in his letter, the text on Jesus Christ, the cornerstone, of which we are 'living stones making a spiritual house' to offer spiritual sacrifices acceptable to God.

All that means nothing else than to answer, always and constantly, with tenacity and consistency, this one question: Do you love? Do you love me? Do you love me more? It is in fact, this answer, namely, this love, which makes us 'a chosen race, a royal priesthood, a people set apart'.

It is this that makes us proclaim the wonderful deeds of him who called us out of darkness into his wonderful light.

Paris 30.5.80

ST. PETER AT ROME   June 28

Somebody else will take you where you would rather not go.

(John 21:18)

Peter came to Rome!
What else but obedience to the inspiration received from *the Lord*

guided him and brought him to this city, the heart of the Empire? Perhaps the fisherman of Galilee did not want to come here. Perhaps he would have preferred to stay there, on the shores of the lake of Genesareth, with his boat and his nets. But guided by the Lord, obedient to his inspiration, he came here.

According to an ancient tradition (given magnificent literary expression in a novel by Henry Sienkiewicz), *Peter wanted to leave Rome during Nero's persecution*. But the Lord intervened: he went to meet him. Peter spoke to him and asked: *'Quo vadis, Domine?'* — 'Where are you going, Lord?' and the Lord answered him at once: 'I am going to Rome to be crucified again.' Peter went back to Rome and stayed here until his crucifixion.

Rome 22.10.78

SAINT PETER AND SAINT PAUL   June 29

All there is to come now is the crown of righteousness reserved for me, which the Lord will give to me on that Day.

(2 Tim. 4:8)

On this day the Roman Church recalls the day of their death: the day that united them with the Lord, whose Coming they awaited, whose Law they observed, and from whom they received 'the crown of life'.

The day of death was for them the beginning of the New Life. The Lord himself revealed this to them with his own resurrection, to which they became witnesses by means of their words and deeds and also by means of their death. Everything together: the words, the deeds, and the death of Simon of Bethsaida, whom the Lord called Peter, and of Saul of Tarsus, who after his conversion was called Paul, is, as it were, the complement of Christ's Gospel, its penetration into the history of mankind, into the history of the world, and also into the history of this city.

And really there is matter for meditation in these days, which the Lord, by means of the death of his Apostles, permits us to fill with a special memory of their lives.

Rome 27.6.79

This man is my chosen instrument to bring my name before pagans and before the people of Israel.

(Acts 9:15)

Paul came to Rome as a prisoner, after appealing to Caesar against the sentence of a condemnation passed in Palestine. He was a Roman citizen, and he had the right to appeal in this way. Therefore, it is possible that he spent the last two years of his life in the Rome of Nero.

He continued to teach by means of the spoken and written word (that is, by means of the letters), but he was probably no longer able to leave the city. His missionary journeys, which had brought him to the main towns of the Mediterranean world, were over. In this way the Lord's announcement about the 'chosen instrument to bring my name before the pagans . . .' was fulfilled.

In the course of just over thirty years since Christ's death, his Resurrection and ascension to the Father, the land around the Mediterranean Sea and therefore the Roman Empire had gradually been populated with the first Christians. This was, to a considerable extent, the result of Paul's missionary activity.

In all this time, the desire 'to be gone and be with Christ' never left him (Phil. 1:23) and it was right here in Rome that his desire came true.

Rome 27.6.79

July

THE MISSION OF PETER
July 1

Then Simon Peter spoke up; 'You are the Christ,' he said, 'the Son of the Living God.'

(Matt. 16:16)

These words of personal faith and divine inspiration mark the beginning of Peter's mission in the history of the People of God. *These words also mark the beginning of a new era in the history of salvation.* From the moment these words were spoken at Caesarea Philippi, the history of the People of God was linked to the man who had pronounced them: 'You are Peter and on this rock I will build my church.'

These words have a special meaning for me. They express what is the heart of my mission as the Successor of Peter at the end of the twentieth century.

Jesus Christ is the centre of the universe and of history. He alone is the Redeemer of every human being. In God's inscrutable providence I have been chosen to continue the mission of Peter and to repeat with similar conviction: 'You are the Christ — the Son of the living God.'

Nothing in my life and ministry can take precedence over this mission: to proclaim Christ to all the nations, to speak of his marvellous goodness, to tell of his power to save, and to assure every man and woman that whoever believes in Christ will not die but will have eternal life.

Rome 22.2.80

THE MISSION OF PETER'S SUCCESSOR
July 2

God has made this Jesus whom you crucified both Lord and Christ.

(Acts 2:36)

In the course of two thousand years, these words 'You are Peter' have been spoken 264 times to the ears and conscience of a fragile and sinful man. *Two hundred and sixty-four times a new Peter was set at the side of the first one to be the foundation stone of the Church.* The last in time, it was to me that the promise of Caesarea Philippi was repeated, and it is in the office of Peter that I am in your midst. With what message?

The same one that Peter proclaimed. Peter, ardent but fearful, the friend, the renegade, the penitent, had just received the Holy Spirit. And with the force of the Spirit he proclaims to a Jerusalem full of pilgrims: 'God has made this Jesus, whom you crucified both Lord and Christ.'

All that Peter will say up to the last confession on the hill of the Vatican, which crowns that of Caesarea Philippi, is reduced to this sentence: *All that the Successor of Peter must say is perhaps contained in these simple words: 'God made him Lord.'* Fundamentally, it is what the Pope feels: the sweet and urgent duty of proclaiming, wherever he passes, with the power and fervour of one who announces good news.

Rome 6.7.80

THE CHURCH'S THREEFOLD MISSION   July 3

You will receive power when the Holy spirit comes on you, and then you will be my witnesses.

(Acts 1:8)

In past centuries, when the Successor of Peter took possession of his See, the triregnum or tiara was placed on his head. The last Pope to be crowned was Paul VI in 1963, but after the solemn coronation ceremony he never used the tiara again and left his Successors free to decide in this regard.

The Second Vatican Council has reminded us of the fact that Christ's mission as Priest, Prophet-Teacher and King continues in the Church.

Everyone, the whole People of God, shares in this threefold mission. Perhaps in the past, the tiara, this triple crown, was placed on the Pope's head in order to express by that symbol the Lord's plan for his Church. Namely that all the hierarchical order of Christ's Church, *all 'sacred power' exercised in the Church, is nothing more than service*, service with a single purpose; that purpose is to ensure that the whole People of God shares in this threefold mission of Christ and always remains under the power of the Lord; a power that has its source not in the powers of this world but in the mystery of the Cross and Resurrection.

Rome 22.10.78

After I have been there, Paul said, I must go on to see Rome.

(Acts 19:21)

Entering the history of man, becoming Man, God made human history, in its entirety, the history of salvation. What was fulfilled at Nazareth, Bethlehem and Jerusalem is a part of history and, at the same time, it is a ferment working throughout history.

Although the history of men and peoples has developed and continues to develop along paths of its own, even though the history of Rome — then at the peak of its ancient splendour — passed alongside the birth, the life, the passion, the death and the resurrection of Jesus of Nazareth almost without noticing it, these salvific events became new leaven in the history of man.

They became new leaven particularly in the history of Rome. It can be said that at the time when Jesus was born, at the time when he died on the Cross and rose again, ancient Rome, then the capital of the world, experienced a new birth. It is not by chance that we already find it so deeply integrated into the New Testament.

In the Acts of the Apostles St. Luke, who plans his Gospel as the path of Jesus to Jerusalem, where the paschal mystery is accomplished, takes Rome as the point of arrival of the apostolic journeys where the mystery of the Church will be manifested.

Rome 25.4.79

BUILT UPON THE EUCHARIST   July 5

These remained faithful . . . to the breaking of bread and to the prayers.

(Acts 2:42)

The Church was founded, as the new community of the People of God, in the apostolic community of those Twelve who, at the Last Supper, became partakers of the Body and Blood of the Lord under the species of bread and wine.

But the Church is not brought into being only through the union of people, through the experience of brotherhood to which the Eucharistic banquet gives rise. In Eucharistic Communion we receive Christ, Christ himself; and our union with him, which is a gift and grace for each individual, brings it about that in him we are also associated in the unity of his Body which is the Church.

Rome 24.2.80

THE PEOPLE OF GOD July 6

Those he called he justified, and with those he justified he shared his glory.
(Rom. 8:30)

We are not a faceless and nameless mass in the Church. We are not impersonal numbers, unknown to one another. We are the People of God. *We are loved one by one by the Father, in the Son, through the Holy Spirit.*

We are persons capable of answering the call of eternal love of this God, who has always known us, and has predestined us to be in conformity with the image of his Son, who called, justified, and glorified us; therefore, *we are brothers, who love one another and form one body.*

Rome 6.7.80

THE GOOD NEWS OF CHRIST'S LOVE July 7

By this love you have for one another, everyone will know that you are my disciples.
(John 13:35)

When I am travelling in my pastoral visits, with the mission of representing Christ to the whole Church scattered throughout the world, I always remember that Christ himself asked St. Peter, and therefore those who were to take his place in the 'Church that presides over the universal assembly of charity' (St. Ignatius of Antioch), for a profession of love.

Love for this Christ, without which it is impossible to feed well the Christian faithful, whom he called his 'lambs' and his 'sheep'. And love for one's neighbour, and especially one's brothers in the faith. By this love, everyone will know that we are his disciples.

To obey this commandment, I do my utmost to meet everyone: rich and poor, those who live in comfort, at least relative comfort, and those who have to cope with great difficulties in order to live. *To all of them I wish to speak of, and bear witness to, the love of Our Lord Jesus Christ in order that they may believe in him and arrive at salvation.*

But the underprivileged of the earth, since they are in greater need of help and comfort, always have a special place in this concern of mine to continue faithfully the mission of Christ: 'to bring the good news to the Poor', the salvation of God.

Favela dos Alagados 7.7.80

CHRIST IS ALIVE IN HIS PEOPLE July 8

The proof that you are sons is that God has sent the Spirit of his Son into our hearts.

(Gal. 4:6)

Of paramount importance in the mystery of the Church is the fact that *Christ is alive in his people.* His life goes on in the communities of the faithful throughout the world, in all those who by faith and Baptism have received justification in his name.

And because Christ is living, his love above all is kept alive in the Church. Jesus continues to love his Father, and the Father continues to love his Son in all those whom the Son has taken to himself as brothers and sisters. And the mystery of a love received from the Father and given back to the Father is the legacy of all Christ's disciples: 'By this love you have for one another, everyone will know that you are my disciples.'

Rome 23.5.80

SOLIDARITY WITH THE POOR July 9

The only thing they insisted on was that we should remember to help the poor, as indeed I was anxious to do.

(Gal. 2:10)

The Church herself is a big community, within which there are different situations in the individual communities. There is no lack of people suffering material deprivation, but there is also no lack of people suffering oppression and persecution. In the whole Catholic community, and in the individual Churches, *there must be an increase in the sense of particular solidarity with these brothers and sisters in the faith.*

Here the *'rich and free' Church* (if one may use the expression) *has enormous debts and commitments towards the 'poor and constricted' Church* (if one may use that expression as well).

Solidarity means above all a proper understanding and then proper action, not on the basis of what corresponds to the ideas of the person offering help, but on the basis of what corresponds to the real needs of the person being helped, and what corresponds to his or her dignity.

Rome 5.11.79

MISSIONARIES OF LOVE   July 10

Serve one another in works of love.

(Gal. 5:13)

Let us not forget that fundamental principle of the plan of salvation, according to which *the person who offers to others saves himself or herself.* Therefore it might be that the remedy for many internal difficulties from which some local Churches and some Christian communities are suffering is to be found precisely in the practice of this solidarity.

Difficulties will be effectively overcome when — in a certain sense taking the gaze off themselves — they begin to serve others 'in truth and charity'. This principle interprets in a simpler way the missionary function of the Church — indeed this principle offers a stimulating idea and, in a certain sense, a missionary imperative for our generation.

Providence has entrusted to our generation a great work of renewal.

Rome 5.11.79

THE LEAVEN OF THE GOSPEL   July 11

If the Lord does not build the house, in vain the masons toil.

(Ps. 127:1)

This is the answer that the Church must give particularly today; society cannot be constructed without God, without the help of God. It would be a contradiction. *God is the guarantee of a society fit for man.* This is so in the first place because he has impressed the supreme nobility of his image and likeness within man; and then because Christ came to reconstitute this image, sullied by sin, and, as 'Redeemer of man', brought him back to the insuppressible dignity of his fundamental origin.

External structures – International Communities, States, Cities, activities of individuals – must highlight this reality, and give it the necessary space; otherwise they collapse, or are reduced to a lifeless façade.

The Church, founded by Christ, indicates to modern man the way he must follow to construct the earthly city, which is a prelude – although not exempt from conflicts and contradictions – to the heavenly city. The Church indicates how to build society in accordance with man in respect for man. *Her task is to put the leaven of the Gospel in all fields of human activity.* It is in Christ that the Church is an 'expert in humanity'.

Rome 6.7.80

OUR HOPE FOR UNITY July 12

In the one Spirit we were all baptized, Jews as well as Greeks, slaves as well as citizens.

(1 Cor. 12:13)

Our times are marked by a great expectation. All who believe in Christ and worship the true God are seeking ways of coming closer to one another. They are seeking paths leading to unity, and their cry is: 'Christ sets us free and unites us.'

The Church, the People of God, senses ever more profoundly that she is being called to this unity. The Church, the People of God, is at the same time the Mystical Body of Christ. St. Paul likened the Church to the Human Body in order to describe more clearly its life and its unity. The human body is given its life and its unity by the mother.

Mary, by the working of the Holy Spirit, gave unity to the human body of Christ. And that is why our hope today turns in a special way towards her, in these times of ours when the Mystical Body of Christ is being more fully reconstituted in unity.

S. of C.

How beautiful on the mountains are the feet of one who brings good news.

(Is. 52:7)

Good news, in particular the Good News par excellence, God's love revealed in Jesus Christ: the joy of having a Saviour and of being called by him to be sons of God and brothers of one another . . .

Be heralds of this good news to all. Proclaim it in all circumstances offering it for the acceptance of men's hearts, in full respect of freedom of conscience, and in this way you will contribute to the transformation of humanity from within, renewing it with the perennial newness of Jesus Christ, the Redeemer of Man.

Belem 8.7.80

CHRIST MEANT US TO BE FREE   July 14

When Christ freed us, he meant us to remain free.

(Gal. 5:1)

To evangelize means making Christ present in the life of man as a person, and at the same time in the life of society. *To evangelize means doing everything possible, according to our capacities, so that man 'may believe'*; so that man may find himself again in Christ; so that he may find again in him the true meaning of his own life.

This rediscovery is what will bring about man's liberation. St. Paul expressed it when he writes: 'When Christ freed us, he meant us to remain free.' So liberation, then, is certainly a reality of faith, one of the fundamental biblical themes, which are a deep part of Christ's salvific mission, of the work of Redemption, of his teaching.

Rome 21.2.79

NO PROGRESS WITHOUT LOVE   July 15

You must love the Lord your God with all your heart . . . and your neighbour as yourself.

(Luke 10:27)

We see the progress of material things, we see the progress of industry, production, all of which is but a means to man and not an end.

But on what does the progress of man depend?

And here, my dear friends, we can see that where the progress of man is concerned, no one has gone further than Jesus Christ. No one has gone further and no one will go further. Jesus Christ has determined the end point of the progress of Man. He is, as the Apostle says, 'the Alpha and Omega', the beginning and the end of human progress.

For, where his own progress is concerned, no one can tell man more than Jesus Christ did when he taught, 'You must love the Lord your God . . . you must love your neighbour as yourself.'

Cracow 11.9.66

THE GLORIFICATION OF CHRIST   July 16

This is my Son, the Chosen One. Listen to him.

(Luke 9:35)

We hear these words at the moment when Peter, John and James, the Apostles chosen by Christ, are on Mount Tabor; at the moment of the Transfiguration.

It is, therefore, an unusual moment. *A moment in which Christ wishes in a way to tell the elect Apostles something more about himself and his mission.* And let us not forget that they are the same three Apostles that he will take with him, some time afterwards, to Gethsemane, so that they may witness the moment when he is a prey to anguish and when the sweat of blood appears on his face.

On Mount Tabor we are, however, witnesses with them of the exaltation of the glorification of Christ in that human aspect of his, in which the Apostles and the crowds were able to see him on earth.

'This is my Son, the Chosen One, Listen to him!'

For the second time the Voice from above bears witness to him: in this witness the Father speaks of his Son, his beloved, Eternal Son, who is of the same substance as the Father – of him who is God from God and Light from Light, and who became a man like each of us.

The first time this witness was borne at the Jordan, at the moment of John's Baptism. This happened at the Jordan – at the beginning of Christ's Messianic mission. Now it happens on Mount Tabor – before the approaching Passion: before Gethsemane, Calvary. And at the same time, in witness of the future Resurrection.

Rome 2.3.80

The Lord Jesus Christ will transfigure these wretched bodies of ours into copies of his glorious body.

(Phil. 3: 21)

When the Father comes, in that mysterious voice, from above, he bears witness to the Son and, at the same time, lets us know that in him and through him is enclosed the new and definitive Covenant with man. This Covenant had been concluded in ancient times with Abraham, who is the father of our faith and this was the beginning of the Old Covenant.

However, the Covenant had been concluded even before with Adam, with the first man Adam and, not having been kept by our ancestors, it was waiting for Christ, the second one, 'the last Adam' (1 Cor. 15:45) in order to acquire in him and through him – its definitive, perfect form.

God the Father concludes the Covenant with man, with the humanity of his Son. This is the climax of the economy of salvation, of the revelation of God's love for man. *The covenant was concluded in order that human beings might become sons of God in God the Son.* Christ 'gave (us) power to become children of God' (John 1:12) regardless of race, language, nationality and sex.

Christ reveals to every man his dignity as God's adopted son, a dignity to which his supreme vocation, earthly and eternal, is bound.

And Christ definitively carries out this work of the Covenant: the work of bringing man to the dignity of adopted son, or daughter, of God, through the Cross.

Rome 2.3.80

LISTENING TO CHRIST   July 18

This is my Son, the Beloved; he enjoys my favour. Listen to him.

(Matt. 17:5)

What does it mean, to listen to Christ?

The whole Church must always give an answer to this question in the dimensions of the generations, periods and changing social, economic and political conditions. The answer must be true, it must be sincere – just as the teaching of Christ, his Gospel, and then Gethsemane, the Cross – and the Resurrection, are true and sincere.

Each of us must always give an answer to this question: whether his Christianity, his life, are in conformity with faith, if they are true and sincere.

The answer will be a little different every time: the answer of the father and mother of a family will be different, that of engaged couples different, that of the child will be different, and that of the boy and the girl different, that of the old person will be different, and that of the sick person confined to his bed of pain will be different, that of the man of science, of politics, of culture, of economy will be different, that of the man who does hard physical work will be different, that of the Religious Sister or Brother will be different, that of the priest, of the pastor of souls, of the Bishop and of the Pope, will be different.

And even if these answers must be as many as are the men who confess Christ – yet they will be in a way only one, characterized by internal likeness to him, whom the Heavenly Father urged us to listen to.

Rome 2.3.80

CHRIST'S AUTHORITY   July 19

Jesus said: 'All authority in heaven and earth has been given to me.'
(Matt. 28:18)

He says so when earthly power – the Sanhedrin, the Power of Pilate – has shown its supremacy over him, by decreeing his death on the Cross. He says so also after his resurrection.

'Authority in heaven and earth' is not an authority against man. It is not even an authority of man over man. *It is the authority that enables man to be revealed to himself in his royalty, in all the fullness of his dignity.*

It is the authority the specific power of which man must discover in his heart, through which he must be revealed to himself in the dimensions of his conscience and in the perspective of eternal life.

Then the whole power of baptism will be revealed in him, he will know that he is 'plunged' in the Father, the Son and the Holy Spirit; *he will find himself again completely in the eternal Word, in infinite Love.*

Le Bourget 1.6.80

Know that I am with you always; Yes, to the end of time.

(Matt. 28:20)

So that also means: today, and for the whole of the era.

The problem of the absence of Christ does not exist. The problem of his moving away from man's history does not exist. God's silence with regard to the anxieties of man's heart and his fate, does not exist.

There is only one problem that exists always and everywhere: the problem of our presence beside Christ. Of our remaining in Christ. Of our intimacy with the authentic truth of his words and with the power of his love.

There exists only one problem, that of our faithfulness to the covenant with eternal wisdom, which is the source of true culture, that is, of man's growth, and that of *faithfulness to the promises of our baptism* in the name of the Father and of the Son and of the Holy Spirit!

Le Bourget 1.6.80

EDUCATING THE APOSTLES   July 21

Jesus said to Simon, 'Put out into deep water and pay out your nets for a catch.'

(Luke 5:4)

The event, which might seem a usual one, shortly takes on an extraordinary character. The catch, in fact, turns out to be particularly abundant, which surprises Simon and the other fishermen, whose preceding effort, which had lasted the whole night, had not yielded any result. 'We toiled all night and took nothing,' Simon says, when Jesus asks him to let down the nets. They do so merely out of respect for the words of Jesus, moved by a motive of esteem and obedience.

The unexpected abundant catch, such as to require the help of their companions in the other boat, arouses in Simon Peter a typical reaction. He falls down at Jesus' feet, saying: 'Leave me, Lord; I am a sinful man.'

The other witnesses of the miraculous event, the brothers James and John, do not react in the same way, but they too are greatly astonished by the extraordinary catch they had taken.

Jesus then addresses to Simon the words which give the whole event a prophetic sense: 'Do not be afraid; from now on it is men you will catch.'

Jesus educates them to the task of future witnesses to his power and of reliable teachers of that truth which he has brought to the world from the Father, the truth that is himself.

Rome 11.2.80

THE CHURCH'S DESTINY   July 22

A servant is not greater than his master. If they persecuted me, they will persecute you too.

(John 15:20)

The Church in its destiny is similar to Christ, it is and must be similar to Christ. Christ said so to the Apostles, to those first witnesses, and they have handed it on to us.

Christ said: 'The disciple is not superior to his teacher', and 'if they persecuted me, they will persecute you too. If they kept my word they will keep yours as well.' In these sentences *he defined the fate of the Church forever.* He linked the fate of the Church to his own fate, for he knew that only with great toil will be created that which the Gospel has brought to mankind.

But he told them too, while foretelling the persecutions and hardship, that to him and to the Church belongs in the end the victory of ideas. 'If they kept my word, they will keep yours as well.'

Cracow 9.4.62

THE MEANING OF DIALOGUE   July 23

Remember this, my dear brothers: be quick to listen but slow to speak and slow to rouse your temper.

(James 1:19)

What does dialogue mean? We know the word, we use it fairly often and it seems to us that it is more or less the same as a conversation. When two people speak together, it is a dialogue, when one person speaks alone, it is a monologue.

But such explanations of the concepts dialogue and monologue are rather superficial. Dialogue is something more than just a conversation, just the exchange of thoughts, *dialogue is a certain attitude*, a human attitude, which flows from the concept that man is a person, and at the

149

same time, is a being called to live together with others, a social being.

Dialogue involves the ability not only to speak but also to listen, the ability to speak in such a way that the other person can hear and understand, and the ability to hear in such a way as to understand the other person.

It involves a certain attitude, a human attitude, an attitude characteristic of the reasoning and social being which man is; it is also an attitude which is profoundly Christian. Why? Because it can serve to defuse hatred between people, to defuse conflict. One can say that *the principle of dialogue is the antithesis of the principle of conflict.*

Cracow 25.12.65

RECONCILIATION July 24

Leave your offering there before the altar, go and be reconciled with your brother first.

(Matt. 5:23)

There is another word that must be part of the vocabulary of every Christian, especially when barriers of hate and mistrust have been constructed. This word is reconciliation. 'Leave your offering and be reconciled with your brother.'

This command of Jesus is stronger than any barrier that human inadequacy or malice can build. Even when our belief in the fundamental goodness of every human being has been shaken or undermined, even if long-held convictions and attitudes have hardened our hearts, *there is one source of power that is stronger than every disappointment, bitterness or ingrained mistrust, and that power is Jesus Christ*, who brought forgiveness and reconciliation to the world.

Drogheda 29.9.79

THE UNITING POWER OF REDEMPTION July 25

The human race has nothing to boast about to God, but you, God has made members of Christ Jesus and by God's doing he has become our wisdom, and our virtue, and our holiness, and our freedom.

(1 Cor. 1:30)

The source of Christian unity is rooted in the mystery of the Redemption. We firmly believe that the Lord Christ, the Son of God, the Eternal Word became man and died on the Cross to redeem all mankind. And so *in the act of redemption there is from the beginning, from the foundation, and from first principles, an intrinsic unity.*

The act of redemption is in its deepest essence the portion of all mankind. It was intended for them and tries to win them all. And if we look through the prism of the mystery of the Redemption, then we receive a clear vision not only of the unity of the Church but also the unity of all mankind.

In this very act, in this mystery, and in this person who is Christ, the redeemer of all, and in this mystery of his Redemption he embraces all mankind, without exception. He is open to all. The mystery of the Redemption has its own inner dynamic. A dynamic which has its origin in Christ himself, God-made-Man.

Cracow 25.1.63

THE ORGANIC UNITY OF THE CHURCH   July 26

Now you together are Christ's body; but each of you is a different part of it.
(1 Cor. 12:27)

On what do the future prospects of ecumenism depend? It is in the hands of God, but it is also in our own hands.

It depends on deriving the unity of Christians and the unity of the Church from the proper beginnings and the proper sources. We cannot become united simply on the basis of some compromise. The Church is not simply a society of people who exercise mutual toleration. The Church is an organic unity.

It is a body, the Mystical Body of Christ. But the unity of this mystical body, which is also the social unity of all God's people, must gradually grow and ripen, until it is ripe and full.

Cracow 25.1.63

CHRISTIAN UNITY; CO-OPERATING WITH GRACE   July 27

We beg you once again not to neglect the grace of God that you have received.
(2 Cor. 6:1)

Praying for Christian unity is a great act of grace, but also, if we play our part, it is a great act of man united with grace and acting under the influence of grace.

151

There are also wider perspectives to the matter about which we are praying. Pastoral perspectives. If Christ and the Gospel have to reach souls universally and widely, then the unity of Christians is a great and fundamental way of accomplishing this.

Cracow 25.1.63

TRUTH GUIDES FREEDOM   July 28

If you make my word your home . . . you will learn the truth and the truth will make you free.

(John 8:32)

Man by his nature possesses freedom, he is endowed with free will. But this freedom is subordinated in man to reason, and through reason to the truth. This freedom does not mean licence and arbitrariness, that man is free to profess anything at all, free to believe anything at all, free in religious matters to assert anything at all.

There exists a close connection between freedom and truth, by which truth guides freedom. *Freedom is subordinated to the truth.* And when we Christians, separated brethren, on the one hand declare our mutual respect for each others' convictions, and proclaim religious freedom, we must on the other hand at the same time stress the higher laws of truth.

If we did not do so, then we would be acting contrary to the idea of Christian unity. For Christians, in accordance with the spirit of the Gospel, must first of all unite in respect for the human person, in respect for human convictions, but must strive towards the truth.

Cracow 25.1.65

CHRIST IN OUR NEIGHBOUR   July 29

'Who are you, Lord?' he asked, and the voice answered, 'I am Jesus, and you are persecuting me.'

(Acts 9:4)

Let us recall what Christ said: 'Whatever you do to one of the least of these, you do to me.' *The Lord Jesus acts on both sides*: on one side he is the person who requires help and on the other the one who gives help.

Through our meetings and our actions of love for our neighbour, in works of charity, in care for the needy, the Lord Jesus is present among us.

Cracow 12.1.69

THE SELF-DISCOVERY OF YOUTH July 30

Do not let people disregard you because you are young, but be an example to all believers in the way you speak and behave.

(1 Tim. 4:12)

Youth is the time when a person 'sees' himself more clearly, his own self, matures his 'I'. Even a child sometimes shows his own 'I', but a child still lives completely in the environment of adults, the environment of his parents; it lives to a large extent their life.

A young person, on the other hand, begins to break away: he sees his own 'I'. And this is quite reasonable, a person cannot remain a child his whole life through. A person cannot just depend on his parents all his life, nor count only on them: a person must acquire his own 'I', his own self. He must become 'someone'. And youth is precisely when a person begins to become this 'someone'.

It is not easy to become 'someone', and that is why youth is a time both of temptation and hesitation. But a young person through all these temptations and hesitations becomes 'someone' because he finds his own way.

Cracow 21.6.70

PRAYER IN YOUTH July 31

If there is anything you need, pray for it, asking God for it with prayer and thanksgiving.

(Phil. 4:6)

A child prays like a child; he prays the way his parents taught him. When he grows up and becomes an adult, he begins to find that this is rather beneath him — to pray the way his parents taught him, the way he prayed as a child. And so sometimes he stops praying. He prays without putting his heart into it.

But we know quite well, from the experience of every generation that *prayer is the greatest support a person can have.* And it is precisely in

153

all these difficulties, in all the various struggles of our youth that we have to make the right choice and follow the path of good. *When it is necessary to overcome evil and choose good, prayer is our greatest support.*

Cracow 21.6.70

August

YOUNG PEOPLE ON PILGRIMAGE

Shout for joy to the Lord, all virtuous men, . . . sing a new song in his honour.

(Ps. 33: 1–3)

'The beauty of joy' is as important for man as 'the beauty of love'. The special expression of this joy is always song. Today, there still resound in my ears the voices of young people singing which has given rise to the new style of religious songs popular today.

Some groups like to go on pilgrimages. *Modern man, more than in preceding generations, is a man 'on his way'.* This applies particularly to the young. There are many of these groups of young pilgrims (in the strict sense of the word). Their pilgrimage often becomes the completion of a tourist trip, even though its character is different.

I am thinking particularly of the pilgrimage which starts out from Warsaw to Jasna Gora every year at the beginning of August. Young people make up the vast majority of the pilgrims, who walk for ten days, sometimes in difficult conditions, covering about two hundred miles.

Rome 25.7.79

THE WITNESS OF FLOWERS

Listen to me, devout children, and blossom like the rose . . . flower like the lily, spread your fragrance abroad.

(Eccl. 39:13)

In their delicate and perfumed elegance, flowers bear witness to the magnificence of the Creator. Sacred Scripture often avails itself of the language of flowers, to call upon man to the praise of God.

But, above all, how could I fail to remind you of the unforgettable reference that the Lord Jesus made to them in the Gospel to call us to confidence in God the Father? 'Think of the flowers growing in the fields, they never have to work or spin . . . Now if that is how God clothes the grass in the field which is there today and thrown into the furnace tomorrow, will he not much more look after you, you men of little faith?' (Matt. 6: 28–30).

The wild flower, nourished only by the fruitful sap of the earth that sustains it, is pointed out by the Lord as the image and example of serene and courageous abandonment to Providence, an attitude necessary to men in all ages, subjected as they always are to the temptation of mistrust and discouragement owing to personal adversities and natural and historical upsets.

Rome 24.11.79

THE REAL MEANING OF REST   August 3

'Martha, Martha,' Jesus said, 'You worry and fret about so many things.'
(Luke 10:41)

What Christ had to say to Mary and Martha always gives us food for thought. However, I wish today particularly to think of all those who now, in the course of the summer, are taking advantage of rest in the various places of Italy and of other countries.

Rest means leaving everyday occupations, withdrawing from the normal toil of the day, the week, and the year. Leaving and withdrawing from everything that could be expressed by the symbol 'Martha'. It is important that rest should not be a going into emptiness, that it should not be only a emptiness (in this case it would not be a real rest). It is important that rest should be filled with meeting. I am thinking of the meeting with nature, the mountains, the sea, and the forests.

Man, in wise contact with nature, regains quietness and reaches inner peace. But that is still not everything that can be said of rest. It must be filled with a new content, with that content which is expressed in the symbol 'Mary'. 'Mary' means the meeting with Christ, the meeting with God. It means opening the inner eye of the soul to his presence in the world, opening the inner ear to the Word of his Truth.

I wish everyone such a rest.

Rome 20.7.80

YOUNG PEOPLE AT REST August 4

It is Mary who has chosen the better part; it is not to be taken from her.

(Luke 10:42)

In particular, I wish the young this rest; boys and girls who, free from school or university tasks, are travelling in this period, getting to know the world and people, living in holiday camps. They are experiencing the beauty of the world and their own youth with particular intensity. I know that among them there are some for whom the period of summer rest is, at the same time, the period of a special meeting with the Lord, in the brotherly community of those of their own age. These holidays are precious, how very precious! I know from my personal experience, because in my life I have spent many holidays as Pastor with the young.

With all my heart, therefore, I wish all the young that this time of rest may become for them the time of the Meeting, of a meeting in which they may find 'the better part of Mary', the part which shall not be taken away from them.

Rome 20.7.80

CO-OPERATION WITH OUR FRIEND August 5

You are my friends if you do what I command you.

(John 15:14)

A human being, a young person, at times gets lost in himself, in the world about him, and in all the network of human affairs that wrap him round.

Allow Christ to find you. Let him know all about you and guide you. It is true that following someone requires also making demands on ourselves. That is the law of friendship. If we wish to travel together, we must pay attention to the road we are to take.

If we go walking in the mountains, we must follow the signs. If we go mountain climbing, we cannot let go of the rope. *We must also preserve our unity with the Divine Friend whose name is Jesus Christ. We must cooperate with him.*

Cracow 8.6.79

THE ANNIVERSARY OF POPE PAUL VI

August 6

Come, let us praise the Lord joyfully, acclaiming the Rock of our safety.

(Ps. 95)

Today is the anniversary of the death of Pope Paul VI, which took place at Castel Gandolfo, on 6 August.

Among the many images that characterized the figure of this great Bishop of Rome and Successor of St. Peter there is one that is particulary striking. During his pilgrimage in the Holy Land, Paul VI, immersed in prayer, deeply bent, is kneeling on the naked earth, in the place where the feet of the Son of God once passed.

Visiting the various other places of the earth, Pope Paul was accustomed, after alighting from the plane, to begin his visit by kissing the ground on which he had arrived. I have adopted this habit from him and I observe it faithfully.

I think that this gesture expressed precisely what the Psalm proclaims: 'Let us bow, prostrate ourselves, and kneel in front of the Lord our Maker.'

There are moments in which man feels the need of particular prostration before God, present in the world and in men, of a particular manifestation of veneration for the Majesty of the Creator, for him who is the 'rock of our safety': only Love and only Holiness.

All Paul VI's life was full of such worship and veneration of the infinite Mystery of God. This is precisely how we see his figure in the light of everything he did and taught; and the further his earthly life and his ministry recede from us in time, the more clearly we see it.

Rome 3.8.80

YOUNG PEOPLE ON HOLIDAY

August 7

Do not let people disregard you because you are young, but be an example to all the believers.

(I Tim. 4:12)

It is holiday time. Young people and children are free from the commitments of school and university and dedicate this period to rest. Rest is not just part of the human order, it is also part of the divine programme of human life. *He rests well who works well and in turn, he who works well must rest well.*

158

My thoughts go, in particular, to those numerous groups of young people who use their summer rest to deepen their relationship with God and to enrich their spiritual life.

Certainly, in various countries of Europe and the world *we can see a marked search for spiritual and religious values in the young*. The fact that it is impossible to fill one's life with only material things and values seems to be felt very deeply by the young. From this realization aspirations and quests have developed which can only be a source of comfort and hope to us.

Rome 25.7.79

LOVE IN SOCIETY August 8

Where two or three meet in my name, I shall be there with them.

(Matt. 18:20)

The demand for righteousness and love, although it relates to the life of people together in society, is also presented to every man and woman.

Every one of us, according to the conditions under which he lives, the job he does, the environment to which he belongs, is bound to reflect on how best he can fulfil these demands. We know from the Gospel the great value that pertains to all common ventures to instil into human life the spirit of righteousness and love, the spirit of Jesus Christ. 'Where two or three meet in my name, I shall be there with them.'

Cracow 15.1.78

CHRIST OUR HOPE August 9

See that you are dressed for action and have your lamps lit.

(Luke 12:35)

Sometimes we are lamps without light, extinguished, but with possibilities not realized. Well, *I have come to light a flame in your hearts*, should the disappointments you have suffered, the expectations that have not come true, have put it out. I want to say to each of you that you have capacities of goodness, honesty and industry; real, deep

159

capacities, often unsuspected, sometimes made even greater and more vigorous by hard experience.

Rest assured that I have come in your midst because I love you, and have confidence in you; to show you personally this affection, this trust I have in you, and to tell you that *I do not fail to raise my prayer to God so that he may always sustain you* with that love which he manifested by sending us his only-begotten Son, Jesus Christ, our Brother. He, too, experienced suffering and need, but he indicated to us the way and offers us his help to overcome them.

Rome 6.1.80

DREAM OF A NEW WORLD August 10

I saw the holy city, and the new Jerusalem, coming down from God out of heaven.

(Rev. 21:2)

Dream, now and always, of making your life and that of others successful! A life always in search of truth, freedom, rightly understood, and above all, continual dedication to others!

Such a conception of existence, referred to by Christ, who came to give life in abundance cannot but put you on the way to a real development of your personalities and a noble service of mankind.

You are dreaming of a new world! You are right! This longing for a world increasingly freed of what weighs down spirits and hearts, of what compromises or degrades, certainly helps to renew the dynamism of society, which, alas, is more inclined to settle down in comfort than to climb to the peaks.

But dream in a realistic way! *Only faithfulness to the present, in fact, will deliver you from the fear or disappointments of the future.* This exacting faithfulness is necessarily incarnated in the daily pursuit of a solid human formation and, in belonging to Jesus Christ, in a more and more conscious way.

This faithfulness will involve marvellous moments and bursts of enthusiasm, but also difficulties in relationships, with others. But *never doubt your capacities or the power of Jesus Christ* which accompanies your faithfulness in a mysterious but real way.

Rome 1.5.80

LOVE, NOT VIOLENCE, TRANSFORMS

I give you a new commandment; love one another; just as I have loved you.
(John 13:34)

Sharing as priest, bishop and cardinal the lives of innumerable young people at university and in youth groups, I learned that a youth begins to grow old in a dangerous way; when he lets himself be deceived by the facile and convenient principle that 'the end justifies the means'. When a young person adopts the belief that the only hope of improving society is to promote struggle and hatred between social groups, then he ceases to be young and has not been a Christian for a long time.

I became convinced that *only love draws closer things that are different, and brings about union in diversity.* Christ's words: 'Love one another, as I have loved you', then appeared to me, as the seed and principle of the one transformation radical enough to be appreciated by the young. The seed and principle of the one revolution that does not betray man. *Only true love constructs.*

Rome 1.7.80

THE NEW SLAVERY

You are slaves of no one except God, so behave like free men, and never use your freedom as an excuse for wickedness.
(1 Pet. 2:16)

Pervading materialism imposes its dominion on man today in many different forms and with an aggressiveness that spares no one. The most sacred principles, which were the sure guides for the behaviour of individuals and society, are being hollowed out by false pretences concerning freedom, the sacredness of life, the indissolubility of marriage, the true sense of human sexuality, the right attitude towards the material goods that progress has to offer.

Many people now are tempted to self-indulgence and consumerism, and *human identity is often defined by what one owns.* Prosperity and affluence, even when they are only beginning to be available to larger strata of society, tend to make people assume that they have a right to all that prosperity can bring, and thus they can become more selfish in their demands.

Everybody wants a full freedom in all the areas of human behaviour and new models of morality are being proposed in the name of would-be freedom. When the moral fibre of a nation is weakened, when the sense of personal responsibility is diminished, then the door is open for the justification of injustice, for violence in all its forms, and for the manipulation of the many by the few. *The Challenge that is already with us is the temptation to accept as true freedom what in reality is only a new form of slavery.*

Dublin 29.9.79

THE SICKNESS OF MODERN SOCIETY   August 13

A man's life is not made secure by what he owns, even when he has more than he needs.

(Luke 12:15)

The more you possess – you may be tempted to think – the more you will feel liberated from every type of confinement. In order to make more money and to possess more, in order to eliminate effort and worry, you may be tempted to take moral shortcuts where honesty, truth and work are concerned. The progress of science and technology seems inevitable and you may be enticed to look towards the technological society for the answers to all your problems.

The lure of pleasure, to be had whenever and wherever it can be found, will be strong and it may be presented to you as part of progress towards greater autonomy and freedom from rules. The desire to be free from external restraints may manifest itself very strongly in the sexual domain, since this is an area that is so closely tied to a human personality.

The moral standards that the Church and society have held up to you for so long a time, will be presented as obsolete and a hindrance to the full development of your own personality. Mass media, entertainment, and literature will present a model for living where all too often it is every man for himself, and where the unrestrained affirmation of self leaves no room for concern for others.

Do not close your eyes to the moral sickness that stalks your society today, and from which your youth alone will not protect you. How many young people have already warped their consciences and have substituted the true joy of life with drugs, sex, alcohol, vandalism and the empty pursuit of mere material possessions.

Galway 30.9.79

162

You are not your own property, that is why you should use your body for the glory of God.

(1 Cor. 6:20)

Young men and women, have very great respect for your body and for the bodies of others! *Let your body be in the service of your inner self!* Let your gestures, your looks, always be the reflection of your soul!

Worship of the body? No, never! Contempt for the body? Again no! Control of the body? Yes! Transfiguration of the body! Even more! It often happens that you admire the marvellous transparency of the soul in many men and women in the daily accomplishment of their human tasks.

Think of the student or sportsman who put all their physical energies in the service of their respective ideal. *Think of the father and the mother whose faces, bending over their child, reveal so deeply the joys of fatherhood and motherhood.* Think of the musician or the actor identified with the authors whom they bring to life again. See the Trappist or the Carthusian, the Carmelite or the Poor Clare, radically abandoned to contemplation and letting God shine through them.

Paris 16.6.80

MARY'S ASSUMPTION   August 15

Christ has been raised from the dead, the first fruits of all who have fallen asleep . . . after the coming of Christ, those who belong to him.

(1 Cor. 15:20,23)

The assumption of Mary is a special gift of the risen Christ to his Mother. If 'those who belong to Christ' 'will be made alive' 'at his coming', then it is correct and understandable that this sharing in the victory over death should be experienced first precisely by her, his Mother; she who is 'of Christ' in the most complete way.

In fact, he also belongs to her as a son does to a mother. And she belongs to him: she is in a special way 'of Christ', because *she has been loved and redeemed in the most unique fashion.*

She, who in her human conception was Immaculate – that is, free from sin, whose consequence is death – for that very fact, should she not be free from death, which is the consequence of sin?

Castel Gandolfo 15.8.80

Since sex is always a danger, let each man have his own wife and each woman her own husband.

(1 Cor. 7:2)

I really hope that you will take up the challenge of the times and be, one and all, champions of Christian mastery of the body. *Sport rightly understood, is a very great help.*

Mastery of the body is decisive for the integration of sexuality in your lives as young people and adults. It is difficult to speak of sexuality at the present time, marked by a lack of inhibitions which is stimulated by a real exploitation of the sexual instinct.

The union of bodies has always been the most forceful language in which two beings can communicate with each other. That is why this language, which touches the sacred mystery of man and woman, demands that the gestures of love should never be performed without the complete assumption of responsibility for the partner. And that commitment should be undertaken publicly in marriage.

Contemplate more Christ the Redeemer of man! He is the Word made flesh whom so many artists have painted with realism in order to signify to us clearly that he assumed everything of human nature, including sexuality, sublimating it in chastity.

Paris 16.6.80

IN SEARCH OF HAPPINESS   August 17

A man came to him and asked: 'Master, what good deed must I do to possess eternal life?'

(Matt. 19:16)

Now you ask the question: *Is it possible to be happy in the modern world?*

As a matter of fact, you ask the same question as this young man! Christ answers – to him and also to you, to each of you – it is possible. That is, in fact, what he answers, even if his words are the following. 'If you wish to enter into life, keep the commandments.' And he will reply further: 'If you wish to be perfect, go and sell what you own and give the money to the poor . . . and follow me.'

These words mean that *man cannot be happy except to the extent to which he is capable of accepting the requirements that his own humanity, his dignity as a man, set him.* The requirements that God sets him.

In this way, therefore, Christ does not only answer the question whether it is possible to be happy — but he says more: how we can be happy, on what condition. This answer is absolutely original, and cannot be outdated, or superseded. You must think about it carefully and adapt it to yourselves.

Paris 16.6.80

YOUNG PEOPLE'S SEARCH   August 18

Go and sell everything you own and give the money to the poor . . . then come, follow me.

(Mark 10:21)

Again and again I find in young people the joy and enthusiasm of life, a searching for truth and for the deeper meaning of the existence that unfolds before them in all its attractions, and potential.

I want to repeat what I keep telling youth: *you are the future of the world, and 'the day of tomorrow belongs to you'.* The Gospels preserve for us a striking account of a conversation Jesus had with a young man. We read there that the young man put to Christ one of the fundamental questions that youth everywhere ask: 'What must I do . . .?' and he received a precise and penetrating answer: 'Jesus looked steadily at him and loved him and he said . . . Come follow me.'

But see what happens: the young man, who had shown such interest in the fundamental question, 'went away sad, for he was a man of great wealth'. Yes, he went away, and — as can be deduced from the context — he refused to accept the call of Christ.

Boston 1.10.79

WHAT MUST I DO?   August 19

Jesus looked steadily at him and loved him.

(Mark 10:21)

This deeply penetrating event, in its concise eloquence, expresses a great lesson in a few words: it touches upon substantial problems and basic questions that have in no way lost their relevance.

Everywhere young people are asking important questions — questions on the meaning of life, on the right way to live, on the true scale of values: 'What must I do . . .?' 'What must I do to share in everlasting life?' This questioning tells the world that young people, carry within them a special openness with regard to what is good and what is true.

This openness is, in a sense, a 'revelation' of the human spirit. And in this openness to truth, to goodness and to beauty, each one can find him or herself, indeed, in this openness one can experience in some measure what the young man in the Gospel experienced: 'Jesus looked steadily at him and loved him.'

Boston 1.10.79

REAL LOVE IS DEMANDING   August 20

If you keep my commandments, you will remain in my love.

(John 15:10)

The sadness of the young man makes us reflect. We could be tempted to think that many possessions, many of the goods of this world, can bring happiness. We see instead in the case of the young man in the Gospel that his many possessions had become an obstacle to accepting the call of Jesus to follow him. He was not ready to say *yes* to Jesus, and *no* to self, to say *yes* to love and *no* to escape.

Real love is demanding. I would fail in my mission if I did not clearly tell you so. For it was Jesus who said: 'You are my friends if you do what I command you' (John 15:14). *Love demands effort and a personal commitment to the will of God.* It means discipline and sacrifice, but it also means joy and human fulfilment.

Do not be afraid of honest effort and honest work; do not be afraid of the truth. With Christ's help, and through prayer, you can answer his call, resisting temptations and fads, and every form of mass manipulation. *Open your hearts to the Christ of the Gospels — to his love and his truth and his joy.*

Boston 1.10.79

CHRIST'S MESSAGE OF LOVE

Everyone who loves is begotten by God and knows God.

(1 John 4:7)

The message of love that Christ brought is always important, always relevant. It is not difficult to see how today's world despite its beauty and grandeur, despite the conquests of science and technology, despite the refined and abundant material goods that it offers, is yearning for more truth, for more love, for more joy. *And all of this is found in Christ and his way of life.*

Do I then make a mistake when I tell you that it is part of your task in the world and the Church to reveal the true meaning of life where hatred, neglect or selfishness threaten to take over the world?

Faced with problems and disappointments, many people will try to escape from their responsibility: escape in selfishness, escape in sexual pleasure, escape in drugs, escape in violence, escape in indifference and cynical attitudes. But today, I propose to you the option of love, which is the opposite of escape. *If you really accept that love from Christ, it will lead you to God.*

Boston 1.10.79

CHRIST MUST CONQUER

Whoever remains in me, with me in him, bears fruit in plenty; for cut off from me you can do nothing.

(John 15:5)

Does man have within himself the strength to face with his own forces the snares of evil, selfishness and — let us say so clearly — the disintegrating snares of the 'prince of this world', who is always active to give man, first, a false sense of his autonomy, and then to bring him, through failure, to the abyss of despair?

All of us, the young and adults, must have recourse to Christ, the eternally young; Christ, the conqueror of every expression of death; Christ who rose again for ever; Christ, who communicates in the Holy Spirit the continuous, irrepressible life of the Father; we must do so in order to found and ensure the hope of tomorrow, which you will build, but which is already potentially present today.

Christ Jesus must conquer; whenever his Grace defeats in us the forces of evil, he renews our youth, widens the horizons of our hope, and strengthens the energies of our confidence.

Rome 15.11.78

LOVE IS IMMORTAL August 23

Over all these clothes, to keep them together and complete them, put on love.
(Col. 3:14)

Man's greatest vocation is the call to love. *Love also gives human life its definitive meaning.* It is the essential condition of man's dignity, the proof of the nobility of his soul. It is the greatest thing in man's life, because *true love bears within it the dimension of eternity.* It is immortal: 'Love never ends' we read in the first letter to the Corinthians.

Man dies as regards the body, because such is the destiny of everyone on earth, but this death does not harm the love that has matured in his life. Certainly, it remains above all to bear witness to the man before God, who is love. It designates the man's place in the Kingdom of God.

Rome 4.11.78

THERE IS ONLY ONE LOVE August 24

A man who does not love the brother that he can see cannot love God, whom he has never seen.

(1 John 4:20)

There are two commandments of love, as the Master expressly states but *there is only one love.* One and the same love embraces God and one's neighbour. God: above everything, because he is above everything. One's neighbour: with the measure of man, and so 'as oneself'.

These two loves are so closely connected with each other that one cannot exist without the other. It is not possible, therefore, to separate one love from the other.

True love of one's neighbour, for the very reason that it is true love, is, at the same time, love of God. Some people may be astonished by this. It is certainly astonishing.

168

When the Lord Jesus presents to his listeners the vision of the Last Judgement, he says: 'I was hungry and you gave me food, I was thirsty and you gave me drink.' Those who listen to these words are surprised, since we hear them ask: 'Lord, when did we see you hungry and feed you?' And the answer: 'I tell you, solemnly, in so far as you did this to one of the least of these brothers, you did it to me' (Matt. 37:40).

Drogheda 29.9.79

THE LORD'S CALL   August 25

Jesus said to them, 'Follow me and I will make you fishers of men.'
(Matt. 4:19)

In the treasure of the Gospel there are preserved the beautiful responses given to the Lord's call. The response of Peter and Andrew, his brother: 'They left their nets at once and, followed him.'

The response of Levi the publican: 'And leaving everything he got up and followed him' (Luke 5:28). The response of the Apostles: 'Lord, who shall we go to? You have the message of eternal life' (John 6:68).

From the time when the Gospel was first proclaimed right up to our time, a very large number of men and women have given their personal response, their free and deliberate response, to the call of Christ. They have chosen the priesthood, the religious life, life in the Missions, as the reason for, and the ideal of existence. They have served the People of God and humanity, with faith, intelligence, courage and love.

Rome 6.5.79

THE MYSTERY OF VOCATION   August 26

God's choice is free, since it depends on the one who calls, not on human merit.

(Rom. 9:11)

Vocation is, therefore, a mystery that man accepts and lives in the depths of his being. A gift and a grace, it depends on supreme divine freedom and, in its total reality, it escapes our understanding.

We cannot demand explanations from the Giver of all goods – because he who calls is also 'He who is'.

The vocation of each person merges, up to a certain point, with his very being: it can be said that *vocation and person become just one thing*. This means that in God's creative initiative there enters a particular act of love for those called not only to salvation, but also to the ministry of salvation.

Therefore from all eternity, since we began to exist in the plans of the Creator, and he willed us to be creatures, he also willed us to be 'called', preparing in us the gifts and conditions for the personal, conscious, and opportune response to the call of Christ and of the Church. *God who loves us, who is love, is also 'He who calls'.*

Rome 5.7.80

THE CALL TO THE PRIESTHOOD   August 27

Lord who shall we go to? You have the message of eternal life.

(John 6:68)

Our life is a gift from God. We must do something good with it. There are many ways of living well, of using it for serving human and Christian ideals. My reason for speaking to you today about total dedication to God in the priesthood, in the religious life, in life as a missionary, is that Christ calls many from among you to this extraordinary adventure. He needs, and he wants to need, your persons, your intelligence, your energy, your faith, your love, your holiness.

If it is to the priesthood that Christ is calling you, it is because he wishes to exercise his priesthood through your dedication and priestly mission. He wants to speak to the people of today through your voice. He wants to consecrate the Eucharist and forgive sins through you. He wants to live with your heart. He wants to help with your hands. He wants to save through your efforts.

Think about it carefully. The response that many of you can give is given personally to Christ, who is calling you to these great things.

Rome 6.5.79

Glory be to him whose power, working in us, can do infinitely more than we can ask or imagine.

(Eph. 3:20)

If you hear and answer this call, you will meet difficulties. Do you think perhaps that I do not know about them? I am telling you that love overcomes all difficulties.

The true response to every vocation is the work of love. *The response to the priestly, religious and missionary vocation can only spring from a deep love of Christ.* He himself offers you this power of love, as a gift that is added to the gift of his call and makes your response possible.

Trust in him who 'can do infinitely more than we can ask or imagine'. And, if you can, *give your life with joy and without fear, to him who first gave his for you.*

Rome 6.5.79

THE LAY VOCATION August 29

I, the prisoner in the Lord, implore you therefore to lead a life worthy of your vocation.

(Eph. 4:1)

Today we are living through an enormous revival of consciousness of the lay vocation. Is medicine, for example, a profession? Engineering a profession? Law a profession? But at the same time, they are vocations.

What does it mean, a vocation? It means that everything you do in your life, for reasons of knowledge, education, practice and skill will become at the same time, a realization of some part of the good ordained in the world by God himself, worked out in the world, paid for in the world by Christ himself.

Cracow 24.3.64

My Beloved lifts up his voice, he says to me, 'Come then, my love, my lovely one, come'.

(Song of Songs 2:10)

Love has still another meaning. Namely, it is closely connected with the direction of a person's vocation.

A person goes in the direction which his love chooses. How else, for example, can we understand the vocation of a nun? There's a young girl, just like all her class-mates: she goes to the school-leaving party, on excursions and I don't know what else, then suddenly, one day, she knocks at the novitiate door.

After that, what will she do in life? She'll do what I often see just looking round Cracow: run up and down stairs from six in the morning till ten at night, nursing the sick, the ones who have no one to take them in, whom the hospitals have discharged and left to their families. But the families very often don't get on with them. And in all this she will be so serene, a bride, a very bride.

She has chosen a very great love. And it is always a cause for astonishment when the voice of the Bridegroom is heard, overwhelming all else and bidding one follow him.

Cracow 14.4.62

THE BRIGHT FLAME OF LOVE   August 31

The Lord Jesus was rich, but he became poor for your sake, to make you rich out of his poverty.

(2 Cor. 8:9)

The religious vocation is derived from a living faith. It is coherent to the very end; it gives mankind a vision of his ultimate objective, that is, meeting with God himself, who alone is worthy of a love 'above everything', an exclusive and nuptial love.

This love consists in the giving of our whole human being, body and soul, to him who gave himself completely to us men by means of the Incarnation, the Cross and annihilation, by means of poverty, chastity, obedience.

In this way, therefore, the religious vocation takes life from these riches of living faith. This vocation is, as it were, the spark which lights a 'bright flame of love' in the soul, as St. John of the Cross wrote. This vocation, once accepted, once solemnly confirmed by means of vows, must continually be nourished by the riches of faith; not only when it brings with it inner joy, but also when it is accompanied by difficulties, aridity, and inner suffering, which is called the 'night' of the soul.

Rome 10.11.78

September

THE BEGINNING OF WORLD WAR TWO September 1

You fight to get your way by force. Why you don't have what you want is because you don't pray for it.

(James 4:2)

September 1 is the anniversary of the beginning of World War Two, a war that caused enormous material and moral damage, and which does not cease to be a painful wound in the history of nations, above all the European nations.

In a particular way, it is a painful wound in the history of our nation which, during the events of the war, beginning in September 1939, was not only subjected to the terrible occupation, as we know, but also sacrificed in the holocaust six million of its sons and daughters on the various fronts, in the camps and in the prisons. We cannot forget this date.

In these first days of September, which every year remind us of the horrible violence wrought on our nation, only twenty years after regaining independence, we must particularly pray that international moral order be respected in Europe and in the whole world. We must pray lest our homeland or any other nation become the victim of aggression or violence on the part of anybody. One must pray for this — and bear witness to this.

Rome 1.9.80

THE VIRTUE OF PRUDENCE September 2

To the man of discretion, wisdom means a watch on his own conduct.

(Prov. 14:8)

The ancients spoke a great deal of the virtue of prudence. We owe them, for this reason, deep gratitude and thanks. In a certain

175

dimension, they taught us that *the value of man must be measured with the yardstick of the moral good which he accomplishes in his life.* It is just this that ensures the virtue of prudence first place.

The prudent man, who strives for everything that is really good, endeavours to measure everything, every situation and his whole activity according to the yardstick of moral good.

So a prudent man is not one who — as is often meant — is able to wangle things in life and draw the greatest profit from it; but one who is able to construct his whole life according to the voice of upright conscience and according to the requirements of sound morality.

So prudence is the key for the accomplishment of the fundamental task that each of us has received from God. This task is the perfection of man himself.

Rome 25.10.78

HELPING OTHERS MAN SAVES HIMSELF   September 3

He has let us know the mystery of his purpose, the hidden plan he so kindly made in Christ from the beginning.

(Eph. 1:9)

The Christian has the right and the duty to look at the virtue of prudence also in another perspective. It is, as it were, the image and likeness of the Providence of God himself in the dimensions of concrete man.

For man — as we know from the Book of Genesis — was created in the image and likeness of God. *And God carries out his plan in the history of creation, and above all in the history of mankind.* The purpose of this plan is the ultimate good of the universe.

The same plan in the history of mankind becomes simply the plan of salvation, the plan that embraces us all. *At the central point of its realization is Jesus Christ,* in whom was expressed the eternal love and solicitude of God himself, the Father, for the salvation of man. This is at the same time the full expression of Divine Providence.

Well, man who is the image of God, must in some way be providence: but within the proportions of his life. He can take part in this great march of all creatures towards the purpose, which is the good of creation.

He must — expressing ourselves even more in the language of faith — take part in the divine plan of salvation. He must march towards salvation, and help others to save themselves. *By helping others, he saves himself.*

Rome 25.10.78

THE VIRTUE OF COURAGE September 4

Put your hope in the Lord, be strong, let your heart be bold, put your hope in the Lord.

(Ps. 27:14)

Speaking from the loggia of St. Peter's Basilica, on the day after his election, Pope John Paul I recalled, among other things, that during the Conclave on August 26, when everything already seemed to indicate that he himself would be chosen, the Cardinals beside him whispered in his ear: 'Courage!' Probably this word was necessary for him at that moment and had been imprinted on his heart, since he recalled it immediately the next day.

John Paul I will forgive me if I use this story of his now. I think it can better introduce all of us present here to the subject which I intend to develop.

Whom do we regard as a strong, courageous man? This word usually conjures up the soldier who defends his homeland, exposing his health to danger, and in wartime risking even his life. We realize, however, that we need fortitude also in peacetime.

And so we highly esteem persons who distinguish themselves for so-called 'civil courage'. A testimony of fortitude is offered to us by anyone who risks his own life to save someone who is about to drown, or by one who provides help in natural calamities, such as fire, floods, etc.

St. Charles, my patron saint, certainly distinguished himself for this virtue when, during the plague in Milan, he carried out his pastoral ministry among the inhabitants of that city.

Rome 15.11.78

In love there can be no fear, but fear is driven out by perfect love.

(1 John 4:18)

The virtue of fortitude always calls for a certain overcoming of human weakness and particularly of fear. Man, indeed, by nature, fears danger, affliction and suffering. Therefore courageous men must be sought not only on battlefields, but also in hospital wards or on a bed of pain. Such men could often be found in concentration camps or in places of deportation. They were real heroes.

Fear sometimes deprives of civil courage men who are living in a climate of threats, oppression or persecution. *The men who are capable of crossing the so-called barrier of fear, to bear witness to truth and justice, have then a special value.*

To reach such fortitude, man must in a certain way go beyond his own limits and transcend himself, running the risk of an unknown situation, the risk of being frowned upon, the risk of laying himself open to unpleasant consequences, insults, degradation, material losses, perhaps imprisonment or persecution.

To attain this fortitude, man must be sustained by a great love for truth and for good, to which he dedicates himself.

Rome 15.11.78

SELF-SACRIFICING COURAGE September 6

A man can have no greater love than to lay down his life for his friends.

(John 15:13)

The virtue of fortitude proceeds hand in hand with the capacity of sacrificing oneself. This virtue already had a well-defined content among the ancients. With Christ it acquired an evangelical, Christian content.

The Gospel is addressed to weak, poor, meek and humble men, peacemakers and to the merciful, but, at the same time, it contains a constant appeal to fortitude. It often repeats: 'Fear not.' *It teaches man that, for a just cause, for truth, for justice, one must be able to 'lay down one's life'.*

Rome 15.11.78

Be strong, let your heart be bold, all you who hope in the Lord.

(Ps. 31:24)

Allow me to draw your attention to examples that are generally not well known, but which bear witness in themselves to great, sometimes even heroic, virtue.

I am thinking, for example, of a woman, already mother of a large family, who is 'advised' by so many to suppress a new life conceived in her womb, by undergoing 'the operation' of interruption of pregnancy; and she replies firmly, 'No'. She certainly feels all the difficulty that this 'no' brings with it, difficulty for herself, for her husband, for the whole family, and yet she replies: 'No'. The new human life conceived in her is a value too great, too sacred, for her to be able to give in to such pressure.

Another example; a man who is promised freedom and also an easy career if he denies his own principles, or approves of something that is against his sense of honesty towards others. And he, too, replies 'No', though faced by threats on the one side, and attractions on the other. Here we have a courageous man!

There are many, a great many, manifestations of fortitude, often heroic, of which nothing is written in the newspapers, or of which little is known. *Only human conscience knows them . . . and God knows!*

Rome 15.11.78

WHY DO I PRAY?   September 8

If there is anything you need, pray for it asking God for it with prayer and thanksgiving.

(Phil. 4:6)

Why do I pray? Why do you pray? Why do people pray? Why do Christians, Muslims, Buddhists, pagans pray? Why do people pray, even those who think that they do not pray?

The answer is very simple, *I pray because God exists.* I know that God exists, therefore I pray. Some people answer boldly: 'I know that God exists.' Some people have rather a different answer to the question: 'Why do you pray?' Maybe they do not say with such certainty: 'I know.' Maybe they say rather, 'I believe.' Maybe the answer is even: 'I am seeking.'

Cracow 9.4.62

FINDING GOD IN NATURE September 9

For he it was who formed the mountains, created the wind, reveals his mind to man.

(Amos 4:13)

I recall a letter which I once received from a great and undoubtedly learned naturalist. A letter which moved me very greatly.

He wrote (I'm quoting from memory, for I lost the original somewhere, but I shall surely remember it until I die) that *'on the paths of my learning I have not found God*. But there are moments — they come very frequently when one is face to face with the majesty of nature, for example, face to face with the beauty of the mountains — when something strange happens to me. I, who have never found God on the paths of my learning, at that moment *feel a sense of certainty that he is*. And then I begin to pray.'

Cracow 10.4.62

THE EXISTENCE OF GOD September 10

Lord God, what variety you have created, arranging everything so wisely! Earth is completely full of things you have made.

(Ps. 104:24)

How do you know that God exists? There are certain ways of thought. The way is sometimes very short.

However, I always recall the answer of Einstein — I'm quoting from memory, not exactly. He said that penetration into the mysteries of nature and working them out scientifically shows us and reveals that everything has been magnificently thought out. *It reveals to us the thought and wisdom of one who is 'beyond' and 'above'* that which we find in the orbit of our experience and in the cognitive studies based on that experience.

Cracow 10.4.62

When he had finished talking to Abraham the Lord God went away, and Abraham returned home.

(Gen. 18:33)

Prayer is a conversation. We know quite well that it is possible to hold all sorts of conversations. Sometimes conversation is simply an exchange of words: we remain, as it were, on the surface.

But our conversations are truly profound when we do not simply exchange words, when we do not simply toss words about, but when we exchange thoughts. When, too, we exchange our hearts, our feelings, when we exchange in some measure our own 'I'.

People's prayers, *too, have very different dimensions, very different depths.* Not just different outward forms. When Muslims pray, for example, they pray with such great courage, everywhere at the appointed times calling upon their Allah. When Buddhists pray, they enter into complete concentration, as if to lose themselves completely in this concentration.

When Christians pray, they take from Christ the word 'Father', which through the Spirit covers everything their spirit needs.

Cracow 12.4.62

What is man, that you should notice him? A human being, that you should think about him?

(Ps. 144:3)

'Man' means a very great deal. Today, perhaps, the deciding factor in our thinking about man is numbers.

We talk about countries, continents, the human race, and we express everything in figures. Thousands, millions, billions. And these numbers, this numerical method of looking at man conceals the heart of the matter from us.

And here, at this point, the Gospel, Christianity, will always bring us back to the heart of the matter. For the truth is that among those thousands, millions and billions, *there is always, in the end, a man.* More precisely, there is my concrete human 'I', one and unique.

Cracow 12.4.62

The Son of Man himself did not come to be served but to serve, and to give his life as a ransom for many.

(Mark 10:45)

When we Christians go through the experience of pain, we must be careful to give it the right meaning. *It is not a punishment*, but an occasion for purification of our sins; in particular, its end is the good of men, our brothers: as it was for Jesus, who gave his life as a ransom for all.

Therefore, through faith, join your tribulations to those suffered by him. We should carry our crosses in his footsteps, otherwise they become too heavy. But with Jesus Christ before us, we walk more quickly, since he *gives meaning and strength to every pain of ours.*

Siena 14.9.80

THE EXALTATION OF THE HOLY CROSS   September 14

'Take him away, take him away!' they said: 'Crucify him!'

(John 19:15)

In that same Jerusalem in which the words had rung out: 'Hosanna! Blessings on him who comes in the name of the Lord! Hosanna to the son of David!' they will cry: 'Crucify him!'

Pilate will wash his hands and say: 'I am innocent of this man's blood . . .' The same voices will answer: 'His blood be on us and on our children.' And in this way the condemnation to death on the Cross will be sealed. Christ will take the Cross on his shoulders.

This Cross will remain through all the generations of mankind, inseparable from Christ. *It will become his memorial and his sign.* It will become an answer to the question that man asked God, and will remain a mystery.

The Church will surround it with the body of her living community, she will surround it with men's faith, with their hope and with their love.

The Church will carry the Cross with Christ through the generations. She will bear witness to it. She will draw life from it. From the Cross she will grow with that mysterious growth of the Spirit, which has its beginning in the Cross. We cannot forget those who, in the course of our age, have suffered death for the faith and for love of Christ; who, in so many different ways have been imprisoned, tortured, tormented, condemned to death; and also mocked, despised, humiliated and relegated to the fringes of society.

Men who live in conditions of freedom and well-being cannot turn their eyes from this Cross and ignore the testimony of those who belong to what is usually called 'the Church of silence'. The Church, forced to keep silent, in conditions of obligatory atheism, continues to grow from Christ's Cross and, by her silence, to proclaim the greatest truth.

Rome 30.3.80

THE SICK; CO-WORKERS WITH CHRIST   September 15

In my own body to do what I can to make up all that has still to be undergone by Christ for the sake of his body, the Church.

(Cor. 1:24)

The Gospels are filled with instances where our Lord shows his particular love and concern for the sick and for all those in pain. Jesus loved those who suffered, and this attitude has been passed on to his Church. To love the sick is something that the Church has learned from Christ.

By suffering and death Jesus took on himself all human suffering, and he gave it a new value. As a matter of fact, *he calls upon the sick, upon everyone who suffers, to collaborate with him in the salvation of the world.*

Because of this, pain and sorrow are not endured alone or in vain. Although it remains difficult to understand suffering, Jesus has made it clear that its value is linked to his own suffering and death, to his own sacrifice. In other words, *by your suffering you help Jesus in his work of salvation.* This great truth is difficult to express accurately, but St. Paul puts it this way . . . 'in my own body to do what I can to make up all that has still to be undergone.'

Knock 30.9.79

183

Happy those who mourn; they shall be comforted.

(Matt. 5:4)

What, then, is the value of your suffering. You have not suffered or do not suffer in vain.

Pain matures you in spirit, purifies you in heart, gives you a real sense of the world and of life, enriches you with goodness, patience and endurance, and — hearing the Lord's promise re-echo in your heart: 'Happy those who mourn; they shall be comforted' — gives you the sensation of deep peace, perfect joy, and happy hope.

Succeed, therefore, in giving a Christian value to your suffering, succeed in sanctifying your suffering, with constant and generous trust in him who comforts and gives strength.

Rome 22.5.79

THE MYSTERY OF SUFFERING September 17

We are . . . heirs of God and coheirs with Christ, sharing his sufferings so as to share his glory.

(Rom. 8:17)

Man, created by God and raised by him to the sublime dignity of a son, bears within him an irrepressible aspiration to happiness and feels a natural aversion to any kind of suffering.

Jesus, on the other hand, in his evangelizing work, though bending over the sick and suffering to cure them and to console them, did not suppress suffering itself, but wished to subject himself to all possible human pain, moral and physical, in his passion up to his agony at Gethsemane, being abandoned by the Father on Calvary and his long agony and death on the Cross. For this reason he declared blessed those who mourn and those who hunger and thirst for righteousness. Redemption is achieved in practice and through the Cross!

This attitude of Jesus reveals a deep mystery of justice and mercy, which involves us all, and because of which every man is called to take part in Redemption.

The mystery of Christ's Redemption is essentially a mystery of love and divine life, being a manifestation of the love of the Father who 'so much loved the world that he gave his only Son' (John 3:16). And it is at the same time the expression of the Son's love for the Father and for men (John 10:11).

You are offered the extraordinary opportunity of touching the peak of human possibilities, that of being able to accept and willing to support sickness and the difficulties that accompany it in a gift of sublime love and of complete abandonment to the Father's will.

Rome 26.11.79

SUFFERING: A BAPTISM OF GRACE September 18

He has given you the privilege not only of believing in Christ, but of suffering for him as well.

(Phil. 1:29)

This is the special mystery of your life, that suffering, the pain of desolation, loneliness is always like some Baptism of penance through which a person must pass as if being tried and tested.

He must go alone along the roads where God's Providence leads him, and very often he finds bitter experience, suffering, loneliness, desolation. This is often penance. Penance does not mean only punishment. Penance means first and foremost conversion.

When I have an occasion to look into your souls, my friends who are suffering – and I try to devote as much time to this as possible – then I can see how great is the truth about the Baptism of penance through which they pass. This is first and foremost conversion, the discovery of God. For it is precisely in suffering that so many people discover God more than ever before.

This is as it were a summing up of all my experience and meetings with the sick and lonely. The Baptism of penance becomes for them a Baptism of revelation, a Baptism of Grace.

Cracow 12.1.69

THE VALUE OF OLD AGE September 19

The crown of the aged is their children's children.

(Prov. 17:6)

The elderly are meant to be part of the social scene; their very existence gives an insight into God's creation and the functioning of society.

The life of the aging helps to clarify a scale of human values; it shows the continuity of generations and marvellously demonstrates the interdependence of God's people. *The elderly often have the charism to bridge generation gaps before they are made*: how many children have found understanding and love in the eyes and words and caresses of the aging? And how many old people have willingly subscribed to the inspired word that 'the crown of the aged is their children's children'.

To point out the resources that belong to the elderly is to sensitize the elderly themselves and to highlight the riches inherent in society — riches which society itself does not appreciate.

Old age is able to enrich the world through prayer and counsel, its presence enriches the home; its immense capacity for evangelization by word and example, and by activities eminently adapted to the talents of the elderly is a force for the Church of God yet to be thoroughly understood or adequately utilized.

Rome 5.9.80

AUSCHWITZ; VICTORY THROUGH FAITH   September 20

This is the victory over the world — our faith.

(1 John 5:4)

These words from the letter of St. John come to my mind and enter my heart as I find myself in this place in which a special victory was won through faith, through the faith that gives rise to love of God and of one's neighbour. The unique love, the supreme love that is ready to 'lay down (one's) life for (one's) friend' (John 15:13).

A victory, therefore, through love enlivened by faith to the extreme point of the final definitive witness.

This victory through faith and love was won in this place by a man whose Christian names are Maximilian Mary. Surname: Kolbe. Profession (as registered in the books of the concentration camp): Catholic priest. Vocation: a son of St. Francis. Birth: a son of simple, hard-working, devout parents, who were weavers near Lodz (Poland). By God's grace and the Church's judgement: Blessed.

Auschwitz 7.6.79

AUSCHWITZ; SELF-SACRIFICE

Anyone who loves God must also love his brother.

(1 John 4:21)

The victory through faith and love was won by Maximilian Kolbe in this place, which was built for the negation of faith — faith in God and faith in man — and to trample in a thorough-going way not only on love but on all signs of human dignity, of humanity.

A place built on hatred and on contempt for man in the name of a failed ideology. A place built on cruelty. On the entrance gate, which still exists, is placed the inscription *Arbeit Macht Frei* (Freedom Through Work), which has a sardonic sound, since its meaning was radically contradicted by what took place within.

In this site of the terrible slaughter that brought death to four million people of different nations, Father Maximilian Kolbe voluntarily offered himself for death in the hunger bunker for a brother and so won a spiritual victory like that of Christ himself. This brother still lives today in the land of Poland.

Auschwitz 7.6.79

AUSCHWITZ; VICTORIES OF LOVE

Let us thank God for giving us the victory through our Lord Jesus Christ.
(1 Cor. 15:58)

Was Father Maximilian Kolbe the only one? Certainly he won a victory that was immediately felt by his companions in captivity and is still felt today by the Church and the world. However, there is no doubt that many other similar victories were won.

I am thinking, for example, of the death in the gas chamber of a concentration camp of the Carmelite Sister Benedicta of the Cross, whose name in the world was Edith Stein, who was an illustrious pupil of Husserl and became one of the glories of contemporary German philosophy, and who was a descendant of a Jewish family living in Wroclaw.

The dignity of man was so horribly trampled on. *Victory was won through faith and love.*

Auschwitz 7.6.79

All those died in faith, before receiving any of the things that had been promised.

(Heb. 11:13)

It is well known that I have been here many times. And many times I have gone down to Maximilian Kolbe's death cell and stopped in front of the execution wall and passed among the ruins of the cremation furnaces of Birkenau. It was impossible for me not to come here as Pope.

I have come then to this special shrine, the birthplace, I can say, of the patron of our difficult century, just as nine centuries ago Skalka was the place of the martyrdom of St. Stanislaus, patron of the Poles.

I have come to pray, I have come to pray with all of you and with the whole of Poland and the whole of Europe. Christ wishes that I, who have become the successor of Peter, should give witness before the world to what constitutes the greatness and the misery of contemporary man, to what is his defeat and his victory.

Auschwitz 7.6.79

AUSCHWITZ; SLAUGHTER OF THE JEWS   September 24

Beside the streams of Babylon we sat and wept at the memory of Zion.

(Ps. 137:1)

I have come and I kneel on this Golgotha of the modern world, on these tombs, largely nameless like the great Tomb of the Unknown Soldier.

I kneel before all the inscriptions that come one after another bearing the memory of the victims of Auschwitz in the languages: Polish, English, Bulgarian, Romany, Czech, Danish, French, Greek, Hebrew, Yiddish, Spanish, Norwegian, Russian, Romanian, Hungarian and Italian.

In particular, I pause before the inscription in Hebrew. This inscription awakens the memory of the people whose sons and daughters were intended for total extermination. This people draws its origin from Abraham, our father in faith, as was expressed by Paul of Tarsus.

The very people who received from God the commandment 'Thou

shalt not kill' itself experienced in a special measure what is meant by killing. It is not permissible for anyone to pass by this inscription with indifference.

Auschwitz 7.6.79

AUSCHWITZ; MANKIND'S CONSCIENCE   September 25

God knows us for what we really are, and I hope that in your consciences you know us too.

(2 Cor. 5:11)

Finally, the last inscription: that in Polish. Six million Poles lost their lives during the Second World War: a fifth of the nation.

Yet another stage in the centuries-old fight of this nation, my nation, for its fundamental rights among the peoples of Europe. Yet another loud cry for the right to a place of its own on the map of Europe. Yet another painful reckoning with the conscience of mankind.

Auschwitz is such a reckoning. It is impossible merely to visit it. It is necessary to think with fear of how far hatred can go, how far man's destruction of man can go, how far cruelty can go.

Auschwitz 7.6.79

EACH MAN'S PLACE IN CHRIST   September 26

Come to me, all you who labour and are overburdened, and I will give you rest.

(Matt. 11:28)

Jesus Christ on the Cross. His wide-open arms do not close. They cannot close, they must be open, for every man must find room in them, he must find his place in them.

He must find in them his own humanity, his dignity, his position as a son of God, which he carries in his soul and in his vocation.

Every man must find in Christ's arms his own freedom and the truth about himself. New people, new generations are always coming, but Christ's arms must be open, they can never close.

Cracow 3.5.74

189

Too long have I lived among people who hate peace, who, when I propose peace, are all for war.

(Ps. 120:6)

If we look at the modern world, we perceive in it two problems which make themselves immediately apparent. One is the problem of progress and development.

There is the progress and development of technology, of civilization, and a multitude of other things. But within the compass of this progress and development which is external to man, man achieves, or at least ought to achieve, the inner development which is essential to him: the development of his human nature, his development as a person. For man is a person – in the image of God. That is the first problem.

And as a converse to the first problem, there has grown up, even before our eyes, a multitude of threats to man and to humanity with all its progress and development. A multitude of threats, but it seems that the greatest threat to modern man and to modern society is war, with the use of means of destruction to which man has now attained in the course of his progress in science and also in technology and civilization.

Cracow 25.12.65

ONE AND THE SAME LOVE   September 28

This is my blood, the blood of the covenant, which is to be poured out for many.

(Mark 14:24)

When Christ broke the bread at the Last Supper, he wanted in this way to show his great love, his love for souls. This was a different way of expressing it than the way he would take on the morrow, by shedding his blood on Calvary.

That terrifying and awesome way was a different way of expressing it, but it was the same love. If it were possible to translate the Cross into bread or the Cross into the Eucharist, we would just be translating Love into Love. *Two ways of expressing love, but the love is one and the same.*

It is just that the way of the Cross, that sacrifice of Christ's blood, is something that we cannot encompass. We cannot participate in it in a direct and immediate manner. However, this bloodless sacrifice, this sacrifice of bread and wine, the Last Supper, permits us to encompass it, permits us to respect it, and we can take part in it by our sacrifice.

Cracow 25.3.64

THE COURAGE OF THE INDWELLING CHRIST   September 29

Sir, I am not worthy.

(Matt. 8:8)

My dear friends, love is always courageous. Love is always courageous, and never spares itself.

Christ is like that. He did not spare himself here on earth in Galilee. He who said of himself that the foxes have holes and the birds have nests but that he had nowhere to lay his head. He who was constantly on the road, constantly beset and persecuted. He who spent the nights in prayer. He who went with all willingness to torment and death. Never did he spare himself. And always to the same end, always for me.

Love is courageous, love never spares itself. And it is still the same, today too he is courageous in his love, and never spares himself. For he constantly gives himself. He gives himself to man, he gives himself to me. And in this there is great courage. 'Lord, I am not worthy' is all we can say, and then keep silence.

Cracow 9.4.62

PRAYER IS POSSIBLE   September 30

Jesus told them a parable about the need to pray continually and never lose heart.

(Luke 18:1)

We often say that we don't know how to pray. How to pray? This is a simple matter. I would say: *Pray any way you like, so long as you do pray.* Say prayers that your mother taught you. Pray any way you like, but you must pray.

And never say: 'I don't pray because I don't know how to pray!'

because this simply isn't true. Everyone knows how to pray. The words of prayer are simple and the rest follows.

To say: 'I don't know how to pray' means that you are deceiving yourself. Yourself and who else? Who can you deceive about this? It always means some smallness of heart. Some lack of good will. Or sometimes of courage. It is possible to pray, and necessary to pray.

Pray any way you like. From a book or from memory, it's all the same. Maybe just in thought. A person can pray perfectly when, for example, he is out on the fells or on a lake and he feels at one with nature. Nature speaks for him or rather speaks to him. He prays perfectly.

Cracow 9.4.62

October

THE IMPORTANCE OF PRAYER   October 1

Ask, and it will be given to you; search, and you will find; knock, and the door will be opened to you.

(Luke 11:9)

A model of such perservering prayer, humble and, at the same time, confident, is found in the Old Testament in Abraham, who beseeches God for the salvation of Sodom and Gomorrah, if there were at least ten righteous men to be found there.

In this way, therefore, *we must encourage ourselves more and more to prayer.* We must often remember Christ's exhortation: 'Ask, and it will be given to you.' In particular, we must remember it when we lose confidence or the desire to pray.

We must also learn anew to pray, always. It often happens that we dispense ourselves from praying with the excuse that we are unable to do so. If we really do not know how to pray, then it is all the more necessary to learn. That is important for everyone, and it seems to be particularly important for the young, who often neglect the prayer they learned as children, because it seems to them too childish, naïve, and superficial.

Such a state of mind is, on the contrary, an indirect incentive to deepen one's prayer, to make it more thoughtful, more mature, *to seek support for it in the Word of God himself and in the Holy Spirit*, who 'expresses our plea in a way that could never be put into words' (Rom. 8:26).

Rome 27.7.80

Pray constantly, and for all things give thanks to God.

(1 Thess. 5:17)

There are several definitions of prayer. But it is most often called a talk or a conversation, with God. When we hold a conversation with some one, we not only speak but we also listen. *Prayer, therefore, is also listening.*

It consists of listening to hear the interior voice of grace. Listening to hear the call. And then, as you ask me how the Pope prays, I answer you: like every Christian: he speaks and he listens. Sometimes, he prays without words, and then he listens all the more. The most important thing is precisely what he 'hears'. And he also tries to unite prayer with his obligations, his activities, his work, and *to unite his work with prayer.*

In this way, day after day, he tries to carry out his 'service', his 'ministry', which comes to him from the will of Christ and from the living tradition of the Church.

Rome 8.6.80

THE PROBLEM OF PRAYER   October 3

One of his disciples said: 'Lord, teach us to pray.'

(Luke 11:1)

These words addressed directly to Christ do not belong just to the past. These are words repeated by men continually; this is a problem that is always relevant: the problem of prayer.

What does it mean to pray? How can we pray? And so the answer given by Christ is always relevant. And how did Christ answer?

In a certain sense, to those who asked he taught words they were to utter when they prayed, when they addressed the Father. These words are found in the two Gospel versions: the text of Luke's Gospel is slightly different from the one to which we are accustomed in our daily prayer; in fact we remember the Our Father according to St. Matthew's version.

Therefore, Christ taught the words of the prayer: the most perfect words, the most complete words; everything is contained in them.

Christ's answer, however, is not limited exclusively to the text, to the words we are to utter when we pray. It is a question of a far more pressing problem and, it could be said, also a far more complex one.

Castel Gandolfo 27.7.80

THE MEANING OF PRAYER October 4

Abraham replied, 'I am bold indeed to speak like this to my Lord, I who am dust and ashes.

(Gen. 18:27)

What does praying mean? *Praying means feeling one's own insufficiency*, feeling one's own insufficiency through the various necessities which man has to face, necessities that are part of his life. Such as, for example, the need for bread to which Christ refers in the example of that man who wakes up his friend at midnight to ask him for bread.

Similar necessities are numerous. The need for bread is, in a way, a symbol of all material necessities, the necessities of the human body, the necessities of this existence which springs from the fact that man is a body. But the range of these necessities is wider.

To the answers of Christ, there also pertains the marvellous event in Genesis, of which Abraham is the main character. And the main problem is that of Sodom and Gomorrah; or in other words, that of good and evil, of sin and guilt; namely, it is the problem of justice and mercy. This conversation between Abraham and God is splendid and proves that praying means moving continually in the sphere of justice and mercy; between justice and mercy, it is penetrating into God himself.

Therefore *praying means being aware, being completely aware, of all man's necessities, of the whole truth about man.* And in light of this truth, whose direct subject is I myself, and not only I but also my neighbour, all men, the whole of mankind; and in light of this truth, addressing God as Father.

Castel Gandolfo 27.7.80

What father among you would hand his son a stone when he asked for bread?

(Luke 11:11)

So, according to Christ's answer to the request: teach us to pray, everything is reduced to this single concept: *to learn to pray means 'to learn the Father'*. If we learn the Father reality in the full sense of the word, in its full dimension, we have learned everything.

To learn the Father means finding the answer to the question about how to pray, because to pray also means finding the answer to a series of questions that, for example, arise from the fact that I pray and in some cases my prayer is not granted.

Christ gives indirect answers to these questions as well. He gives them in the whole Gospel and in the whole of Christian experience. *To learn who the Father is means learning what absolute trust is.*

To learn the Father means acquiring the certainty that he absolutely cannot refuse anything. He does not refuse you even when everything, materially and psychologically, seems to indicate refusal. He never refuses you.

Castel Gandolfo 27.7.80

OUR PRAYER ALWAYS ANSWERED   October 6

How much more will the heavenly Father give the Holy Spirit to those who ask him!

(Luke 11:13)

So learning to pray means 'learning the Father' in this way; learning to be sure that the Father never refuses you anything, but that on the contrary, he gives the Holy Spirit to those who ask him.

The gifts we ask for are various; they are our necessities. *We ask according to our needs* and it cannot be otherwise. Christ confirms this attitude of ours: yes, it is so: you must ask according to your needs, as you feel them. As these necessities shake you, often painfully, so you must pray.

On the other hand, when it is a question of the answer to every request of yours it is always given through a substantial gift: *the Father gives us the Holy Spirit*. And he does so in consideration of his Son.

For this reason he gave his Son, gave his Son for the sins of the world; he gave his Son facing all the needs of the world, all the needs of man, so as to be able always to give the Holy Spirit in this crucified and risen Son. This is his gift.

Castel Gandolfo 27.7.80

THE GIFT OF THE FATHER   October 7

On the day I called, you answered me, O Lord.

(Ps. 138:3)

Learning to pray means learning the Father and learning absolute trust in him who always offers us this greatest gift. And in offering it he never deceives us. If sometimes, or even often, we do not directly receive what we ask for, *in this so great gift — when it is offered to us — all other gifts are contained*, even if we do not always realize this.

The example that struck me most in the past is that of a man whom I met in a hospital. He was seriously ill as a result of wounds suffered during the Warsaw Insurrection. In that hospital he spoke to me of his extraordinary happiness.

This man achieved happiness by some other way because visibly, judging his physical state from the medical point of view, there was no reason to be so happy, to feel so well, and to consider himself heard by God. Yet he was heard in another aspect of his humanity. He recalled the gift in which he found his happiness despite so much unhappiness.

Castel Gandolfo 27.7.80

PRAYER GROUPS   October 8

God gives power and strength to his people.

(Ps. 67:36)

There are many communities that pray, pray as perhaps they have never done before, in a different way, a more complete and richer way, *with a greater receptiveness for that gift which the Father gives us.* Also with a new human expression of this receptiveness and I should say with a new cultural programme of new prayer. Such communities are numerous. I wish to unite with them wherever they may be: all over the earth.

This great revolution of prayer is the fruit of the gift, and it is also the testimony of the vast needs of modern man and of the threats looming over him and over the modern world.

I think that Abraham's prayer and its content is very relevant in the times in which we live. Such a prayer is so necessary, to negotiate with God for every just man, to redeem the world from injustice. *A prayer that makes its way into God's heart*, so to speak, between what is justice and what is mercy in it, is indispensable.

Castel Gandolfo 27.7.80

ALL PRAYER IS OUTGOING   October 9

Pray for one another, and this will cure you; the heartfelt prayer of a good man works very powerfully.

(James 5:16)

Prayer has a social significance. Let us never think that someone who devotes a great deal of time to prayer serves only himself and his own inner longings. He also serves the Church, the community, society, because that is the sense of his prayer, he shares himself with others.

Let us remember that prayer shares itself with others. It never remains in isolation; it always penetrates the walls of the soul and reaches others.

Cracow 7.11.70

MAN'S CALL TO HOLINESS   October 10

God the Father chose us, chose us in Christ, to be holy and spotless.

(Eph. 1:4)

Holiness is the most perfect reflection of God in man, according to the design of the Son of God, Jesus Christ, under the action of the Holy Spirit. *Holiness is the mystery of God in the human soul; it is the mystery of the human soul itself.* Holiness is the fullest realization of man's vocation on earth, man's pilgrimage to the homeland of his Eternal Father.

A person's holiness is at the same time, a historical fact, visible, bounded to a place and a time, to character, temperament, vocation and the style of the age. And, being a visible fact, it always has linked to it the pattern of holiness which the whole people of God, at that time and in future generations, nourishes in its heart.

Holiness is finally a special good of the Church who watches over it in every one of her children. And also pronounces on it with an enormous feeling of responsibility, for this is truly a matter of her greatest treasure.

Cracow 22.3.64

ACTION AND CONTEMPLATION October 11

It is Mary who has chosen the better part; it is not to be taken from her.
(Luke 10:42)

The Gospel episode recounts the hospitality offered to Jesus by Martha and Mary. These two sisters, in the history of Christian spirituality, have been understood as symbolic figures, representing action and contemplation respectively. Martha is bustling around with household tasks, while Mary is sitting at Christ's feet to listen to his words. We can draw two lessons from this Gospel text.

First of all we should note the final sentence of Jesus: "Mary has chosen the better part." In this way he strongly emphasizes the fundamental and irreplaceable value that listening to the Word of God has for our existence: it must be our constant reference point, our light, our strength. But it is necessary to listen to it.

It is necessary to know how to keep silent to make room for solitude, or rather for a meeting reserved for intimacy with the Lord. It is necessary to be able to contemplate.

Castel Gandolfo 20.7.80

CONTEMPLATION PURIFIES October 12

'Martha, Martha', he said, 'you worry and fret about so many things.'
(Luke 10:41)

Today man feels deeply the need of not limiting himself to mere material concerns, and of integrating his own technical culture with superior and purifying contributions coming from the world of the spirit.

Unfortunately, in our everyday life we risk interior pollution. But the contact of faith with the word of the Lord purifies us, elevates us, and restores energy to us.

Therefore, we must always keep before our heart's eyes the mystery of love, with which God came to meet us in his son, Jesus Christ. The object of our contemplation is entirely here, and from here comes our salvation, redemption from every form of alienation and sin.

Essentially, we are invited to act like the other Mary, the mother of Jesus, who 'kept all these things, pondering them in her heart'. It is on this condition that we shall not be men of one dimension, but rich in the very greatness of God.

Castel Gandolfo 20.7.80

ACTION AND CONTEMPLATION   October 13

A woman named Martha, welcomed him into her house.

(Luke 10:38)

But there is a second lesson to learn; and it is that we must never see a contradiction between action and contemplation. In fact, we read in the Gospel that it was 'Martha' (and not Mary) who received Jesus Christ 'into her house'.

Let us recall St. Benedict's famous motto: 'Pray and work'. These words contain a whole programme: not of opposition but of synthesis, not of contradiction but of the fusion of two equally important elements.

The result is a very concrete lesson for us which can be expressed as a question: to what extent are we able to see in contemplation and prayer a moment of real thrust for our daily tasks? And, vice versa, to what extent are we able to strengthen our work to its very core with a leavening communion with the Lord?

These questions can serve as an examination of conscience and become a stimulus for a renewal of our daily life, which will be at the same time more contemplative and more active.

Castel Gandolfo 20.7.80

When you pray, go to your private room and, when you have shut your door, pray to your Father.

(Matt. 6:6)

When he says 'Go to your room and shut your door', he is talking about an ascetic effort of the human spirit which must not be confined within oneself. *This shutting-in of oneself is, at the same time, the deepest opening of the human heart.*

It is indispensable for the purpose of meeting the Father, and must be undertaken for this purpose. 'Your Father who sees in secret will reward you.'

Here it is a question of acquiring again the simplicity of thought, of will, and of heart which is indispensable if one is to meet God in one's own 'self'. And God is waiting for this, in order to approach man who is absorbed interiorly and at the same time open to his word and his love!

God wishes to communicate himself to the soul thus disposed. He wishes to give it truth and love, which have their real source in him.

Rome 28.2.79

RESIST EVIL WITH GOOD   October 15

Resist evil and conquer it with good.

(Rom. 12:21)

It is no use complaining of the wickedness of the times. As St. Paul wrote, we must overcome evil by doing good. *The world esteems and respects the courage of ideas and strength of virtues.*

Do not be afraid to refuse words, acts, and attitudes which are not in conformity with Christian ideals. Be courageous in rejecting what destroys your innocence or damages the freshness of your love of Christ.

To seek, love and bear witness to Jesus — this is your commitment; these are the instructions I leave you! By doing so, not only will you keep real joy in your lives, but you will also benefit the whole of society, which needs, above all, consistency with the evangelical message.

Rome 8.11.78

The word of God is something alive and active.

(Heb. 4:12)

The Gospel is precisely about trust. God trusts in man. And if we do not grasp this, if we do not read this in the Gospel, then we have not read it properly.

God speaks to man about himself but not in a reference book manner. One cannot talk about oneself in a reference book manner. *God speaks about himself, putting himself into what he says.*

In the Gospel, it is not even what is said that is the most important thing; the most important thing is the reality. Of course, its form is the form of speech, or rather of writing, but through the writing and the written speech is revealed the reality: God speaks about himself.

Cracow 16.4.62

GOD SPEAKS HIS DESIRES   October 17

God is love and anyone who lives in love lives in God, and God lives in him.

(1 John 4:16)

In the Gospel, God speaks about himself, he says what he is. He takes us into his confidence about what he is, what he is in his divinity, in his deepest being. *He tells us that he is love.* And he tells us in what manner he is love.

He is love in such a manner that he is Father, Son and Holy Spirit. And in that manner he is in himself love.

Further: God speaks about himself, he not only speaks, but throughout the Gospel, he desires. He tells us what he desires, what he desires from us. But first and foremost, he tells us what he desires for us.

Cracow 16.4.62

I call you friends, because I have made known to you everything I have learnt from my Father.

(John 15:15)

Why do I say that we have to meet him in the Gospel? If this meeting does not come about, the Gospel has not been read properly. It is the word of God, his word to man. He can call me 'My friend'. I can call him 'My Friend'.

It is the word of God to man. And not just an oration. It is not rhetoric. It is not just talking to the empty air, it is not a lecture. It is inner speech, it is speech which waits for an answer. For the answer of man. For the answer of every one of us.

The Gospel is not something to be read. The Gospel is something to be answered. What does it mean: to answer? How are we to answer?

We answer by choosing. For *in the Gospel there is a proposal; the proposal of God addressed to man.* Addressed to each one of us, addressed to every human being. And we have to answer this proposal. To choose him.

Cracow 16.4.62

THE CHOICE OF GOD October 19

If anyone declares himself for me in the presence of men, I will declare myself for him in the presence of my Father.

(Matt. 10:32)

Christianity is a religion of choice. The choice of God in Christ. *The outward profession of this choice of God in Christ is the creed.* I choose God, I choose God through the fact that I profess him. I do not simply think about him in the abstract like an idea. I choose God through the fact that I profess him.

I choose Christ through the fact that I profess him. *Christ pronounced on this matter in no uncertain terms.* In no uncertain terms, he stressed the importance of this profession, for he said: 'The man who disowns me in the presence of men, will be disowned in the presence of God's angels.'

He did not speak from the position of a severe judge, but spoke from his own position, he spoke as Christ, but he spoke in such a manner because he had in mind the essential condition: the answer to God, the choice of God.

Cracow 16.4.62

THE HONOUR DUE TO PARENTS   October 20

Honour your father and your mother so that you may have a long life in the land.

(Ex. 20:12)

We repeat this commandment very often, and I do not know whether we really think about the fact that no other commandment is put together in this way. The ten commandments usually take the form of a prohibition. 'Thou shalt not kill, thou shalt not commit adultery, thou shalt not steal.' But here we have simply 'Honour'. And then comes a purpose clause: 'that you may have a long life in the land'.

It is very possible that the Israelites understood this 'long life in the land' as earthly prosperity first and foremost, in a material sense. But there is certainly another, deeper sense to this purpose clause. A deeper sense. Honour! *To honour means to perceive human value.* To learn what it means to be a man. That is a human being.

Now maybe, at this moment, some of you are thinking with bitterness in your hearts; 'How am I to learn, how am I to learn when my father has left my mother, when the man whom I have to call my mother's husband is not my father? Or, conversely, when the woman I have to call my father's wife is not my mother? Honour! God is very demanding!'

'That you may have a long life.' Is this really to be understood in the material sense, is this really earthly prosperity? *Is it not most important that one draws from the family a profound sense of the value and dignity of man?* Or that, even if one only lives a short while, one has had a full life?

Cracow 16.4.62

Foxes have holes and the birds of the air have nests, but the Son of Man has nowhere to lay his head.

(Matt. 8:20)

The home is not simply a dwelling – a place in which people exist. *The home is the climate which these people create in that dwelling*, within the four walls of their earthly abode, their housing, by their work, by their encounters, by their joy and sorrow. All this is truly the home.

An enormous task for a human being. Especially important at the present time, for the present time is sick with the breakup of the home.

It is not easy today to create the home of the human community. Not just in the sense of the housing shortage we are constantly hearing about in the press for young couples and families, but especially in the form of a lack of climate, community and sense of union.

It is not without reason that the Son of God, Jesus Christ, spent the thirty years of his hidden life at home. *He wanted to point out in this way that the home is a power*, the fundamental power of man, that a homeless man is in some way shaken in his humanity, in his human vocation, in his most important gift, the gift of married love between parents and the love of children for their parents.

Cracow 19.3.78

LOVE YOUR FAMILY   October 22

Jesus then went down with them and came to Nazareth and lived under their authority.

(Luke 2:51)

Remember that you are part of a family. Love your family! Love your parents and all those who loved you!

The family, as you know, is the historic and visible expression of the love of God, who in his way wished to make people capable of loving and giving their lives, precisely because they are created 'in his image and likeness'.

It is sad to think that certain ideologies want to destroy the family, spreading alienation and causing disputes! It is distressing to think that so many young people leave their own homes, casting their parents into bitterness and despair! That is not the way. Love your families with generosity, patience, tact, tolerating those imperfections which are not lacking in any person whatsoever. *Make your home an oasis of peace and confidence:* pray with your families.

And prepare yourselves also to form families of your own in the future: do it in such a way that your love will always remain pure and serene through intimate friendship with Jesus!

Rome 18.9.80

THE DIGNITY OF THE HUMAN PERSON   October 23

You were called to liberty; but be careful, or this liberty will provide an opening for self-indulgence.

(Gal. 5:13)

Every human being has inalienable rights that must be respected. Each human community — ethnic, historical, cultural or religious — has rights which must be respected.

Peace is threatened every time one of these rights is violated.

The moral law, guardian of human rights, protector of the dignity of man, cannot be set aside by any person or group, or by the State itself, for any cause, not even for security or in the interests of law and order. The law of God stands in judgement over all reasons of State.

As long as injustices exist in any of the areas that touch upon the dignity of the human person, be it in the political, social or economic field, be it in the cultural or religious sphere, true peace will not exist.

The causes of inequalities must be identified through a courageous and objective evaluation, and they must be eliminated *so that every person can develop and grow in the full measure of his or her humanity.*

Drogheda 29.9.79

DIALOGUE BETWEEN NATIONS   October 24

Speak the truth to each other; let the judgements at your gates be such as conduce to peace.

(Zech. 8:16)

The word 'dialogue' is a correlate of the word 'freedom'. Dialogue is the principle of forming relations between people on all kinds of scales;

206

on the international scale, between people of different convictions and groups of different convictions — on the principle of a common search for truth.

Dialogue cannot be a unilateral dictating of terms, nor action from a position of power, using that power to curtail the authentic existence of another.

Dialogue is an offshoot of freedom, it establishes freedom and serves it in relationships between people, between nations. *Dialogue is at once the source and the guarantee of peace on every scale.*

Cracow 31.12.66

THE DEMANDS OF MARRIED LOVE October 25

Follow Christ by loving as he loved you.

(Eph. 5:1)

Christian spouses have promised to share with each other all they are and all they have. It is the most audacious contract that exists, the most marvellous one too!

The union of their bodies, willed by God himself as the expression of the even deeper communion of their minds and their hearts, carried out with equal respect and tenderness, renews the dynamism and the youth of their solemn commitment, of their first 'yes'.

The union of their characters: to love a being is to love him such as he is, it is to love him to the extent of cultivating in oneself the antidote of his weaknesses or his faults, for example, calm and patience, if the other manifestly lacks them.

The union of hearts! There are innumerable fine shades of difference between the love of man and that of woman. Neither of the partners can demand to be loved in the same way as he or she loves.

To share the joys and, even more so, the sufferings of the heart, is a strong bond of unity.

Kinshasa 3.5.80

This is why a man leaves his father and mother and joins himself to his wife, and they become one body.

(Gen. 2:24)

Life is also precious because it is the expression and the fruit of love. *This is why life should spring up within the setting of marriage*, and why marriage and the parents' love for one another should be marked by generosity in self-giving.

The great danger for family life, in the midst of any society whose idols are pleasure, comfort and independence, lies in the fact that people close their hearts and become selfish. The fear of making permanent commitments can change the mutual love of husband and wife into two loves of self — two loves existing side by side until they end in separation.

Washington 7.10.79

RESPONSIBILITY FOR THE GIFT OF LOVE   October 27

The love of God has been poured into our hearts by the Holy Spirit.

(Rom. 5:5)

Only those are capable of responsible love in marriage who are imbued with deep responsibility for the gift of love itself. *For love is above all a gift*, and that is the basic content of its first and continued experience.

Although everything seems to confirm that love is a thing 'of the world', that it is born in souls and bodies as the fruit of emotional sensitivity and sensuous attraction, reaching to the hidden depths of the sexual constitution of the organism, yet through all this and as if over and above all this, love is a gift.

It comes as a gift to those who are in love, allows them to discover and identify each other, then to develop until they reach the suitable point of maturity, and in turn confirm the marriage covenant.

F.R.L.

THE GIFT OF PARENTHOOD

Husbands must love their wives as they love their own bodies.

(Eph. 5:29)

Married love is fulfilled by parenthood. Responsibility for this love from the beginning to the end is at the same time responsibility also for parenthood. The one participates in the other, and they both constitute each other.

Parenthood is a gift that comes to people, to man and to woman, together with love, that creates a perspective of love in the dimension of a reciprocal life-long self-giving, and that is the condition of gradual realization of that perspective through life and action.

Parenthood, the gift, is therefore at the same time a rich task whose receiving and successive fulfilling is synonymous with receiving a gift; a gift, moreover, which the persons themselves become for each other in marriage: the woman for the man, the man for the woman.

Their reciprocal offering to each other of what they are as man and woman reaches its full sense through parenthood, through the fact that as husband and wife they become father and mother.

F.R.L.

FAMILY RESPONSIBILITY FOR EACH OTHER

You should carry each other's troubles and fulfil the law of Christ.

(Gal. 6:2)

In order that Christian marriage may favour the total good and development of the married couple, it must be inspired by the Gospel, and thus be open to new life — new life to be given and accepted generously.

The couple is also called to create a family atmosphere, in which children can be happy, and lead full and worthy human and Christian lives.

To maintain a joyful family requires much from both the parents and the children. *Each member of the family has to become, in a special way, the servant of the others and share their burdens.*

Each one must show concern, not only for his or her own life, but also for the lives of the other members of the family: their needs, their hopes, their ideals.

Washington 7.10.79

Samuel ran to Eli and said: 'Here I am, since you called me.' Eli said: 'I did not call. Go back and lie down.'

(1 Sam. 3:5)

What then shall be the attitude of responsible Christians, and especially of parents and mass media workers conscious of their duties in regard to children? They ought, before all else, to take charge of the human growth of the child; any pretence of maintaining a 'neutral' position in his regard and of letting him grow up in his own way merely disguises a dangerous lack of interest under the appearance of respect, for the child's personality.

No such disengagement in relation to children can be accepted; for *children really have a need for help in their development towards maturity.* There are great natural riches and vitality in a child's heart; however, he is not capable, all by himself, of resolving the diverse mysteries and longings that assail him from within.

It is on the adults that the duty falls — on the parents, teachers and communicators — and it is also they who are capable of enabling the child to sort things out and find himself. Does not every child in some way resemble the boy Samuel, mentioned in sacred Scripture? Unable to interpret the call of God, he sought help from his master, who at first replied: 'I did not call.'

Now, shall we adopt this kind of attitude, and smother the inspirations that impel the child to higher things? Shall we not rather help him to understand and respond, as the priest Eli eventually did with Samuel.

Rome 27.5.79

CHRIST'S LOVE OF CHILDREN   October 31

Anyone who is an obstacle to bring down one of these little ones who have faith in me, would be better drowned in the depths of the sea.

(Matt. 18:6)

Like soft wax on which even the tiniest pressure leaves a mark, so the child is responsive to every stimulus that plays upon his imagination, his emotions, his instincts and his ideas. *And the impressions received at this age are the ones which are destined to make the deepest mark* on the psychology of the adult human being and to condition, often in a lasting way, his later relationships with himself, with others, and with his environment. We must regard Christ's warning, with its reasoned severity, in the light of these facts, 'Anyone who is an obstacle . . . would be better drowned.'

For the believer who intends to base the conduct of his own life on the Gospel, the example of Christ has to be the norm. Now, Christ presents himself as one who lovingly welcomes little children, as the one who defends them in their spontaneous desire to come close to him, who praises their typical and trusting simplicity as being worthy of the Kingdom.

He does not hesitate to make a surprising equation: 'Anyone who welcomes a little child in my name welcomes me.' As I had occasion to write myself recently, *'The Lord identifies himself with the world of young children . . . Jesus does not condition children, he does not use children. He calls them, and brings them into his plan for the salvation of the world.'*

Rome 27.5.79

November

MAKE YOURSELVES SAINTS! November 1

May the God of peace make you perfect and holy; and may you all be kept safe and blameless.

(1 Thess. 5:23)

The spiritual necessities of the present-day world are immense! If we look at the boundless forests of buildings in modern metropolises, invaded by numberless multitudes, we cannot but be frightened. *How can we reach these persons and bring them to Christ?*

We are helped by the certainty of being only instruments of grace: it is God Himself who acts in the individual soul, with his love and his mercy.

Our real and constant goal must be that of personal sanctification, to be suitable and effective instruments of grace.

The truest and most sincere wish I can form for you is just this: *'Make yourselves saints and do so quickly!'*

Let us be happy to live in these times of ours and let us commit ourselves courageously to the plan that Providence carries out mysteriously, through us.

Rome 28.10.79

REMEMBERING THE DEAD November 2

If anyone believes in me, even though he dies he will live, and whoever lives and believes in me will never die.

(John 11:26)

The necessity of dying, the truth of death, Christ explained to us not only by these words: Christ also explained this truth to us by the very fact of his death and resurrection.

213

And so, when in the spirit of faith and with prayers on our lips we stand among the graves of our dear ones, then reality itself speaks to us in a different manner; the reality of death speaks to us the truth of eternal life. The reality of death, suffering and the Cross speaks to us the truth of Christ's Resurrection. On the basis of this, truth speaks to us of faith in the resurrection of the body and life everlasting.

Cracow 1.11.67

THE VALUE OF LONELINESS November 3

A woman who is really widowed . . . can give herself up to God and consecrate all her days and nights to petitions and prayer.

(1 Tim. 5:5)

In the Church today, there is a constant need for service, acts of mercy to soul and body. And this need is, as it were, an unceasing call going out to all Christians, and especially to lonely people, for whom God's providence has ordained a life of widowhood or some other form of loneliness.

The example of the early Church is very eloquent here and provides a constant lesson for our times too. And in our times, *it is necessary to make good use of loneliness*, and the best use of loneliness is service, the diaconate.

There are various forms of diaconate. First there is service through prayer, which is very important in the Church. When we read the Acts of the Apostles, and the Epistles, we can confirm that the founders of *the Church called lonely people, widows and widowers, to special prayer*. This is reasonable because they are often free from the many human duties associated with the family; they can rather open their hearts to the things of God.

And so the life of loneliness is always linked in the Church with a special God-mindedness. It is necessary to fill one's soul, one's heart, with thoughts of God, to think deeply about the Divine mysteries. Some people, we know, even choose loneliness specially for this purpose, so that they can fill their minds with thoughts of the Divine mysteries, with contemplation.

Cracow 8.12.70

ST. CHARLES BARROMEO

Each one of us has been given his own share of grace, given as Christ allotted it.

(Eph. 4:7)

My beloved parents gave me the name Karol (Charles) which was also my father's name. Certainly, they could never have foreseen (they both died young) that this name would open up for their child a path to the great events of today's Church.

St. Charles! How often I have knelt before his relics in Milan Cathedral; how often I have thought about his life, contemplating in my mind the gigantic figure of this man of God and servant of the Church, Charles Barromeo, Cardinal, Bishop of Milan, and a man of the Council. He is one of the great protagonists of the deep reform of the sixtenth-century Church, carried out by the Council of Trent, which will always remain linked with his name.

Moreover, he was a servant of souls, who never let himself be intimidated, a servant of the suffering, of the sick, of those condemned to death.

My patron saint!

In his name my parents, my country, intended to prepare me right from the beginning for an extraordinary service of the Church, in the context of today's Council, with the many tasks united with its implementation, and also in all the experiences and sufferings of modern man.

Rome 4.11.78

THE VIRTUE OF PATIENCE

November 5

Your endurance will win you your lives.

(Luke 21:19)

Patience is a virtue which, according to the teaching of St. Thomas Aquinas, is extremely close to fortitude. Fortitude tells us to take on difficult tasks, and not to give way under adversity.

Patience teaches us how to endure in difficult circumstances, teaches us to endure even when this entails suffering. Patience is the opposite of impatience, haste.

Patience, as the Lord Jesus described it, is always the ability to look forward. It is endurance in the endeavour for great ends. It is the ability to endure, which is born from the premise that *great ends can only be achieved thoroughly, achieved with great efforts, at the cost of great devotion and great work.*

Cracow 24.1.71

LOVE AND TRUTH November 6

Love takes no pleasure in other people's sins but delights in the truth.

(1 Cor. 13:6)

Love is always linked to the truth. *The love of one's neighbour must always be guided by the truth about him.* It is this love which as St. Paul says, 'delights in the truth'.

First and foremost love must perceive the good in another, but must also see the bad — sins and defects. And according to the sense of duty, it is capable of calling this evil by name and, above all, is able to repair it.

This is the most important manifestation of love and its touchstone, its ability to repair evil in another. Such is the love of God towards us, such is the love of Christ.

Cracow 16.4.73

LOVE DEMANDS THE TRUTH November 7

Do not judge, and you will not be judged; because the judgements you give are the judgements you will get.

(Matt. 7:1)

The love of our neighbour demands that we should always be guided by the truth in making judgements about people. This is a very important and fundamental demand of the Gospel. The Lord Jesus says, 'Do not judge' and these words of his give us a great deal to think about.

First of all, they indicate that it is not an easy thing for one person to judge another. *Only God knows all the secrets of the human heart and can find out all the truth.* In the judgement of men, there is always a need to appeal to the judgement of God.

Cracow 16.4.73

Speak the truth to each other; let the judgements at your gates be such as conduce to peace.

(Zech. 8:16)

Truth in judging others is also a fundamental condition of social morality. This is linked with the question of what is known as public opinion, which is nothing else but a judgement about human beings and human problems, felt by wider or narrower circles of society.

One can say that here the responsibility for truth is even greater, if we treat public opinion as a matter of conscience — and we cannot treat it otherwise.

For opinion is created from statements expressed verbally in some public place, or from judgement proclaimed in writing or by the mass media. We live in an era of very great advances in these forms of communication and this in turn, creates a particular responsibility for those who use them. This responsibility is all the greater if the other party has no possibility of using the media in self-defence.

Cracow 16.4.73

CHRIST; THE ANSWER TO OUR ANXIETY   November 9

None of the disciples was bold enough to ask. 'Who are you?'; they knew quite well it was the Lord.

(John 21:12)

When his disciples were perturbed, Christ's answer was very simple: my presence among you, my physical presence among you should wipe out your anxiety, put an end to it: I am; I am the same person whom you remember, right up to the moment of the Crucifixion. And he invites them, as it were, to test his identity.

Christ is the answer to the anxieties of man, and I think that he is also the answer to the anxiety which you have to live with today. He is. He is the same. If you link your calling, your calling to a creative communication with him, with his truth, with his Gospel, his Church — he is, the same. And his identity was and will be — must be — the basis of your identity.

Cracow 23.4.73

DO NOT FEAR, GOD IS WITH US November 10

Know that I am with you always; Yes, to the end of time.

(Matt. 28:20)

You must be strong, dear brothers and sisters. *You must be strong with the strength that comes from faith.* You must be faithful. Today more than in any other age you need this strength. *You must be strong with the strength of hope*, hope that brings the perfect joy of life and does not allow us to grieve the Holy Spirit.

You must be strong with love, which is stronger than death. You must be strong with the love that 'is patient and kind; . . . is not jealous or boastful: . . . is not arrogant or rude . . . Does not insist on its own way; . . . is not irritable or resentful . . . does not rejoice at wrong but rejoices in the right . . . Bears all things, believes all things, hopes all things, endures all things. Love never ends' (1 Cor. 13:4–8).

You must be strong with the strength of faith, hope and charity, a charity that is aware, mature and responsible and helps us to set up the great dialogue with man and the world rooted in the dialogue with God himself, with the Father through the Son in the Holy Spirit, the dialogue of salvation. Yes, we must work for peace and reconciliation between the people and the nations of the whole world.

Warsaw 16.7.79

THE SPIRIT OF OPENNESS November 11

We have received the Spirit that comes from God, to teach us to understand the gifts that he has given us.

(1 Cor. 2:12)

We must try to come close to one another. We must open the frontiers. When we are strong with the spirit of God, we are also strong with faith in man, strong with faith, hope and charity which are inseparable, and ready to give witness to the cause of man before the person who really has this cause at heart. The person to whom this cause is sacred. The person who wishes to serve this cause with his best will. There is therefore no need for fear.

We must open the frontiers. There is no imperialism in the Church, only service. There is only the death of Christ on Calvary. There is the activity of the Holy Spirit, the fruit of that death, the Holy Spirit who is always with all of us, with the whole of mankind.

Warsaw 16.7.79

CHRIST REVEALS THE FATHER — November 12

No one has ever seen God; it is the only Son, who is nearest to the Father's heart who has made him known.

(John 1:18)

Although God dwells in unapproachable light, he speaks to man by means of the whole of the universe: 'ever since the creation of the world his invisible nature, namely, his eternal power and deity, has been clearly perceived in the things that have been made' (Rom. 1:20). This indirect and imperfect knowledge, achieved by the intellect seeking God by means of creatures through the visible world, falls short of 'vision of the Father'.

'No one has ever seen God,' writes St. John, in order to stress the truth that 'the only Son, who is nearest to the Father's heart has made him known.' This 'making known' reveals God in the most profound mystery of his being, one and three, surrounded by 'unapproachable light' (1 Tim. 6:16).

Nevertheless, through this making-known by Christ we know God above all in his relationship of love for man: in his 'philanthropy' (Titus 3:4). It is precisely here that his invisible nature becomes in a special way 'visible', incomparably more visible than through all the other 'things that have been made'. It becomes visible in Christ and through Christ, through his actions and his words, and finally through his death on the Cross and his Resurrection.

Rome 9.12.80

GOD'S REVELATION — November 13

At various times in the past and in various different ways, God spoke to our ancestors.

(Heb. 1:1)

Revelation consists of the initiative of God, who personally came to meet man, in order to open with him a dialogue of salvation. *It was*

God who began the talk, and it is God who carries it forward. Man listens and answers.

But the answer that God expects from man is not reduced to a cold intellectual evaluation of an abstract content of ideas. God comes to meet man and speaks of him, because he loves him and wants to save him. Man's answer, therefore, must be, in the first place, grateful acceptance of the divine initiative and confident abandonment to the antecedent power of his love.

To enter upon a dialogue with God means letting oneself be enchanted and won over by the luminous figure of Jesus the revealer and by the love of him who sent him.

Rome 15.10.79

THE SCRIPTURES REVEAL GOD November 14

The Word was made flesh, he lived among us, and we saw his glory.
(John 1:14)

The same divine Word had previously become human language, assuming the ways of expression of different cultures which, from Abraham to the seer of the Apocalypse, offered the adorable mystery of God's salvific love the possibility of becoming accessible and understandable for successive generations — in spite of the multiple diversity of their historical situations.

Thus, 'in various different ways', God was in contact with men and, in his benevolent and immense condescension, he dialogued with them through the prophets, the Apostles, sacred writers, and above all through the Son of Man.

Rome 26.4.79

THE HOLINESS OF SCRIPTURE November 15

Man does not live on bread alone, but on every word that comes from the mouth of God.

(Matt. 4:4)

'Every word that comes from the mouth of God', is also, like the Eucharist, the true 'food of eternal life', capable of nourishing the new life of the baptized person.

Of divine reality, although expressed in human words, *Scripture is therefore infinitely authoritative.* It is a source of faith, according to Paul's words, it is the foundation of a certainty that is full, sure, not hesitating. As it is completely from God, it is entirely, even in its slightest parts, of immense importance and worthy of the most careful observance.

For this reason, too, the Scripture is rightly called holy. Just as it would be a terrible sacrilege to profane the Eucharist so too *it would be a sacrilege to tamper with the integrity and purity of the word of God.*

Rome 2.1.80

THE PRE-EMINENCE OF SCRIPTURE   November 16

All Scripture is inspired by God and can profitably be used for teaching, for refuting error, for guiding people's lives and teaching them to be holy.

(2 Tim. 3:16)

It is vitally necessary, in fact, that one's approach to the word of God should always be worshipful, faithful and loving.

The Church must draw essentially from it for her proclamation, letting herself be guided by the very words of her Lord, in order not to run the risk of 'reducing to human words the words of religion'.

Every Christian must refer 'always and everywhere' to the Scriptures for all his choices, becoming 'like a child' before it, seeking in it the most effective remedy against all his various weaknesses, and *not daring to take a step without being illuminated by the divine rays of those words.*

Rome 2.1.80

THE WORDS OF THE WORD   November 17

In the beginning was the Word: the Word was with God and the Word was God.

(John 1:1)

From the word of Jesus we learn, first and foremost, the very nature of God, who is Life, Light, Love, Trinity. No philosopher and theologian can penetrate the essence of God; only Jesus, the Word Incarnate, can reveal and guarantee this fundamental truth.

And because of this we are certain that there is a relationship of love between God the creator and man: *every human being is an eternal heart-beat of God's love.*

From the word of Jesus we know our eternal destiny: only Jesus, with his divine word, can assure us absolutely concerning the immortality of the soul and the final resurrection of the body, as a result of which it is worthwhile being born, living, and projecting our existence beyond time towards endless happiness.

Rome 24.7.80

THE WORD OF JESUS   November 18

If anyone loves me he will keep my word, and my Father will love him.
(John 14:23)

Furthermore we learn from the word of Jesus, where the true dignity of man lies, namely, in participation in divine life itself by means of grace. True joy, real greatness, supreme dignity, are found only in the life of grace.

From the word of Jesus we learn how we must behave, because he reveals to us that the will of God is expressed in the moral law and in the supreme commandment of mutual charity.

The will of God, in fact, is the absolute determinant between good and evil, the guideline for correct behaviour and for true pedagogy.

Finally, from the word of Jesus we know also his presence, always current and alive in time and in history, by means of the Church, willed and founded by him, which gives us certainty about the truths to believe and to practise, and offers us the Eucharist, a mystery of faith and at the same time a supreme manifestation of love.

Rome 24.7.80

THE TREASURY OF GOD'S WORD   November 19

Mary treasured all these things and pondered them in her heart.
(Luke 2:19)

God's word is the centre of all theological study; *it is the chief instrument for handing down Christian doctrine* and it is the perpetual source of spiritual life.

Speaking to seminarians in America, I said: 'The intellectual formation of the priest, which is so vital for the times in which we live, embraces a number of the human sciences as well as the various sacred sciences. These all have an important place in your preparation for the priesthood. But the first priority for seminaries today is the teaching of God's word in all its purity and integrity, with all its demands and in all its power' (Address at Saint Charles Seminary, Philadelphia).

It is my hope that in your reverence for the word of God you will be like Mary – like Mary whose response to God's word was, 'Let what you have said be done to me' (Luke 1:38), like Mary 'who believed that the promise made her by the Lord would be fulfilled' (Luke 1:45); like Mary who treasured those things which were said of her Son and pondered them in her heart.

May you treasure God's word always and ponder it each day in your heart, so that your whole life may become a proclamation of Christ, the Word made flesh.

Rome 22.2.80

CHRIST'S MISSION   November 20

I came into the world for this; to bear witness to the truth.

(John 18:37)

When Jesus was about thirty – the age prescribed by the Law for participation in public life – he went to the synagogue in Nazareth to read a passage from the prophet Isaiah. After reading it he said: 'This text is being fulfilled today, even as you listen' (Luke 4:20).

We know that 'his own people did not accept him': they were unwilling to accept that the carpenter's son was truly the one he claimed to be. That is how it is: 'no prophet is ever accepted in his own country.' He then left Nazareth and began to teach in towns and villages all over Galilee, bearing witness everywhere to the truth for the sake of which he had been sent by the Father.

We know how the ordinary people welcomed and accepted him, and we know too that the witness he bore to the truth brought him in the end before two tribunals, first a Jewish and then a Roman one.

S. of C.

'Truth?' said Pilate. 'What is that?'

(John 18:38)

Pilate's tribunal was the setting for an encounter that brought into the full light of day the nobility of truth and the dignity of the man who bore witness to it.

Pilate suspects Jesus of claiming sovereignty over Israel. 'Are you the king of the Jews?' he asked. When the imputation is denied he puts the question in a different form: 'So you are a king?' Then Jesus replies: 'It is you who say it, I am a king. For this I came into the world, to bear witness to the truth.'

Even though Pilate the sceptic interrupts him to ask: 'What is truth?', there is no doubt that *truth emerged from that encounter as something real constituting both Jesus's kingship and the dignity of man.*

S. of C.

THE KINGSHIP OF CHRIST   November 22

Jesus replied: 'Mine is not a kingdom of this world.'

(John 18:36)

These words remind us of past events, which took place in the distant outskirts of the great Roman Empire. They are not, however, without significance. Perhaps present-day, topical problems still resound in them. In this dialogue, perhaps, there could be found, at least from certain standpoints, the same discussions that happen today.

Christ answers the judge's questions and shows that the accusation brought against him is groundless. He does not aim at temporal power.

Shortly afterwards he will be scourged and crowned with thorns. He will be mocked and insulted, with the words: 'Hail, King of the Jews!' But Jesus is silent, as if he wished, by his silence, to express to the end what he had already replied to Pilate.

Rome 26.11.78

'So you are a king then?' said Pilate.

(John 18:37)

A strange question, strange after all that Christ had declared so firmly. But Pilate felt that the accused man's denial did not exhaust everything: in the depth of this denial an affirmation was hidden. What? And here Christ helps Pilate, the judge, to find it:

'Yes, I am a king; I was born for this, I came into the world for this; to bear witness to the truth.'

We must all reflect carefully on Christ's denial and affirmation.

Jesus' affirmation does not belong to the trial that was once held in the distant territories of the Roman Empire, but is always at the centre of our lives. It is relevant today. Those who issue laws, and those who govern states and those who judge, must think it over.

Every Christian, every man, who is always a citizen, and who consequently belongs to a definite political, economic, national and international community, must reflect on this affirmation.

Rome 26.11.78

A REIGN OF TRUTH AND LOVE   November 24

Yes, I am a king, I was born for this, I came into the world for this.

(John 18:37)

The times in which we live require us to think more and more often of this answer. They ask us to seek that unusual King, to desire him more and more fervently.

How marvellous he is, in fact, this King who renounces all the signs of power, the instruments of dominion, force and arrogance, *and wishes to reign only with the power of truth and love*, with the power of interior conviction and sheer abandonment.

How unusual this King is! How much modern man must long for him, weary as he is of those systems of exercising power which, in so many places of the globe, do not spare man oppression and violence.

They are forms of power which try to condition man even in his most interior dimensions; they subordinate him to ideological systems, without taking into account whether or not they correspond to his convictions, and they make his civil and social life depend more on acceptance of those systems than on the real merits of the person.

How marvellous is this King, Jesus Christ, who refused such methods of leading man.

Rome 25.11.79

SYSTEMS OF OPPRESSION AND PERSECUTION   November 25

If my kingdom were of this world, my men would have fought to prevent my being surrendered to the Jews.

(John 18:36)

He not only rejected all means of exercising power over others by means of force and violence, but *he even deprived himself of the legitimate support of defence against his persecutors.* All that in order to enter man's life with the power of truth and love alone, to reign in human hearts, in all those who are capable of listening to his voice and perceiving his call.

And there is no lack of them; in fact, they are numerous even where there is absolute silence with regard to them, where they are treated as if they did not exist, where they are deprived of elementary human rights, even though, theoretically, the latter are mostly guaranteed, where *they are imprisoned and tried because they gather together to pray and read the Word of God,* or because they have transcribed liturgical texts for the use of the faithful who wish to pray.

Nor, certainly, can human hearts be won by those systems which do not recognize equality among men, who are all children of God, and which, to deny it, avail themselves of pretexts of race, culture and opinions, even if expressed peacefully, or do not respect the requirements of the physical and moral dignity of persons, beginning with the right, when they are accused, to defend themselves.

In all systems of oppression, and persecution, there are men who, at the cost of courage and suffering, bear witness to Christ and *choose this unusual King, who reigns in human hearts with the power of truth and love alone.* Let us join them, particularly in prayer.

Rome 25.11.79

Your word is a lamp to my feet, a light on my path.

(Ps. 119:105)

Each one of you is individually called by Christ, called to be part of his Kingdom and to play a role in his mission of salvation.

These are the great realities of your Confirmation. Having called you by name, God sends you forth to accomplish what he wants you to do. He says to each of you what he said to Jeremiah the Prophet: 'I am with you to protect you.'

He seals his protection over you by putting his words into your mouth. In the expression of the Psalmist, the word of God becomes for you a lamp for your feet and a light for your path. *Christ calls you to lead a new life based on the Beatitudes*, with new criteria of judgement, a fresh spiritual outlook and a transformed pattern of life.

Incorporated into the newness of Christ's own life, *only a constant turning to him will give you fulfilment and joy*. A repeated conversion of heart becomes the condition for the usefulness of your activities and for the attainment of your destiny.

Rome 25.8.80

REVEALING CHRIST TO OTHERS   November 27

Always have your answer ready for people who ask you the reason for the hope that you all have.

(1 Pet. 3:15)

As you pursue your fundamental Christian calling, you will be summoned to perform joyfully and faithfully the activities of each moment, each day, each week.

For most of you, the field of your activities is the secular world itself in need of the Gospel leaven. Your task is crystal clear: *to bring Christ to the world and to bring the world to Christ*.

You are called to understand each other, to work together, to walk together the path of life — together with each other and with Christ — to respect humanity in everyone, even in those who have lost a sense of their own dignity.

You must find Christ in others, and give Christ to others — the Christ who alone is the hope of the world. In all the circumstances of your lives you are called to be bearers of a message of hope, called to be ready, in the words of St. Peter, with an answer for anyone who asks you 'the reason for the hope that you all have'.

Rome 25.8.80

'THERE IS NO GOD!' November 28

The Lord is looking down from heaven to see if a single one is wise, if a single one is seeking God.

(Ps. 14:2)

I shall never forget the impression left with me by a Russian soldier in 1945. The war was only just over. A conscript knocked at the door of the Cracow seminary. When I asked: 'What is it you want?' he replied that he wished to enter the seminary.

Our conversation went on for a long time. Even though he never in fact entered (incidentally he was far from clear in his mind about what a seminary really is) our meeting taught me, personally, one great truth: how wonderfully God succeeds in penetrating the human mind even in the extremely unfavourable conditions of systematic denial of him.

In the whole of his adult life that man had scarcely ever gone inside a Church. At school, and then later at work, he had continually heard people asserting, 'There is no God!' And in spite of all that he said more than once: 'But I always knew that God exists . . . and now I would like to learn something about him . . .'

S. of C.

CHRIST'S CONTINUAL COMING November 29

Blessed be the Lord, the God of Israel, for he has visited his people, he has come to their rescue.

(Luke 1:68)

The truth of Christianity depends on two fundamental realities which we can never lose sight of. Both are closely connected. The first reality is called 'God', the second one 'man'. *Christianity arises from a special mutual relationship between God and man.* In recent times there have been long discussions as to whether this relationship is God-centred or man-centred. There will never be a satisfactory answer to this question if we continue to consider the two terms of the question separately.

In fact, Christianity is man-centred precisely because it is fully God-centred; and simultaneously it is God-centred, thanks to its being so unusually man-centred. It is just the mystery of the Incarnation which, in itself, explains this relationship.

It is for this reason that Christianity is not only a 'religion of Advent', but Advent itself. *Christianity lives out the mystery of God's real coming to man*; this is the reality which gives it life.

Rome 29.11.79

THE MEANING OF ADVENT   November 30

People of Zion, the Lord will come to save all nations, and your hearts will exult.

(Is. 30:19)

We are now accustomed to the term Advent; we know what it means, but precisely because we have become so familiar with it, we do not succeed, perhaps, in understanding all the riches hidden in this word.

Advent means 'coming'.

We must therefore ask ourselves: Who comes? And for whom does he come?

We find the answer to this question at once. Even children know that it is Jesus who comes, for them and for all men. He comes one night at Bethlehem. He is born in a grotto, which was used as a cowshed.

The children know this, and so do the adults who participate in the children's joy, and who on Christmas night seem to become children too. Nevertheless many questions are asked. Man has the right, and even the duty, to question in order to know. There are also those who doubt and, although they take part in the joy of Christmas, seem strangers to the truth it contains.

For this very reason *we have the time of Advent, so that every year we can penetrate again into his essential truth of Christianity.*

Rome 29.11.79

December

ADVENT'S ROOTS IN GENESIS   December 1

God said: 'Let us make man in our own image, in the likeness of ourselves.'
(Gen. 1:26)

Advent took shape for the first time on the horizon of man's history, *when God revealed himself as the one who delights in the good, who loves and who gives.* In this gift to man God did not just give him the visible world. God wants to give him himself too, just as man is capable of giving himself to another.

God wants to give himself to him, admitting him to participation in his mysteries, and even to participation in his life. This is carried out in a tangible way in the relationships between members of a family: husband, wife, parents, children. That is why the prophets refer very often to these relationships, to show God's true image.

The order of grace is possible only 'in the world of persons'. It concerns the gift which always aims at the formation and communion of persons; in fact the book of Genesis presents us with such a giving. The form of this 'communion of persons' is portrayed in it right from the beginning.

Man is called to familiarity with God, to intimacy and friendship with him. God wants to be close to him. He wants to share his plans with him. He wants to share his life with him. He wants to make him happy with his own happiness, his own Being.

Rome 13.12.78

231

The Lord God fashioned all the wild beasts, these he brought to the man to see what he would call them.

(Gen. 2:19)

The first 'man' carries out the first and fundamental act of knowledge of the world. At the same time this act enables him to know and distinguish himself, 'man', from all other creatures. It could be said that this first man does what every man of any time usually does; that is: he reflects on his own being and asks himself who he is.

The result of this cognitive process is the realization of the fundamental and essential difference: I am different. I am more 'different' than I am 'similar'. The Bible description concludes: 'no helpmate suitable for man was found for him.'

Why are we speaking of all this today? We are doing so to understand better the mystery of Advent, to understand it from its very foundations – and thus penetrate with greater depth into our Christianity.

Advent means 'the Coming'.

If God 'comes' to man, he does so because in the human being, he has prepared a 'dimension of expectation' through which man can 'welcome' God, and is capable of doing so.

Rome 6.12.78

ADVENT IS NECESSARY   December 3

God wants everyone to be saved and reach full knowledge of the truth.

(1 Tim. 2:4)

Because of all this the coming of God is necessary, as is the expectation of man: the availability of man.

We know that the first man, who enjoyed original innocence and the particular closeness of his Creator, did not show this availability. This first covenant of God with man was interrupted, but *the will to save man did not cease on the part of God.* Therefore Advent lasts always.

The reality of Advent is expressed, among other things, by those words of St. Paul: 'God wants everyone to be saved.'

That 'God wants' is precisely Advent, and it is the basis of every Advent.

Rome 13.12.78

'ROGER AND OVER – ROGER . . .' December 4

What you hear in whispers, proclaim from the housetops.

(Matt. 10:27)

I saw with pleasure the wall poster with its ingenious slogan: 'Roger and over'. This slogan, which you have taken from radio jargon, defines very well the Christian commitment to which each of you is called.

That is, the commitment to listen to the word of God and of men in order to transmit it, in your turn, to others, just as Jesus said to his disciples: 'What I say to you in the dark, tell in the daylight.'

'Roger' – (received and understood!) This first word of your motto means also knowing how to listen . . .

But above all it means being able to accept good inspirations, letting oneself be imbued with God's grace, aspiring to holiness, according to the Lord's words: 'You must, therefore, be perfect just as your heavenly Father is perfect' (Matt. 5:48).

Rome 26.5.79

'ROGER AND OVER – OVER . . .' December 5

Your light must shine in the sight of men, so that, seeing your good works, they may give the praise to your Father.

(Matt. 5:16)

'Over' – all that you receive must not remain lifeless in you, but must also go over, that is, be given, communicated to others, as was done by the Apostles who scattered over the world to communicate and proclaim to all peoples the message of salvation they had received from their Master and ours.

You too will do this, if you feel in your hearts that you are true living witnesses to Christ among your companions.

And such *you will be if you are able to manifest your joy in living, growing and loving*; if you are able to overcome the deceptive lure of the senses; if you succeed in not being proud in relation to others who are not so gifted and who are worse-off as regards social status; if you do not act selfishly; if you are not spiteful; if you do not revenge yourselves, but are able to forgive sincerely those who have offended you; if, in other words, you are able to live in an evangelical way.

In this way you will certainly succeed in putting 'over' your ideals to others, and they, seeing your good works, will give glory to the Father in heaven.

Rome 26.5.79

TURNING TOWARDS THE FATHER December 6

John the Baptist appeared in the wilderness, proclaiming a baptism of repentance for the forgiveness of sins.

(Mark 1:4)

The role of John was to prepare for Christ. It was in the context of conversion that the communion existing in the life of the Most Holy Trinity was revealed. The Baptist was announcing an invitation to turn to God, to be conscious of sin, to repent, to walk in the truth of one's relationship with God.

Meanwhile, Jesus himself had submitted to the penitential rite and was at prayer when the voice of the Father proclaimed him as Son: the one who is totally devoted to the Father and living for him, the one totally enveloped in his love.

We too are called to take on the attitude of Jesus towards his Father. The condition, however, for this is conversion: a daily, repeated, constant, sustained turning to God.

Rome 13.1.80

WE LEARN IN PRAYER December 7

While Jesus after his own baptism was at prayer, heaven opened and the Holy Spirit descended on him.

(Luke 3:22)

In Baptism the vivifying action of the Holy Spirit took place in us, and the Father now sees in us his only Son, Jesus Christ: 'You are my Son, the Beloved; my favour rests on you' (Luke 2:32).

234

The Evangelist points out that it was while Jesus was in prayer that the mystery of the Father's love was manifested and the communion of the Three Divine Persons was revealed.

It is in prayer that we learn the mystery of Christ and the wisdom of the Cross. *In prayer* we perceive, in all their dimensions, the real needs of our brothers and sisters throughout the world; *in prayer* we are strengthened for the choices that lie ahead; *in prayer* we are fortified for the mission that Christ shares with us: to bring 'true justice to the nations . . . to serve the cause of right' (Is. 42: 1,6).

Rome 13.1.80

GOD'S CHOICE OF MARY December 8

The angel Gabriel went in and said to her, 'Rejoice, so highly favoured! The Lord is with you.'

(Luke 1:29)

God in his eternal love has chosen man from eternity: he has chosen him in his Son. *God has chosen man, in order that he may reach the fullness of good by means of participation in his own life, divine life, by means of Grace.* He has chosen him from eternity, and irreversibly.

Neither original sin, nor the whole history of personal faults and communal sin has been able to dissuade the eternal Father from this plan of love of his. They have not been able to cancel the choice of us in the eternal Son, the Word consubstantial with the Father.

Since this choice was to take form in the Incarnation, and since the Son of God was to become a man for our salvation, for this very reason *the eternal Father chose for him, among men, his Mother.* Each of us becomes a man because he is conceived and born from his mother's womb. The eternal Father chose the same way for the humanity of his eternal Son.

He chose his Mother from the people to whom he had entrusted his mysteries and his promises in a special way for centuries. He chose her from the race of David and at the same time from the whole of mankind. He chose her of royal descent, but at the same time from among poor people.

He chose her from the beginning, from the very first moment of conception, making her worthy of the divine motherhood to which she would be called at the appointed time. *He made her the first heir to the holiness of her own Son.* The first among those redeemed by his blood, which he had received from her, humanly speaking. He made her spotless at the very moment of conception.

Rome 8.12.79

OPENING ONESELF TO OTHERS December 9

If you are repentant, produce the appropriate fruits.

(Luke 3:8)

The call to repentance, to conversion, means *a call to an interior opening of oneself to others*. Nothing in the history of the Church and in the history of man can replace this call. This call is universal. It is addressed to everyone, and it is addressed to each person for a specific reason. So everyone must see himself as being called to make this conversion.

Christ demands that I should be open to others. But to whom exactly? To the one who is here, at this moment! It is not possible to postpone this call of Christ until an actual beggar will appear in his rags and stretch out his hand. I must be open to every man, always ready to 'give myself'.

How? It is well known that sometimes we can make a present to someone with a single word. But with a single word we can also strike him painfully, offend him, wound him; and can even 'kill him'.

It is necessary, therefore, to accept this call of Christ in those ordinary everyday situations of co-existence and social contact where each of us can give to others, and at the same time, accept what others offer.

Rome 4.4.79

THE OPENNESS OF GRATITUDE December 10

For all things give thanks to God, because this is what God expects.

(1 Thess. 5:16)

To answer Christ's call to open inwardly to others means always being prepared to find oneself at the receiving end of this call. By showing gratitude, I give to others even while I am accepting things from them.

I cannot be closed and ungrateful. I cannot isolate myself. *To accept*

Christ's call to be open to others requires a fundamental change in the whole style of our daily life.

This openness must become a part of our personality, and not something we adopt on the odd occasions when it becomes necessary. *It is something we must persevere continually in.* Otherwise, when the occasion arises, we may not be equal to it.

Rome 4.4.79

THE BROTHERHOOD OF MAN

December 11

You have only one Master, and you are all brothers.

(Matt. 23:8)

While understanding the practical meaning of Christ's call to give oneself to others in our everyday life, we do not want to limit this dedication only to routine, everyday events.

Our giving of ourselves must also be directed to distant events, to the needs of neighbours with whom we are not in touch every day, but of whose existence we are aware. Today, we know far better the needs, the sufferings, the injustices of men who live in other countries and continents.

We cannot ourselves experience their hunger, their want, the ill-treatment, the humiliation, the tortures, imprisonment and social discriminations, their condemnation to a spiritual exile or to 'proscription'; however, we know that they are suffering, and we know that they are men like us, our brothers.

'Brotherhood' was not inscribed only on the banners and standards of modern revolutionaries. Christ had already proclaimed, a long time ago: 'you are all brothers.' And, what's more, he gave this brotherhood an indispensable point of reference: he taught us to say 'Our Father'. *Human brotherhood presupposes the divine Fatherhood.*

Rome 4.4.79

MAN'S THIRST FOR JUSTICE

December 12

Happy those who hunger and thirst for what is right; they shall be satisfied.

(Matt. 5:6)

Every man lives and dies with a certain sense of insatiable hunger for justice, since the world is not able fully to satisfy a being created in the image of God, either in the depths of his person or in the various aspects of human life.

And thus, by means of this hunger for justice, man turns to God who is 'justice itself'. Jesus expressed this very clearly and concisely in the Sermon on the Mount.

Each of us, then, must be able to live in a context of justice and, even more, *each of us must be just and act justly* with regard to those near us and those who are far away, with regard to the community, to the society of which one is a member . . . and with regard to God.

Let us give our attention, meanwhile, to men. Christ left us the commandment to love our neighbour. In this commandment, everything that concerns justice is also contained. *There can be no love without justice.*

Love stands above justice, but at the same time, it finds itself validated in justice. Even a father and a mother, loving their own child, must be just in his regard. *If justice is uncertain, love, too, runs a risk.*

Rome 8.11.78

THE JUST MAN AND JUSTICE December 13

The amount you measure out is the amount you will be given.

(Matt. 7:2)

To be just means giving each one what is due to him. This concerns temporal goods, of a material nature. The best example here might be one's wages or the so-called right to the fruit of one's own work or of one's own land.

But to man is due also his good name, respect, consideration, the reputation he has deserved. The more we know a man, the more his personality, his character, his intellect and his heart are revealed to us. And the more we realize — and we must realize! — by what criterion to pay him his due and what it means to be just towards him.

It is necessary, therefore, to deepen our knowledge of justice continually. It is not a theoretical science. It is virtue, it is capacity of the human spirit, of the human will and also of the heart. *It is also necessary to pray in order to be just and to know how to be just.*

We cannot forget our Lord's words: 'The amount you measure out is the amount you will be given.'

A just man is a man of a 'just measure'. May we all be so! May we all strive constantly to become so!

Rome 8.11.78

THE RICH MAN AND LAZARUS December 14

At the rich man's gate there lay a poor man called Lazarus.

(Luke 16:20)

Both the rich man and the beggar died, and were carried before Abraham, and there judgement was rendered on their conduct. And scripture tells us that Lazarus found consolation, but that the rich man found torment.

Was the rich man condemned because he had riches, because he abounded in earthly posessions, because he dressed in purple and linen and feasted every day? No, I would say that it was not for this reason. *The rich man was condemned because he did not pay attention to the other man.*

The parable of the rich man and Lazarus must always be present in our memory; it must form our conscience. *Christ demands openness to our brothers and sisters in need — openness from the rich, the affluent, the economically advanced;* openness to the poor, the underdeveloped and the disadvantaged.

Christ demands an openness that is more than benign attention, more than token actions or half-hearted efforts that leave the poor as destitute as before or even more so.

New York 2.10.79

THE RESPONSIBILITY OF RICHES December 15

'My son', Abraham replied, 'remember that during your life good things came your way, just as bad things came the way of Lazarus.'

(Luke 16:25)

All of humanity must think of the parable of the rich man and the beggar. Humanity must translate it into contemporary terms, in terms of economy and politics, in terms of all human rights, in terms of relations between the 'First', 'Second' and 'Third World'.

We cannot stand idly by when thousands of human beings are dying of hunger. Nor can we remain indifferent when the rights of the human spirit are trampled upon, when violence is done to the human conscience in matters of truth, religion, and cultural creativity.

We cannot stand idly by, enjoying our own riches and freedom, if, in any place, the Lazarus of the twentieth century stands at our doors. *In the light of the parable of Christ, riches and freedom mean a special responsibility.* Riches and freedom create a special obligation.

New York 2.10.79

TOWARDS A SIMPLER WAY OF LIVING December 16

You cannot be the slave both of God and of money.

(Luke 16:13)

The life-style of many of the members of our rich and permissive societies is easy, and so is the life-style of increasing groups inside the poorer countries.

It is not a question of slowing down progress, for there is no human progress when everything conspires to give full reign to the instincts of self-interest, sex and power. *We must find a simple way of living.*

For it is not right that the standard of living of the rich countries should seek to maintain itself by draining off a great part of the reserves of energy and raw materials that are meant to serve the whole of humanity. *For readiness to create a greater and more equitable solidarity between peoples is the first condition of peace.*

It is in the joyful simplicity of a life inspired by the Gospel and the Gospel's spirit of fraternal sharing that you will find the best remedy for sour criticism, paralysing doubt and the temptation to make money the principal means and indeed the very measure of human advancement.

New York 2.10.79

THE MAN FOR OTHERS December 17

The Son of Man must be lifted up. . . . so that everyone who believes may have eternal life in him.

(John 3:16)

Love goes hand-in-hand with poverty, its power none other than the utter weakness of the incarnate Word in the stable at Bethlehem and

on the Cross. *He sought nothing except the good of those who were his own.*
An Anglican theologian, John Robinson, has called him 'the man for others'.

Love is a force, the driving force in salvation. Man — even the man who is far distant from the Gospel — is capable of recognizing the close tie between love and salvation.

The concentration camps will always remain in men's minds as real-life symbols of hell-upon-earth; they expressed to the highest degree the evil that man is capable of inflicting on his fellow men. In one such camp Fr. Maximilian Kolbe died in 1941. All the prisoners knew that he died of his own free choice, offering his own life in exchange for that of a fellow-prisoner.

And with that particular revelation there passed through that hell-upon-earth *a breath of fearless and indestructible goodness, a kind of intimation of salvation.* One man died, but humanity was saved! So close is the tie between love and salvation.

S. of C.

HUMAN LIFE IS SACRED   December 18

It was you who created my inmost self, and put me together in my mother's womb.

(Ps. 139:13)

I do not hesitate to proclaim before you and before the world that all human life — from the moment of conception and through all subsequent stages — is sacred, because human life is created in the image and likeness of God.

Nothing surpasses the greatness or dignity of a human person. Human life is not just an idea or an abstraction; human life is the concrete reality of a being that lives, that acts, that grows and develops; a human life is the concrete reality of a being that is capable of love, and of service to humanity.

Let me repeat what I told the people during my recent pilgrimage to my homeland: 'If a person's right to life is violated at the moment in which he is first conceived in his mother's womb, an indirect blow is struck also at the whole of the moral order, which serves to ensure the inviolable goods of man. Among those goods, life occupies the first place.'

Washington 7.10.79

THE UNBORN'S RIGHT TO LIFE

You knew me . . . when I was being formed in secret, knitted together in the limbs of the womb.

(Ps. 139:15)

All human beings ought to value every person for his or her uniqueness as a creature of God, called to be a brother or sister of Christ by reason of the Incarnation and the universal Redemption.

And so, we will stand up every time that human life is threatened. When the sacredness of life before birth is attacked, we will stand up and proclaim that *no one ever has the authority to destroy unborn life.*

When a child is described as a burden or is looked upon only as a means to satisfy an emotional need, we will stand up and insist that *every child is a unique and unrepeatable gift of God, with the right to a loving and united family.*

Washington 7.10.79

THE STRENGTHENING OF VALUES

December 20

Put on the new self that has been created in God's way, in the goodness and holiness of the truth.

(Eph. 4:24)

How then can a Christian, inspired and guided by the mystery of the Incarnation and Redemption of Christ, strengthen his or her own values?

The answer to that question, in order to be complete, would have to be long. Let me, however, just touch upon a few important points. These values are strengthened:

— *When power and authority are exercised in full respect for all the fundamental rights of the human person*, whose dignity is the dignity of one created in the image and likeness of God (Gen. 1:26).

— When freedom is accepted, not as an absolute end in itself, but as a gift that enables self-giving and service.

— *When the family is protected and strengthened*, when its unity is preserved, and when its role as the basic cell of society is recognized and honoured.

Philadelphia 3.10.79

God loved the world so much that he gave his only Son.

(John 3:16)

The Gospel is a message of life. *Christianity bears deeply in its whole content the sense of the value of life and of respect for life.* The love of God as Creator is shown in this, that he is the Giver of life.

The love of God as Creator and Father is shown in this, that man, created in his image and likeness as male and female, is made by him a collaborator from the very beginning, a collaborator of the Creator in the world of giving life.

To such a task is connected a particular dignity of man: the generative dignity, the dignity of father and mother, a dignity fundamental and irreplaceable in the whole order of human life: individual and social at the same time.

The problem of the affirmation of human life from the first moment of its conception, and, necessarily also the problem of the defence of this life, is joined in a very strict way with the most profound order of the existence of man, as an individual being, and as a social being, for whom the first and fundamental environment can not be other than a true human family.

Siena 14.9.80

THE FUNDAMENTAL HUMAN RIGHT   December 22

So that everyone who believes in him may not be lost but may have eternal life.

(John 3:16)

The explicit affirmation of human life from the first moment of its conception under the mother's heart is necessary. Likewise necessary is the defence of this life when it is in any way whatsoever endangered (even socially!).

It is necessary and indispensable, because in the final analysis *we are dealing here with fidelity to humanity itself, with fidelity to the dignity of man.*

This dignity must be accepted from the very beginning. If it is destroyed in the woman's womb, in the mother's womb, it will be difficult to defend it, then, in so many areas and spheres of life and of human society.

How is it possible, in fact, to speak of human rights, when this most primary right is violated? Today many talk about the dignity of man, but then they don't hesitate to trample the human being, when these present themselves, weak and defenceless, on the threshold of life. Isn't there a patent contradiction in all that?

We must not tire of re-affirming it: *the right to life is the fundamental right of the human being*, a personal right that obliges from the very beginning.

Siena 14.9.80

MOTHERHOOD IS SACRED December 23

Rejoice, so highly favoured! The Lord is with you.

(Luke 1:28)

God in fact so loved the world as to give his only-begotten Son, so that whoever believes in him may have life!

And God has so loved human motherhood, the motherhood of a Woman — of the Virgin of Nazareth, through whom he could give the world his only-begotten Son — that in this light all human motherhood acquires an extraordinary dimension. *Is is sacred.*

Life is sacred. *And the motherhood of every mother is sacred.*

Hence the problem of the affirmation of life. The problem of the defence of life already in the mother's womb is, for all those who confess Christ, a problem of faith and a problem of conscience.

And it is also a problem of conscience for others, for all men without exception: it is *by reason of their very humanity*.

Siena 14.9.80

CHRISTMAS EVE December 24

The virgin will conceive and give birth to a son and they will call him Emmanuel, a name which means 'God-is-with us'.

(Matt. 1:23)

There comes unbidden to my mind the memory of my feelings and my experiences, beginning from the years of my childhood in my father's house, through the difficult years of youth, the period of the Second World War. May it never be repeated in the history of Europe and of the world!

Yet, even in the worst years, *Christmas has always brought some rays of light with it.* And these rays penetrated even the hardest experiences of contempt for man, of annihilation of dignity, of cruelty. To realize this we only have to pick up the memoirs of men who have passed through the prisons or concentration camps, the war fronts and the interrogations and trials.

This ray of Christmas Night, a ray of the birth of God, is not only a memory of the lights of the tree beside the crib at home, in the family or in the parish Church. It is something more. *It is the deepest glimpse of humanity visited by God*, humanity newly received and assumed by God himself; assumed in the Son of Mary in the unity of the Divine Person: the Son-Word.

Human nature assumed mystically by the Son of God in each of us who have been adopted in the new union with the Father.

Rome 25.12.78

CHRISTMAS DAY   December 25

She wrapped him in swaddling clothes and laid him in a manger.
(Luke 2:7)

Christmas is the feast of *all the children of the world* — all of them, without distinction of race, nationality, language or origin. Christ is born at Bethlehem for them all. And he represents them all.

His first day on this earth speaks to us of all of them and of each of them individually; the message of the Child of a poor Mother; of the Mother who, after his birth, 'wrapped him in swaddling clothes, and laid him in a manger, because there was no room for them at the inn'.

The child is always a new revelation of the life that is given to man by the Creator. It is a new confirmation of the image and likeness of God, imprinted upon man from the very beginning.

The child is also a great and continuous test of our fidelity to ourselves. Of our fidelity to humanity. *It is a test of our respect for the mystery of life*, upon which, from the very first moment of conception, the Creator places the imprint of his image and likeness.

Rome 25.12.79

245

For there is a child born for us, a son given to us and dominion is laid on his shoulders.

(Is. 9:6)

And so a baby is born to us. A child is born to us. This child bears on his shoulders a special authority: he is the King of all ages.

But still more than authority, *he bears in his heart the Cross of complete humanity.* By this Cross of full humanity, the Divine Child has claimed for all times the rights of a man: his greatness, his dignity, his holiness and peace to men of goodwill.

Cracow 25.12.68

GOD COMES TO US   December 27

While they were there the time came for her to have her child, and she gave birth to a son.

(Luke 2:6)

Christ is born. What does it mean? It means, dear brothers and sisters, that *he himself has come out to meet those strivings inherent in man*: strivings to transcend his own limits, to conquer greater things, to attain greater things, to become in some way greater.

God has come out himself to meet these aspirations, and, by becoming man, reveals to man a certain ultimate limit of a potentiality which is not inherent in creation, not inherent in the visible universe, but is inherent in God himself.

Man can transcend himself not just by travelling further into outer space. *Man can surpass himself by becoming a son of God.*

Cracow 25.12.68

THE DIGNITY OF THE INDIVIDUAL   December 28

A Saviour has been born to you; he is Christ the Lord.

(Luke 2:11)

A human being is born. He is one of the millions and millions of people who have been born, are being born and will be born on earth.

A human being, one item in the vast range of statistics.

It was not inappropriate that Jesus came into the world when a census was being held, when a Roman Emperor wanted to know the number of subjects in his territory. A human being is an object to be counted, sometimes considered under the aspect of quantity, one of many millions.

Yet at the same time he is a single being, unique and unrepeatable. If we celebrate with such solemnity the birth of Jesus, *it is to bear witness that every human being is somebody unique and unrepeatable.* If our human statistics, human categories, human political, economic and social systems, and mere possibilities fail to ensure that man can be born, live and act as one who is unique and unrepeatable, then all this is ensured by God.

For God and before God, the human being is always unique and unrepeatable, somebody thought of and chosen from eternity, someone called and identified by his own name.

Rome 25.12.78

JOY IN THE LORD December 29

I want you to be happy, always happy in the Lord; I repeat, what I want is your happiness.

(Phil. 4:4)

Christ came to bring joy: joy to children, joy to parents, joy to families and to friends, joy to workers and to scholars, joy to the sick and to the elderly, joy to all humanity.

In a true sense, joy is the keynote of the Christian message and the recurring motif of the Gospels. Recall the first words of the angel to Mary: 'Rejoice, so highly favoured, the Lord is with you.' And at the birth of Jesus, the angels announced to the shepherds: 'Listen, I bring you news of great joy.'

Years later as Jesus entered Jerusalem riding on a colt, 'the whole group of disciples joyfully began to praise God at the top of their voices, "Blessings on the king who comes in the name of the Lord!"' We are told that some Pharisees in the crowd complained, saying: 'Master, check your disciples.' But Jesus answered: 'I tell you, if these keep silence the stones will cry out' (Luke 19: 37–40).

Are not those words of Jesus still true today? If we are silent about the joy that comes from knowing Jesus, the very stones of our cities will cry out! *For we are an Easter people and 'Alleluia' is our song.* With St. Paul I exhort you: 'Rejoice in the Lord always, I say it again, rejoice.'

> Rejoice because Jesus has come into the world!
> Rejoice because Jesus has died upon the Cross!
> Rejoice because he rose again from the dead!
> Rejoice because in baptism, he washed away our sins!
> Rejoice because Jesus has come to set us free!
> And rejoice because he is the master of our life!

New York 2.10.79

BE MESSENGERS OF JOY December 30

To give light to those who live in darkness and the shadow of death.
(Luke 1:79)

But how many people have never known this joy? They feed on emptiness and tread the paths of despair. 'They walk in darkness and the shadow of death.' And we need not look to the far ends of the earth for them. They live in our neighbourhoods, they walk down our streets, they may even be members of our own families.

They live without true joy because they live without hope. They live in our neighbourhoods, they have never heard, really heard, the Good News of Jesus Christ, because they have never met a brother or a sister who touched their lives with the love of Jesus and lifted them up from their misery.

We must go to them therefore as messengers of hope. *We must bring to them the witness of true joy.* We must pledge to them our commitment to work for a just society and city where they feel respected and loved.

And so I encourage you, be men and women of deep and abiding faith. Be heralds of hope. Be messengers of joy. Be true workers for justice. *Let the Good News of Christ radiate from your hearts*, and the peace he alone gives remain for ever in your souls.

New York 2.10.79

Of all the names in the world given to men, this is the only one by which we can be saved.

(Acts 4:12)

In the first moments of the New Year, we stand before God, our Creator, the Giver of Truth, the Lord of Time. To him we give honour, to him we say 'Glory', glory which time, and creation in time, and in the world of creation man expresses and proclaims in an imperfect manner. *Glory, which only the Son, who exists from before all ages, can express in a perfect manner*, befitting God, to the Father who exists from before all ages.

When we stand before the Word which exists from before all ages, which is co-existent with the Father, omnipotent as he is, eternal as he is, which entered time, and in time became flesh and dwelt amongst us, that instant our thoughts and our hearts return to him.

With his Name, we are entering into a new period of time, a new year, since only this Name is appointed on earth so that we may be saved. *The name of Jesus Christ means the salvation of man.* The name of Jesus Christ declares and creates the history of the salvation of mankind. History is a matter of time; history is man and time.

Cracow 31.12.68

ACKNOWLEDGEMENTS

The editor and publishers would like to express their gratitude to the Director of *Libreria Editrice Vaticana*, Brenno Bucciarelli, for permission to use excerpts from *L'Osservatore Romano* (The numbers following the newspaper's date of issue are the date references to material used, e.g.: passage on May 24 – 24/5: is taken from issue 5 May 1980 (631))

26 Oct '78 (552) – 28/6: 3/7; 2 Nov '78 (553) – 2–3/9; 9 Nov '78 (554) – 21/6: 23/8: 4/11; 16 Nov '78 (555) – 1/6: 15/10: 12–13/12; 23 Nov '78 (556) – 25/1: 22/8: 31/8: 4–7/9; 30 Nov '78 (557) – 21–22/3; 7 Dec '78 (558) – 22–23/11: 2/12; 14 Dec '78 (559) – 9–10/2: 2/5; 21 Dec '78 (560) – 1/12: 3/12: 8/12; 28 Dec '78 (561) – 2/2; 1 Jan '79 (562) – 24/12: 28/12; 15 Jan '79 (564) – 1/1; 22 Jan '79 (565) – 19/1; 29 Jan '79 (566) – 6/1; 26 Feb '79 (570) – 1/5: 14/7; 5 Mar '79 (571) – 19–20/3: 14/10; 12 Mar '79 (572) – 7/ 2: 28/2; 22–23/6; 19 Mar '79 (573) – 29/2: 1–5/3; 26 Mar '79 (574) – 6–8/3; 2 Apr '79 (575) – 9–15/3; 9 Apr '79 (576) – 11–12/ 2: 9–11/12; 16 Apr '79 (577) – 26/2; 23 Apr '79 (578) – 16–19/4; 30 Apr '79 (579) –4/7; 7 May '79 (580) – 25/6: 14/11; 14 May '79 (581) – 20–23/4: 22/5: 25/8: 27–28/8; 21 May '79 (582) – 24–26/4: 30/4: 30–31/10; 28 May '79 (583) – Ascen: 29/5; 18 June '79 (586) – 11/4: 11–14/6: 16/9: 4–5/12; 25 June '79 (587) – 16–17/6; 2 July '79 (588) –29–30/6; 16 July '79 (590) – 5/8: 20–25/9; 30 July '79 (592) – 1/8: 7/8; 10–11/11; 3 Sept '79 (597) – 18/5; 8 Oct '79 (602) – 3/1: 15/6: 24/6: 23/7: 12–13/8: 15/9: 23/10; 15 Oct '79 (603) – 2/1; 22 Oct '79 (604) – 18–21/8: 13/11: 14–16/12: 20/12: 29–30/12; 5 Nov '79 (606) – 26/10: 29/10: 18–19/12: 12 Nov '79 (607) – 9–10/7; 19 Nov '79 (608) – 13/11; 3 Dec '79 (610) – 17/9: 10/10: 18/10: 1/11: 24–25/11; 10 Dec '79 (611) – 2/8; 31 Dec '79 (613) – 4–15/1; 8/12: 29–30/11; 7 Jan '80 (614) – 25/12: 21 Jan '80 (616) – 26–27/1: 9/8; 28 Jan '80 (617) – 21/1; 4 Feb '80 (618) – 6– 7/12; 11 Feb '80 (619) – 13/5; 18 Feb '80 (620) – 2–4/6: 21/7; 25 Feb

'80 (621) – 15–16/11; 3 Mar '80 (622) – 5/2: 24/2: 1/7: 19/11; 17 Mar '80 (624) –22–23/6: 16–18/7; 24 Mar '80 (625) – 16–18/3; 5/6: 7 Apr '80 (627) – 14/10; 14 Apr '80 (628) – 17/1: 6/2: 14/2: 25/2: 27/2; 21 Apr '80 (629) – 29–30/1: 1/2: 7/4: 15/4: 3/5: 27/5; 28 Apr '80 (630) – 3/5; 5 May '80 (631) – 24/5: 10/8; 19 May '80 (633) – 6/5: 25/10; 2 June '80 (635) – 20/1: 7/5; 9 June '80 (636) – 6/2: 14/2: 26–27/6: 8/7; 16 June '80 (637) – 18/1: 3–4/2: 4–5/5: 15–16/5: 18/5: 31/5: 19–20/7: 14–17/8; 2/10; 23 June '80 (638) –27–29/4; 14 July '80 (641) – 8/6: 11/8; 28 July '80 (643) – 3–4/8: 26/8; 4 Aug '80 (644) –2/7: 6–7/7: 11/7: 1/10; 11 Aug '80 (645) –14/5: 30/5: 5–7/6: 9–10/6: 13/7: 6/8; 25 Aug '80 (646) – 16/1: 11–13/10; 1 Sept '80 (647) – 3–8/10: 15/8; 8 Sept '80 (648) – 1/9; 15 Sept '80 (649) – 26–27/11; 22 Sept '80 (650) – 19/9: 22/10: 17–18/11: 21–23/12; 29 Sept '80 (651) – 13/9; 5 Jan '81 (665) – 12/11.

Scripture texts are taken from the Jerusalem Bible published and copyright 1966, 1967 and 1968 by Darton, Longman & Todd Ltd. and are used by permission of the publishers.

Extracts taken from *Sign of Contradiction* and *Fruitful and Responsible Love* are reproduced with the permission of the publishers, St. Paul Publications.

The editor would like to thank Fr. Andrzej Bardecki, editorial director of ZNAK, for the extracts from the sermons of Pope John Paul II from the time when he was the archbishop of Cracow. These are taken from an anthology called *Kazania 1962–1978*, published by ZNAK, publishing house, in Cracow 1980.

A special 'thank-you' is due to Monsignor Mario Oliveri, Chargé d'Affaires of the Apostolic Delegation, London, without whose assistance and encouragement this book would not have appeared.

Sincere thanks are also due to the Sons of Divine Providence in England and Poland; Mr Olgierd Stepan for advice; Vera Rich for the translation of material collected in Cracow; Elaine Riches for typing the manuscript. Finally all those mentioned in the Introduction who made my visit to Cracow so memorable.